THE
INTENTIONAL
ENTREPRENEUR

THE
INTENTIONAL
ENTREPRENEUR

BRINGING TECHNOLOGY AND
ENGINEERING TO THE REAL NEW ECONOMY

FOREWORD BY RICHARD A. BENDIS

DAVID L. BODDE

M.E.Sharpe
Armonk, New York
London, England

Library of Congress Cataloging-in-Publication Data

Bodde, David L.
   The intentional entrepreneur : bringing technology and engineering to the real new
economy / David L. Bodde.
      p. cm.
   Includes bibliographical references and index.
   ISBN 0-0756-1414-6 (alk. paper); ISBN 0-7656-1415-4 (pbk. : alk. paper)
      1. Technological innovations—Economic aspects. 2. Technological
innovations—Management. 3. Venture capital. 4. Entrepreneurship. I. Title

HD45.B574 2004
658.4′21—dc22

                                                          2003067345

Printed in the United States of America

The paper used in this publication meets the minimum requirements of
American National Standard for Information Sciences   ·
Permanence of Paper for Printed Library Materials,
ANSI Z 39.48-1984.

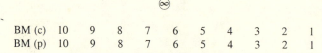

BM (c)   10   9   8   7   6   5   4   3   2   1
BM (p)   10   9   8   7   6   5   4   3   2   1

Contents

List of Tables and Figures

Tables

Figures

Foreword

Reflections on the
Entrepreneurial Journey

Welcome to the joys, heartaches, and complexities of technology-based entrepreneurship. From my experience, both as an entrepreneur and as a coach of entrepreneurs, you will encounter all three in varying proportion over the course of your journey. The only guarantee is that you will not find any of it dull, and that once embarked, the experience will change you forever.

Experience, however, remains the worst kind of teacher—it gives the exam first, and the teaching second. *The Intentional Entrepreneur* seeks to reverse that, at least as far as possible within the limits of the printed word. And so, do not expect a cookbook with step-by-step instructions on how to make your endeavor successful. Plenty of those can be found, and a few will actually prove useful. Instead, David Bodde offers you the best method of instruction there is to give: the stories of others who have walked the entrepreneurial walk and the lessons they have paid so dearly to learn.

The Intentional Entrepreneur leads with the exciting journeys of two companies: EnerTech Environmental and Nth Power Technologies. As you follow their progress, you will note the three key elements shared by all successful ventures: entrepreneurs with good market insight, strong business models, and effective organizations. Technology is important, to be sure—one way to build a business model around capabilities that competitors cannot duplicate. But by itself, technology remains incomplete. Your job as an entrepreneur is to discover the economic value that technology can offer and find a way to capture that value in a profitable company. This is your societal purpose and your economic purpose. Besides, it is both fun and financially rewarding—and in my experience, you can't have fun if you're not making money, and you can't make money if you're not having fun.

The Intentional Entrepreneur observes that a *real* new economy is now emerging from the disastrous dot-com era. Economic value in the real new economy will spring from knowledge of the physical world enabled by advances in science and engineering. Bodde asserts that those who understand it will find rich opportunities to create value for society and wealth for themselves. EnerTech Environmental, the lead story, recognized this opportunity. Reading about how that company hopes to break into the environmental protection industry will help you understand how to break into an industry that you might choose. Nth Power Technologies, the second story, spent three years completing its "6-month" search for investors. Each company dealt with hurdles such as governmental delays, international partners, and the insatiable need for growth capital. As you follow their failures and successes, it becomes clear that success cannot come without initial failure. Entrepreneurship is a journey of trial and error; there is no shortcut to success.

Four persistent trends will shape the opportunities seen by entrepreneurs in the emerging economy: (1) the rise of knowledge as a source of economic value; (2) a growing privatization of markets once thought to be foreclosed by government regulators of one kind or another; (3) the convergence of scientific disciplines once thought distinct and their ascendance as the key source of opportunity in a knowledge-driven world; and, (4) a new set of ethical issues rising from all this to alter the rate and direction of the new economy. And as that great non-technology entrepreneur, Jerry Garcia (The Grateful Dead) once observed about opportunities, "Somebody has to do something, and it's just incredibly pathetic that it has to be us."

Yes, somebody has to do something. Universities and private laboratories in the United States and in aspiring countries everywhere are creating new knowledge at an astonishing pace. But that knowledge will not translate into a better life for billions of people around the globe unless "somebody" does something. That somebody is you. The future prosperity of this nation, and indeed of the world, rests with the ability of entrepreneurs, like you who read this book, to translate the burgeoning knowledge of humankind into economic reality—and that requires successful new ventures.

How "pathetic" that attempt actually turns out to be also depends on you. First, please understand that market context matters—whether you are working to start a new company or invest in one, you must establish yourself as an expert in your market niche, and in the mainstream markets beyond. You must create a competent board of directors, decide how many patents/trademarks/copyrights are needed to protect the company, and create a business model that creates value for paying customers and captures enough of that value for your company to grow. You must persuade a venture capital community that still bears psychic scars from the excesses of the dot-com era that your new enterprise really is different. And all this must be accomplished on the fly with too little time and few resources.

In a business environment like that, you will quickly reach the limits to planning. Thus the central skill of the entrepreneur becomes learning—and taking prompt, effective action based on that learning. And so, I commend this book to your attention as the best point of departure I have seen for this voyage of discovery. And finally, after you have mastered the lessons of *The Intentional Entrepreneur,* come and see me in Philadelphia. We might have a deal for you. But in any case, welcome to the adventure.

Richard A. Bendis
President and CEO
Innovation Philadelphia, Inc.

Preface and Acknowledgments

The urge to write a book dwells deep within the human spirit. Those who successfully resist this urge go on to lead lives uncomplicated by writing schedules and unsullied by grumpiness when the scheduled sessions turn up dry. Those who succumb find the writing process a magnificent obsession, one for which the question, "Why am I doing this?" is self-answering. Even so, just as thoughtful persons should not live unexamined lives, neither should they read unexamined books—and so I offer the thoughtful reader my motivation for this small volume.

About Purpose

The competitive advantage of a free economy springs from its ability to invent what it needs when it needs it. Yet the old order never passes without a fight. The new battles against the established in these wars of creative destruction, and entrepreneurs are the shock troops. And yet, much of the combat training offers only partial preparation—academic knowledge without the behavioral context required to make that knowledge fully useful. I wrote this book explicitly for technologists, whose entrepreneurial experience tends to be long on information and short on behavioral context.

Gordon Moore's noted self-characterization as an "accidental entrepreneur," one who had stumbled haphazardly into success, inspired the book's title, *The Intentional Entrepreneur*. My purpose for the book is to help others find more deliberate routes on their own entrepreneurial journeys. Its subtitle, *Bringing Technology and Engineering to the Real New Economy*, focuses this purpose on the opportunities that are emerging from the dot-com wreckage, opportunities to create lasting value from technology and build the real new economy. And so, I hope that title reflects purpose, and that you who read this find that purpose worthy of your time and energy.

An Appreciation

Neither books nor people make good islands. Rather, facts, understandings, and impressions from countless individuals, both recognized and unrecognized, combine to give a book its shape and substance.

First, I must thank those who have allowed their stories to become the vehicle for communicating the truth of the entrepreneurial experience: Kevin Bolin of EnerTech Environmental; Maurice Gunderson and Nancy Floyd of Nth Power Technologies; and John Voeller and Gerald White of Black & Veatch. Theirs was not the inerrant rise to wealth and fame promoted by the success magazines, but rather the more common experience—apparently promising pathways that yield disappointing results; the struggle to balance constancy and learning; and intelligent persistence in the face of a highly uncertain outcome. All contributed their time and, more importantly, their candor, to the sharing of their experiences. They are fellow seekers of truth.

Other entrepreneurs—Dianne Syme of Light Cicles, Atul Pasricha and Michelle Drage of Delphi Corporation, Richard Marczewski, Stan Lapidus of Exact Sciences Corporation, and George LaMotte—all contributed unique insights into special aspects of the entrepreneurial experience. A number of reviewers were invaluable in shaping the final product: Rodrigo Prudencio, Abel Mojica, Dan Chase, Elizabeth Murry, Caron St. John, Kim Cassady, Richard Linden, and Malcolm Fortson. Their comments, often highly critical, added materially to the quality of the work—and we even managed to remain friends.

I appreciate especially the editorial counsel of Mrs. Betty Clay, that redoubtable foe of the passive voice and "to be" verbs. She has single-handedly improved my writing more than any other teacher except my mother. And if you still don't like it, the fault is fully mine—she has done the best that could be done with the material available to her. Graphic artist Bruce Kay turned the scribblings that I used to illustrate major points into comprehensible figures. Dr. Patricia Greene, now Dean of the Undergraduate Program at Babson College, contributed key insights, especially during the formative stages of this project. My son David Bodde, whose artistic talents went underappreciated for many years, provided the concept for the book cover.

The editors at M. E. Sharpe have been simply superb. I am grateful to Lynn Taylor, Esther Clark, and Angela Piliouras for their energy, enthusiasm, and publishing wisdom. Indeed, I chose M. E. Sharpe because these were the kind of people I wanted to work with. I have not been disappointed—I hope they have not either.

I owe an enormous debt to those teachers who chose to mentor me at a time when that might have looked like an unpromising choice: the late Professor David Rose of MIT; the late Professor William Abernathy of Harvard; Dr. Arden L. Bement Jr., currently Director of the National Institute for Standards and Technology; Dr. Jordan Baruch of Harvard; and Dr. James Utterback of Harvard. This has been a blessing beyond my poor powers to repay—but perhaps I can pass it on.

And finally, I am grateful for the patience and support shown by my wife, Priscilla, and my family. They were always there for me, even when the reverse was not true.

A Closing Observation

The world is informed by those who write; it is built by those who do. This book is respectfully dedicated to those who do.

Introduction

My grandmother, a wise and self-educated woman, once noted that the best way to avoid disillusionment is to avoid the illusions in the first place. Had she lived to see technology markets at the close of the century, their illusory hopes setting the conditions for inevitable disappointment, she would not have been surprised—neither would she have invested.

By the late 1990s, new ventures had proliferated in all fields of technology (especially those enabled by the Internet), born of the conceit that new economic laws would create instant wealth for those who *get it*. The NASDAQ, a commonly accepted yardstick for the technology economy, outperformed the Standard and Poor's (S&P) 500 by a factor of nearly six from mid-1998 until early 2000; and the technology component of the S&P 500 itself rose from 7 percent in the early 1990s to 34 percent by 2000.

Profit performance, however, failed to match inflated stock price, and by late 2002, anyone with a portfolio and a central nervous system had felt the pain. An aggregation of the 100 largest technology companies had lost money for five straight quarters. The NASDAQ Composite had dropped by 75 percent. Venture capital investments declined sharply as volatility and poor performance in public equity markets diminished the likelihood of a successful stock offering. And the level of entrepreneurial activity fell markedly in 2001 and 2002.

But just as the euphoria of the 1990s misled all but the most thoughtful observers, so did the crash that followed. Indeed, a real "new economy" is emerging from the rubble of the dot-com era, and those who understand it will find rich opportunities to create value for society and wealth for themselves. The canonical value of the real new economy will be knowledge, especially knowledge of the physical/biological world enabled by advances in science and engineering. Indeed, science and technology has become the basic fuel for successful economies in the twenty-first century.

The most powerful fuel will be blended and not traditional. For example, convergence in four fields—information technology, the life sciences, nanotechnology, and the cognitive sciences—offers the possibility of a new golden age of invention. In other fields—energy and the environment, for example—emerging societal needs will create a strong and persistent market for a host of inventions.

But invention is not enough. For humankind to reap full benefit from technology, entrepreneurs must recognize the economic value resident in that technology and create enterprises capable of bringing it to market. Whether operating independently or from the platform of an established company, entrepreneurs build the bridge between technical possibility and economic reality.

For all its societal value, however, entrepreneurship remains an uncertain art. According to the National Council on Entrepreneurship, less than 5 percent of all businesses become high-growth companies, achieving compound growth rates in excess of 15 percent per year. Other estimates place the number below 1 percent, about the chance of a good college basketball player reaching the NBA. I am writing this book to help technology professionals and students of science and engineering improve these odds.

Creating Economic Value from Technology

In principle, technologists should have a distinct advantage in creating new ventures from their technology. They have the requisite intellectual horsepower and the deep knowledge. They are energetic. They solve complex problems with grace and elegance.

But in practice, we can observe many successful technology businesses founded by nontechnical people. This is because technological abilities, the capacity to imagine and build the better mousetrap, are incomplete by themselves. Releasing the economic value inherent in technology requires a complete venture, which must include:

- *market insight*—how using the technology confers on customers some advantage that they are willing to pay for;
- a *business model* that packages technology and market insight to build a structural, defensible competitive advantage; and
- an *effective organization* that implements the business model, delivers the service, and collects a fair price for it.

Thus the challenges facing the technology-based enterprise are rarely all technical or all business in character. Instead, creating new ventures with technology requires holistic thinking and a propensity for unified action. But action is a behavioral skill, and those who would gain that skill can benefit from opportunities to practice it—in effect, to try on the relevant behaviors for fit and feel.

Entrepreneurship as a Behavioral Skill

In its remarkable reformation from the army that fought in Vietnam to the force that won the 1991 Gulf War, the U.S. Army built its leadership training around three behavior traits—what a leader must *be*, his or her essential mental and moral character; what a leader must *know*, the leader's base of information and analytical skills; and what a leader must *do*, the willingness to take action and accept the personal risks that action brings.

Successful entrepreneurs practice these same traits. But character and wisdom cannot be taught in linear fashion, and so I use the stories of real entrepreneurs to allow readers to try on the character and behaviors that have worked for these people.

The Logic of the Book

Chapter 1 relates the founding of two new ventures: EnerTech Environmental, an Atlanta company that converts treated sewage into a boiler fuel; and Nth Power Technologies, a San Francisco venture capital firm specializing in energy ventures. We will follow these enterprises throughout the book. The chapter closes with a brief commentary, relating these stories to current research on entrepreneurship.

Chapter 2 is the first of four rather didactic chapters. It addresses the sources of entrepreneurial opportunity—a market insight, a technology insight, or an organizational innovation. Whichever source inspires the new enterprise, the opportunity must be captured in a business model strong enough to confer a sustainable competitive advantage. Understanding the business model is a principal concern of Chapter 2.

Chapter 3 introduces the service concept of technology—that any market offering, from a golf ball to brain surgery, can be understood as a bundle of services. The customer benefits from these services can be measured along a definable set of performance dimensions, the importance of which change as the product matures. The chapter stresses marketing concepts of special relevance to the new venture, in particular establishing the first foothold in an unproven territory.

THE
INTENTIONAL
ENTREPRENEUR

1

A Tale of Two Entrepreneurs

Adams Field, Little Rock, Arkansas
Friday afternoon, December 3, 1998

Anxious travelers packed the terminal at Little Rock's airport, and a dark line of approaching thunderheads promised that the customary delays would be even longer. Two entrepreneurs sat in the crowded terminal awaiting their flights home, one to Atlanta, the other to San Francisco. The waiting did nothing to relieve their depression.

The two had invested their most precious resource, their time, in a sponsored forum intended to link emerging businesses that relate to renewable energy with sources of venture capital. Both were questioning the wisdom of that investment. Kevin Bolin, founder and president of EnerTech Environmental of Atlanta, Georgia, had presented his company to a panel of new venture investors and technology experts. The presentation had been thoughtfully prepared and thoroughly rehearsed. It had elicited spirited discussion during the question period and in the halls afterward. But Bolin also knew that protracted negotiations lay ahead before any solid offers for investment might appear. For Kevin Bolin, unresolved issues of financing his company's growth would accompany him on the flight home to Atlanta.

Maurice Gunderson, a founding partner of Nth Power Technologies, a venture capital firm in San Francisco, had heard the presentations of many start-up companies during the two-day forum. He had tried to contribute helpful suggestions to all the presenters, even when such advice was received with all the enthusiasm of a proposed root canal. He had discovered many interesting business models, some of which might even work, but had found no company that matched his own investment criteria. For Gunderson, an incomplete investment portfolio would accompany him on the long flight to San Francisco.

EnerTech Environmental

Kevin Bolin gazed idly out the window of his homeward flight, the enforced leisure giving opportunity to reflect on the events that had brought him to this place and time. The road to Little Rock had not been the unerring progression of triumph that one reads about in the success magazines. Rather, EnerTech's progress showed the more common experience: promising starts, a rueful learning from events, and a fresh start with an improved business model.

A Family Matter

They got the news in early 1993 while driving north from Atlanta to a family wedding. On their way out the door, Kevin and his wife, Laurel-Ann, had grabbed a stack of letters to open in the car. Among the bills and assorted junk mail was a letter from the National Science Foundation notifying them that the company they had formed in February 1992, EnerTech Environmental, had won a $50,000 federal grant. The grant from the Small Business Innovation Research (SBIR) program[1] would pay for a series of tests needed to validate the new firm's core technology, the SlurryCarb Process.

But the value of the grant reached beyond mere money. This first external confirmation gave hope that the technology developed within Bolin's family might actually offer enough value to support a commercial enterprise. The psychological lift was priceless. The money wasn't bad, either.

The chemical process that came to be known as SlurryCarb had been invented by Norman L. Dickinson, Bolin's maternal grandfather. Dickinson had retired in his mid-fifties from M.W. Kellogg, a large engineering and construction firm, where he had been employed as a chemical engineer. In retirement he had pursued his real ambition, chemical process inventions. The first patent that would become the basis for SlurryCarb was issued in October 1981, and over the next fifteen years, Dickinson broadened and deepened his capture of the relevant technologies with over a dozen U.S. patents.

This would have been an impressive achievement for any person. But Dickinson, born in 1915, created the basic technologies at an age when conventional wisdom suggests that idle reminiscence is one's chief mental activity. His energy and persistence were driven by a fundamental belief in the value of his creation, and a desire to see it put into practice.

Like many process innovations, SlurryCarb is an aggregation of related technology pieces. No single patent covers its entire scope, but the base of intellectual property, taken as a whole, serves to protect this rather simple, flexible chemical process. The process that emerged from this fifteen-year evolution converts municipal sewage sludge (or other organic wastes) into a uniform, pumpable, slurry fuel suitable for combustion, co-firing, or reburning in industrial and utility boilers. The manufactured slurry fuel can be pumped and transported through pipes or tankers to industrial and utility users, where it is stored in tanks and used as needed as a supplement or substitute for conventional fuel sources such as coal or oil. With environmental and economic advantages over current methods, the current EnerTech process can stand alone or mesh with existing or planned waste-disposal strategies.

An Answer in Search of a Question

Neither the growth path that this technology would take nor the business model that would best convert its technical promise into economic reality had been obvious in the beginning. EnerTech had grown out of a company started by Norman Dickinson in the early 1980s called DIPAC, an acronym for Dickinson's Pure Air Combustion. DIPAC would earn its cash by licensing the basic technology and would serve as the platform through which the patent base would be deepened and extended. But after ten years' work, only one license had been signed despite notable technical progress. Like many technologists, Dickinson had little interest in marketing, and so did not pursue it aggressively.

By the early 1990s, Dickinson had become frustrated by the pace of events, and so began a series of discussions with Kevin Bolin, his grandson. Bolin seemed an unlikely candidate to participate in a technology start-up. Graduating from Notre Dame in 1985 with a bachelor's degree in accounting, Bolin had worked in public accounting for KPMG Peat Marwick and as a media salesman for an Atlanta television station. As he grew restless at his TV job, the opportunity that Dickinson had posed began to resonate within him. Bolin had always been an enterprising person, holding three entrepreneurial jobs while in college. The opportunity for another such experience became compelling.

And so in February 1992, EnerTech Environmental was formed as the commercial platform for Dickinson's waste-to-fuel technologies. Bolin remained employed at the TV station until November of that year, and his wife, Laurel-Ann, also left her job practicing corporate law at an Atlanta firm. After a two-month break for travel, both plunged into the EnerTech venture full time.

First Business Model

In the beginning, the business model for EnerTech owed much to the thinking that had founded DIPAC. It would be a licensing company, building a proprietary position through the inventive genius of Dickinson and licensing the technology to developers and users for an appropriate fee. This strategy gained apparent validation when a Canadian company came across a Dickinson patent that matched its own in-house technology. Realizing that they would have to license if they wanted to practice the technology in the United States, the Canadians contacted EnerTech. The license, however, was for a peripheral invention, and not for EnerTech's core technology. Even so, it reinforced Bolin's belief in the licensing model, and Kevin and Laurel-Ann set out to market the company and its capabilities.

The marketing challenge derived from the technological origins of the company. Despite their technological successes, neither the Bolins nor Dickinson were known within the waste disposal industry. Articles in technical publications helped add credibility, as did EnerTech's affiliation with the business incubator at the Georgia Institute of Technology and a second federal grant from the SBIR program. Even so, they found it difficult to attract more than casual attention without a tangible demonstration of the technology.

The Technology Demonstration

Small-scale tests had shown enormous promise for EnerTech's core technologies. But chemical processes are notorious for glitches that appear only in full-sized plants, and Bolin had estimated that a demonstration large enough to be credible might cost as much as $14 million. EnerTech was caught in a classic trap for the early-stage technology company. On the one hand, without a demonstration at near-commercial scale, EnerTech could not convince potential customers that the technology would actually perform. But on the other hand, the company could not raise funds for the demonstration plant in the absence of some confirmation of performance. Customers seemed to hold the philosophy that, while the early bird might get the worm, the second mouse usually gets the cheese.

Rising Sun, Rising Hope

EnerTech's relationship with Mitsubishi began at a trade show in late 1994. The Japanese conglomerate quickly became interested in the core technologies, which offered a solution to two long-standing problems for their crowded island: fuel security and waste disposal. After a year and a half of tough negotiations, Bolin found himself with a shelf filled with well-worn "how-to-negotiate-in-Japan" books and a signed agreement. Mitsubishi, leader of a Japanese consortium of four companies, gained a license to use the EnerTech process throughout Asia. In exchange, Mitsubishi and its partners would: (1) build the demonstration plant; (2) turn over to EnerTech the know-how derived from the plant for use in the U.S. market; and (3) pay EnerTech a cash fee of $500,000.

The plant was commissioned in March 1997, at Ube City, Japan, with Kevin Bolin and Norman Dickinson attending. A three-year technology demonstration would be performed under a research protocol largely dictated by the Japanese government, which had also put money into the project. The project, however, soon encountered difficulties.

First, the Japanese elected to use municipal solid waste as feedstock, following the precedent set by EnerTech, which from the beginning had focused its technology development on that material. However, municipal solid waste in Japan differs significantly from that in the United States, chiefly due to a much higher plastics content. This raised unanticipated technical hurdles, as the plastics tended to clog the pipes of the demonstration plant. And with the technical hurdles, the cost of the project swelled beyond the $14 million originally estimated.

At the same time, the economic recession in Japan deepened, and companies fabled for their patient technology development came to recognize some very near-term constraints. After one of the consortium partners dropped out, others followed quickly. The Japanese companies completed the demonstration, but delayed indefinitely their commercial use of the waste-to-fuel technology.

From Bolin's perspective, however, the demonstration plant proved the effectiveness of the technology and contributed three precious jewels to the EnerTech crown: credibility in the U.S. marketplace, know-how concerning the commercial-scale SlurryCarb process, and strategic insight concerning the real nature of the opportunity.

Rethinking the Opportunity

While the demonstration proceeded, doubt began to grow in Bolin's mind about the ability of the licensing model to capture the value inherent in the technology. Most obviously, there had been no licenses negotiated since Mitsubishi and the original one with the Canadian company, and neither firm appeared likely to make commercial use of the technology any time soon. This hint from the marketplace became increasingly hard to ignore.

But other subtle and powerful forces were also at work. Whether licensing or not, Bolin recognized that the technical credibility was not, by itself, enough. In addition, he needed a marketing capability that would give EnerTech a deep understanding of the U.S. waste-disposal market and a network of contacts in that market. For this, he hired Charles Carter in August 1997.

Carter had thirty years' experience in environmental and waste-conversion markets, previously serving as president and chief executive officer of the Bedminster Bioconversion Corporation, an environmental engineering firm. At Bedminster, Carter had structured and negotiated municipal solid waste and sewage sludge composting projects. In his four years there, he took the company from the development stage to market success, with $40 million in construction revenues and over $200 million in pending negotiations.

Now executive vice president of EnerTech, Carter brought to the company a deep understanding of the culture and economic imperatives of EnerTech's target customers; and he had the gray hair to prove it. Among his first priorities, Carter reexamined the nature of the opportunity afforded by EnerTech's growing technology base. His conclusion matched Bolin's: The licensing model was unlikely to succeed, and EnerTech would have to develop its own plants if they were to be built at all.

Rethinking the Technology

From the beginning, EnerTech had focused its attention on municipal solid waste, and its federal grants had supported technology development for that market. But the accumulating experience from the Mitsubishi demonstration plant led Bolin and Carter to question that focus. While the technical difficulties afflicting that plant could be fixed, the solution would impose higher capital costs. Too few markets in the United States seemed capable of bearing those costs, and in most cases, the alternative disposal method—a municipal landfill—would be more economical. Faced with these stark realities, Bolin and Carter began sniffing around for an alternative feedstock.

The plain candidate was municipal sewage sludge, principally human waste treated by the sewage systems of urban communities. As a feedstock, this material offered several advantages. First, it is relatively uniform in content, thereby eliminating the difficulties imposed by plastics and other materials incompatible with the SlurryCarb Process. Second, it comes in a liquid form, thus saving a costly processing step. And third, EnerTech could compete well against the alternative disposal methods, which tended to be more costly and raised unpleasant social issues.

Armed with a new business model and feedstock, Bolin and Carter then turned to building the company. The push toward commercial-scale plants would also require a much stronger engineering capability, so the company hired two experienced engineers early in 1998. One of these was Heinz Ropers. As senior vice president for engineering and technology, Ropers brought to EnerTech twenty-five years of chemical engineering experience. His Teutonic thoroughness and efficiency would set the tone for technology development in the company. Between Carter and Roper, EnerTech had acquired half a century of engineering expertise and industry experience. By contrast, Kevin Bolin the accountant, was thirty-four years old.

The Road Ahead

Bolin recognized that many aspects of EnerTech had become stable, though not set in stone. The SlurryCarb technology and its implementation in practical, economical plants had plainly become the core capability of EnerTech Environmental. And the business model had centered around building and operating these plants. As he looked to the future, Bolin saw the next great challenge as financial. To be sure, EnerTech was expecting $1 million in new investment capital from a wealthy environmentalist with an interest in new businesses. But EnerTech would need much more capital to grow.

Bolin pondered these financial issues as his plane approached Atlanta in the December dusk. How could EnerTech secure the resources to expand at a pace that matched the scale of the opportunity? Could the company really generate the exponential growth in valuation that was being demanded by professional venture capital investors? And how would EnerTech maintain its progress if the funds were not immediately forthcoming? The questions proliferated. The answers did not.

Nth Power Technologies

Maurice Gunderson squirmed to accommodate his six-foot, five-inch frame to the meager room offered by his coach-class seat. He was not looking forward to the five-hour flight home in a space presumably designed by the interrogation squad of the Bosnian secret police. Not that this act of compression was unusual. To the contrary, Gunderson had spent many hours in airplane seats since launching Nth Power Technologies with partner Nancy Floyd in August 1993.

If EnerTech was born of a technology insight, Nth Power was born of a market insight: that the wave of state and federal deregulation that would follow the Energy Policy Act of 1992 would create enormous opportunities for entrepreneurs in energy. Yet there were no venture capital firms with special expertise in deregulating industries and energy. Nth Power was created to fill that void.

The Founders' Insight

Both Gunderson and his cofounder Nancy Floyd were experienced entrepreneurs, which is to say they had actually made money—lots of money. Prior to cofounding Nth Power, Floyd had built and sold three energy and telecommunications companies. In the energy arena, she founded NFC Energy Corporation, an independent power company utilizing advanced technology developed by NASA and Sandia Labs. She developed over $30 million in projects and sold the company after three years, generating a twenty-five-fold return on the original capital investment. In 1984, while at Pacific Telesis, Floyd helped found and spin off Spectrum Services, a network management company for private voice and data networks. Spectrum Services was ultimately sold to IBM in 1987.

Her experience with Pacific Telesis left Floyd with two insights that were to shape the Nth Power idea. First, she came to understand the scope and power of the opportunities that are created for entrepreneurs when major industries are deregulated. The telecommunications industry offered little prospect for new enterprise prior to deregulation, and the amount of venture capital investment reflected that. In 1978, the year that the antitrust case against AT&T went to court, about $25 million in venture capital was invested in telecom start-ups. In 1984, when competition went into effect by court order, about $475 million was invested. And by 1988, annual venture capital investment in telecommunications had reached its high point, slightly under $800 million. The industry incumbents, though retaining great financial power and a large customer base after deregulation, seemed poorly equipped to recognize the opportunities, especially those created by advanced technology. This insight set the foundation for the company that would be called Nth Power Technologies.

Second, Floyd came to realize her own limitations in penetrating the many subtle, yet decisive, quirks of advanced technology. A political scientist by training, she recognized the need for a partner with deep technical understanding and experience.

The Team and the Opportunity

Maurice Gunderson proved to be that partner. Prior to cofounding Nth Power, Gunderson had launched five companies, the most recent a manufacturer of specialized computer systems for the aerospace industry, which he sold to a European aerospace conglomerate. A specialist in thermodynamics and energy technologies, Gunderson has been instrumental in developing cryogenic equipment, energy systems, turbomachinery, and computer-based control systems for process plants and pipeline systems. He is a NASA Technology Fellow, a patent holder, and a registered professional engineer—not a person who spends much time watching daytime television.

Floyd met Gunderson in 1992 after he had sold his last company. His active mind did not tolerate idleness well, and he was bored and looking for the next new thing. Floyd was working at a consultancy, starting a practice that would manage direct investments for electric utility companies. Gunderson joined that practice, and thus began a professional partnership that would grow to enormous power and durability.

The electric utility industry seemed ideal for the new investment practice. Utility companies, by the nature of their business, generated large cash flows but enjoyed relatively limited opportunities to reinvest that cash in the regulated business. Hence, these companies returned relatively large cash dividends to their shareholders. The stability of these dividend payments in good times and bad had made utility stocks attractive to investors seeking regular cash payments rather than growth in share price.

Even before deregulation began its fitful course, most utilities had been permitted to invest their retained cash in unregulated subsidiaries. Many, however, chose utility-like investments such as housing bonds. But when the president signed into law the Energy Policy Act of 1992, setting the federal government on a path toward deregulation of wholesale electric energy, that situation changed. Many states, principally in New England and California, began developing plans for furthering competition in the retail energy markets, which they controlled. In that business environment, it was reasonable to suppose that utility companies would be willing to consider investment in growth companies related to energy. This was the market that Floyd and Gunderson sought.

But they also saw farther than the consulting company. Both shared the vision that in the early 1990s, the electric energy industry was standing where telecommunications had stood in 1981. Deregulation would advance, although the pace might be slow and the eventual stopping point uncertain. New entrants would come into the market. There would be a surge of innovation. The incumbents would be poorly equipped to respond. Opportunities would abound for investors possessing the requisite skill and courage. And so, when the market for managed utility investment was slow to develop and the consultancy lost interest, Floyd and Gunderson bought the practice from them. Thus began Nth Power Technologies.

The Nth Power Business Model

When Gunderson and Floyd launched Nth Power in August 1993, their point of departure was the business model developed for the consultancy—but with an important difference. In addition to managing direct investments for utility companies, Nth Power would also raise a venture capital fund, make the investments, and grow the companies for the investors of the fund. This would be the classical venture capital model, working with the two distinct markets that define any venture capital company.

The first is the market for "deal flow": the supply of investment-quality companies having sound management, an opportunity to create extraordinary value, and a business model that can capture that value. Such companies offer growth strong enough to allow the venture investors to monetize their holdings in five to ten years at a multiple many times the original investment. Gunderson and Floyd believed that deregulation, together with a host of technical advances that had yet to be realized in the energy marketplace, would provide this deal flow.

But they also recognized that competition among venture capitalists for the best deals can become intense once others recognize the value of an emerging investment area. Floyd and Gunderson wanted to be first into the energy market to capture the best deals and establish a reputation as the investor of choice for the best entrepreneurs. They sensed an inherent advantage in doing so, considering themselves to be entrepreneurs first and financiers second.

To attract deal flow, however, they needed to succeed in the second defining market—that for investment dollars. A venture capital company typically raises a large investment fund, say $100 million, from potential strategic partners, institutions, pension funds, and wealthy individuals. Of the amount raised, an annual budget is taken off the top for operating expenses and to compensate the venture capital partners, typically 2 to 3 percent. Much later, when the portfolio is monetized, the investors in the fund typically receive 70 to 80 percent of the gains, the venture capital partners taking the rest.

Experienced investors would find this classic venture capital model familiar. But utility managers were not experienced investors, and persuading them to turn over large sums in an unfamiliar investment arena to two persons without an investment track record proved an unexpected challenge. As a result, the managed-investment business model would have to define the Nth Power offering, at least until inexperience faded as an issue. Retaining this model would serve four purposes: (1) it would strengthen credibility among investors as the actual deals done began to build a convincing record of accomplishment for Nth Power; (2) it would persuade energy entrepreneurs to seek out Nth Power as a firm connected to real sources of capital; (3) it would provide enough income to defray the very considerable costs of raising a venture fund; and (4) it would build on an established relationship with the first client, a large East Coast electric utility, which was included with the purchase from the consultancy.

Three new utility companies were soon added to the client list, and the investment practice was launched. In exchange for a retainer fee that covered expenses, Nth Power would discover venture capital opportunities, perform the initial vetting of the entrepreneur's company (called "due diligence" in investment parlance), and present the opportunity to the utility. Nth Power paid no salaries in those days; it simply did not have the resources.

Gunderson and Floyd estimated that they would have to continue offering this service for six months to a year before their first fund closed at their goal of $60 million. However, the best plans of mice and men are really about equal, and so it proved here.

Raising the First Fund: Early Lessons

Cycle time posed the first challenge to the managed-investment model. The decision cycle of the client utility companies was just too long for the entrepreneurial ventures that Nth Power brought before them. The small companies would asphyxiate for want of cash—the oxygen of the new enterprise—while the large companies pondered their investment decision. The utility companies had not built a decision process through which timely conclusions could be reached. As Gunderson later observed with a touch of remorse, the entrepreneurs were paying their own way to the meetings, suffering the creation of false hopes, and ultimately wasting their opportunities. At least Nth Power was covering its expenses.

This same inability to reach a conclusion caused problems for Nth Power as well. Gunderson and Floyd had hoped to attract not merely financial investors, but *strategic* investors—those who might recognize a stake in the new venture that reached beyond simple financial return. A strategic investor might be a customer for the new enterprise, for example, or perhaps a supplier. But in any case, the interest in the entrepreneur's success would be strengthened, perhaps even to the point that a mentoring relationship could be established.

In principle, the electric utilities had enormous incentive to embrace such a value proposition. The advent of competition appeared close at hand, and rivals were already emerging. Even so—and to the complete surprise of the Nth Power founders—the incumbent utilities proved to be among the slowest to respond to the emerging competitive environment. Gunderson recalled an incident in which he and Floyd had presented the Nth Power offering to the senior management of a major electric utility. These officers listened attentively, plainly impressed with the depth of industry knowledge of the Nth Power team. At the end, however, they were not interested in the venture capital fund—instead, they wanted to hire Gunderson and Floyd to help them figure out how to slow the onset of competition. Later, Gunderson wryly observed, "They totally missed the point. There they were, sitting on top of the biggest opportunity of a lifetime and trying to figure out how to stop it."

And so it went for the first year and a half of fund-raising—much apparent interest, but no tangible results. In retrospect, Floyd and Gunderson recognized that they had made two strategic mistakes. First, they had focused exclusively on incumbent electric utilities. In 1993–94, most of these companies were culturally unready for Nth Power's value proposition. And those who best understood the Nth Power value proposition saw it as a threat to their established business.

Second, and equally important, Gunderson and Floyd had addressed the wrong level of management within these companies. The consulting model that they had adopted gave them ready access to the managers who could approve consulting agreements. But these were not the people who would shape the strategic intent of the company, and so not the people from whom a commitment to invest could ever be secured. They needed CEO access.

Raising the First Fund: Insight and Persistence

In late 1994, Floyd and Gunderson rewrote the Nth Power business plan to recognize the emerging dynamics of the competitive environment. Many high-value opportunities would not be found within the traditional industry boundaries, but rather within the increasing overlap of these boundaries. Customers were less interested in the form of the energy they purchased (natural gas versus electricity, for example) than they were in the services that the energy provided (light on a desk, power for a computer, heat in the winter, and so forth). Thus competition between electricity and gas would intensify as these sources converged in their ability to provide highly valued services. In addition, information technology would revolutionize the way in which these services could be delivered, and allow many to become unbundled—meter reading and billing services, for example, could be offered separately from energy service.

The new business model made several subtle yet strategic changes. First, it broadened the search for investment partners. In the future, Nth Power would look for the emerging winners in the incipient competitive battles, which might include some of the incumbent electric utilities but would surely include major, nonelectric, nonutility players as well. These emerging players would not be restricted to U.S. companies. In addition, Nth Power would look beyond electricity for its investment opportunities to include energy devices in general and the information infrastructure that adds value to them. And finally, Gunderson and Floyd would become more selective in the way they approached potential strategic investors, seeking CEO access and persons who realized the need for change and wanted to accomplish it.

These changes made a difference, and in June 1995, Nth Power had secured a commitment for $10 million from a lead investor, PacifiCorp, a large West Coast utility headquartered in Portland, Oregon. Even so, the founders' hopes for a quick closure of the fund were not met. In part, the slow progress was due to the layered decision-making process of the large corporations. Nobody was willing to make an initial $5 million commitment without validation by the board of directors, the amount probably being less important than the change in strategic direction that the commitment implied.

As Gunderson and Floyd pursued their funding campaign through 1995 and 1996, a new kind of objection arose. By that time, the emerging competitive environment could not be denied, even by the most atavistic companies. But many whom Nth Power had persuaded of the enormity of the opportunity then concluded that they could simply do it themselves. In the end, the results were mixed. But to the extent that any utility company succeeded with this leap into corporate entrepreneurship, two preconditions could be found.

First, the parent company had to be prepared to intervene effectively when (not if) the new venture got into trouble. Successful incubation requires more than mere money—it requires an ability to add value through management assistance. As skilled entrepreneurs, Gunderson and Floyd understood this. Many utility companies did not.

And second, the more successful utilities had to separate the entrepreneurial venture from the parent company's culture. The prototypical utility culture with its emphasis on reliability and conservatism is exactly what is needed to ensure that the lights go on when customers flip the switch. But the pace of decision making in that culture is simply too measured for the imperatives of an emerging enterprise.

Altogether, Floyd and Gunderson visited 197 utility companies before the first closing[2] of their fund in late 1996. After three years of hard work, Nth Power had raised only $30 million, about half the original goal. Nevertheless, Floyd and Gunderson felt the urgency of getting started while the best investment opportunities were still available. Their first investment was in early 1997, followed by three more that year. At the same time, additional partners joined, convinced of the value of the Nth Power investment thesis, bringing the fund to $65 million by its second closing in late 1997. In 1998, Nth Power made four more investments.

Learning and Moving On

As his flight droned homeward from Little Rock, Gunderson reflected on the five years that had passed since the founding of Nth Power. The intense, often disappointing, often frustrating, focus on fund-raising now appeared to be past. In truth, there had been no villains in this arduous drama. Instead, it seems that the hardest job for persons of good sense and good will is to persuade other persons of good sense and goodwill, but of a different business culture, to trust them with their money. The future challenges would be to invest that money well.

Commentary: Research on Entrepreneurship

Stories allow us deep, personal insight into the behavior of those seeking to create new ventures from technology. But to complete our understanding, we must frame this experience within the larger patterns of entrepreneurial behavior. In particular, three elements of this larger picture can provide a helpful context for technology professionals considering their own enterprise: (1) the personal characteristics of technology entrepreneurs themselves; (2) the need for a capable management team, as distinct from an individual entrepreneur; and (3) the purposeful search for opportunity.

Personal Characteristics of Entrepreneurs

Numerous studies have attempted to identify the personal characteristics most likely to lead to success as an entrepreneur. Indeed, if a definitive profile were to exist, it would hold enormous implications—you could take a simple test, compare yourself with the standard profile, and if you did not fit, drop any further ideas of entrepreneurship.

Fortunately, neither life nor entrepreneurship is so neatly packaged, and no unique profile enables us to distinguish entrepreneurs from nonentrepreneurs. Nevertheless, some personal attributes can be associated with success, and these are illuminating even if they are not causal. For example, Massachusetts Institute of Technology (MIT) professor Ed Roberts studied technology professionals who made the transition to entrepreneurship and found that several characteristics seem dominant (Roberts 1991: 94–97).

The first is family background. Roberts's data suggest that an entrepreneurial heritage, often as the son of a self-employed father, characterizes as many as two-thirds of high-technology entrepreneurs. An achievement-oriented religious and cultural heritage reinforces this. Second, the technology entrepreneurs in Roberts's sample were better educated than entrepreneurs in general, typically with a master's degree in engineering or an applied scientific discipline. They tended to be in their mid-thirties at the founding of their enterprises.

And third, most of the technologists in Roberts's surveys were motivated to start their companies by a strongly felt need for independence. Financial gain, though important, did not appear to be a primary motivation—at least not one that many would claim. But as experienced venture capitalist Robert Kunze once observed, "A few entrepreneurs actually tell me they aren't in it for the money. I always assume that means money is all they want. I haven't been surprised yet" (Kunze 1990: 44). In truth, the financial motivations of entrepreneurs, like those of any of us, dwell deep in the human heart, and are not easily discernible with surveys.

One other demographic characteristic of technology entrepreneurs bears mention: the historic predominance of males. Among the many companies spun off from MIT's laboratories, for example, Roberts found only one started by women. And from another study of 113 high-technology entrepreneurs, he noted only three women (Roberts 1991: 41, 54).

All this is changing, however, in response to two trends: increasing female participation in science and engineering, and increasing numbers of female entrepreneurs. With regard to the first, women make up about 25 percent of the science and engineering workforce in the United States according to National Science Foundation (NSF) data (U.S. NSF 2002: 3–12, 3–13). However, women comprise slightly under 50 percent of the general college-educated workforce, suggesting a historic underrepresentation in technology. This gap appears to be closing, and the NSF finds anecdotal evidence of growing participation by women in the science and technology workforce.

At the same time, women-owned businesses in the United States have increased significantly. The nonprofit Center for Women's Business Research (CWBR) estimates that the number of women-owned businesses in the United States grew by 14 percent from 1997 to 2002. By 2002, women-owned businesses accounted for 28 percent of all privately owned firms (CWBR 2002). Although the CWBR data do not distinguish technology-based enterprises, their estimates together with those of the National Science Foundation imply an increasing participation of women in high-technology entrepreneurship.

For all these central tendencies, however, the diversity of individual entrepreneurs remains striking. For example, the observation that two-thirds of those studied came from self-employed family backgrounds means that one-third did not. That diversity is captured in the stories that launched this book.

Even a technology education does not seem essential. Kevin Bolin has a bachelor's degree in accounting, and Nancy Floyd holds master's and bachelor's degrees in political science. Yet Bolin was able to recognize the economic potential in a technology that he could not possibly have invented, and Floyd employed advanced technology to build successful energy and telecom companies prior to founding Nth Power. By contrast, Gunderson is an accomplished technologist: an inventor, patent holder, and registered professional engineer with a master's degree in thermodynamics in addition to his Stanford MBA.

All this should offer comfort to technical professionals and students of science and engineering. It would appear that the chief qualification for becoming a technology entrepreneur is a burning desire to become a technology entrepreneur.

The Founding Team

Creating a new venture is really a special case of general management; and, as it is for all general managers, you cannot do the whole job yourself. Yet the challenges and sacrifices demanded by a new venture are likely to overmatch the personal commitment of employees. And so in the beginning, you need partners, not employees. Indeed, analyses of successful technology ventures show the majority were launched by founding teams, not individual entrepreneurs (Timmons 1994: 254). The ability to develop an effective founding team is one of the central skills of the successful entrepreneur. At EnerTech Environmental, for example, Kevin Bolin imported the core technology and assembled the experienced leaders required for the step from technology to product. Similarly, Nancy Floyd's technical skills were not equal to the task of founding Nth Power, nor were Maurice Gunderson's political skills. But in combination, the team became formidable.

No specific rules lead inevitably to the building of an effective management team, but several general characteristics appear endemic to those who succeed:

- A *lead entrepreneur* who understands his or her own limitations as well as the capacity and limitations of the other team members.
- *Experience and relevant industry connections*, which are central to attracting the venture capital needed for growth.
- *Cohesion* that allows the team to function well as a unit and that relies on a founding vision as the point of orientation.
- *Integrity* born of shared commitment and mutual respect.
- A *reward and compensation system* that reinforces all the above.

In Search of Opportunity

Jeffrey Timmons, that astute observer of new venture creation, once famously remarked that an idea is not, by itself, an opportunity (Timmons 1994: 20). To be sure, attractive opportunities contain ideas, but these alone are not enough—an observation of special relevance to technology professionals for whom the technology idea can too often seem sufficient.

In addition, entrepreneurs must seek opportunities in special marketplace situations. Timmons characterizes these as market imperfections, the "gaps, asymmetries, and inconsistencies of knowledge and information" that skilled entrepreneurs discern in time to act before they become general knowledge (Timmons 1994: 20).

A classic analysis of entrepreneurial innovation by Peter Drucker suggests the kinds of marketplace anomalies likely to produce the best opportunities, whether one operates independently or from the platform of an established company (Drucker 1985: 68).

From the *internal* perspective of a company or industry, Drucker suggests seeking opportunity in the unanticipated. He notes, for example, the incongruity between expectations and results in the ocean shipping industry in the 1950s. Costs had risen beyond expectation and profitability stagnated despite years of innovation that made ships faster and more efficient. More insightful analysis, however, revealed that the most significant costs did not derive from operating the vessels at sea, but rather from their idle time in port. A set of entirely different innovations, such as the roll-on/roll-off ship and the container ship, transformed profitability in ocean shipping for the next twenty years.

From the perspective of the social and intellectual environment outside the company, Drucker observes opportunity in demographic changes, changes in societal perception, and new knowledge (Drucker 1985: 68). Consider the ongoing revolution in information science and technology—hardware for computation, data manipulation, and data storage; advanced software and networks; and telecommunications—as a generator of discontinuity and hence opportunity.

But whatever the source of insight regarding entrepreneurial opportunity, a long and error-strewn path awaits those who would translate a general observation into a workable business model. None of the entrepreneurs in our opening stories got the model right at the beginning. Rather, their purposeful search took detours they could not foresee at the beginning—but the new insights could be gained only by trying something and learning from the results. Chapter 2 seeks a deeper understanding of opportunity for the technology-based enterprise, and its expression in a business model.

2

Creating the Opportunity

The obscure, we see eventually. The completely
obvious, it seems, takes longer.
—*Edward R. Murrow, broadcaster*

The launch pad for any new enterprise is the recognition of an opportunity: the value that can be created, and the way for some of that value to be retained by its founders and owners. This chapter examines the process of creating the opportunity, focusing especially on its expression as a business model.

The power of any opportunity can be understood best when viewed through the lens of the business model—the complete set of ideas concerning the way that value is to be created and a durable, structural competitive advantage sustained. To be sure, a single insight often serves as the entry point for the business model. But by itself, that single idea rarely suffices. The most successful companies weave around their initial insights a rich system of coherent, mutually reinforcing ideas that guide subsequent actions. While tactics and even strategy must adapt as experience reveals the realities of the competitive environment, these foundation ideas remain firm. This complete set of foundation ideas is what I mean by the term "business model." A powerful business model creates a powerful opportunity for the new enterprise.

The chapter closes by noting the purposeful nature of the creation process itself: that opportunities tend to be found the old-fashioned way—by looking for them. To be sure, some few emerge immediately in a flash of inspired brilliance. But more commonly, it is the purposeful, systematic search for the wealth-creating opportunity that succeeds in discovering it.

Foundation Ideas

A complete business model will encompass two foundation concepts:

- A concept of how customer value will be created.

- A concept of how the new venture will build for itself a structural competitive advantage in providing that value.

Taken together, these concepts articulate for the entrepreneur and his or her stakeholders a rational explanation of the anticipated success of the enterprise (van der Heijden 1997: 59). The basic forces driving that success can be conceptualized as in Figure 2.1 (page 25).[1] Our point of departure is a set of *societal needs*, which derive from the values, aspirations, and worries (real or imagined) of the culture in which the new enterprise must dwell. These surround the new enterprise like water surrounds a fish and are as influential in shaping its prospects.

Societies, of course, have many needs: truth, love, justice, and so forth. But here we are chiefly concerned with those needs that can be expressed in the marketplace—that can be bought and sold. I will call the subset of societal needs that can be recognized in the marketplace *customer value*. This value might be explicit or it might be latent, unrecognized by most entrepreneurs and unarticulated by their putative customers. But above all, the value must be real, not contrived. As Stan Lapidus, a seasoned technology entrepreneur and founder of two highly successful companies notes, no enterprise ever rises above the quality of the problem it chooses to solve. Special insight into high-quality problems and the value of their resolution drives the entrepreneurial process.

But insight alone is never enough. In addition, you must build a competitive enterprise by combining technology that is well matched to customer value and an organization to deliver that value and capture enough of it to become self-sustaining.

Technology can create a powerful lever in building customer value. Indeed, technology that meshes well with the value sought in the marketplace will always trump technology that is highly advanced.

This technology requires a delivery platform: an organization capable of delivering the product or service and capturing enough of the value to retain the interest of its owners, employees, and investors. The organizational platform becomes an *entrepreneurial innovation*, the heart of the business model for the new company. The entrepreneurial innovation adds to the technology the processes, people, skills, and equipment needed to deliver value to its customers and to capture enough of that value to sustain the enterprise.

To the extent that the combined *technology* and *entrepreneurial innovation* are truly unique to the new venture and not available to competitors, they become *distinctive competencies*. This term, overused to the point of becoming a cliché and widely misunderstood, merits some explanation. A core competency, however powerfully established in an enterprise, does not become *distinctive* if rivals can easily duplicate it or buy it in the marketplace. Distinctive competency can arise from intangibles like corporate culture—consider the culture of customer service inherent in the retailer Nordstrom, for example. Or it can arise from business processes—the customer service model of Southwest Airlines. It can even be a gift from the past—a railroad's ownership of a right-of-way, an electric utility's ownership of a fully depreciated nuclear power plant, or an installed customer base like Microsoft's operating system, for example. But whatever the source, rivals can duplicate this only slowly and at great expense.

These distinctive competencies in turn create a *sustainable competitive advantage*. As a result of this advantage, the venture builds a *surplus*. Part of that surplus returns to the stakeholders of the enterprise: chiefly its founders, investors, employees, and community. The remainder becomes a *resource* to reinvest in nurturing the distinctive competency of the enterprise.

The ideal business model establishes the virtuous cycle of Figure 2.1, in which the success of the new venture becomes self-reinforcing—the better the company becomes, the better it can become. The most skilled entrepreneurs organize their ventures to ensure that all elements of the business model work toward this end. To the extent that this harmony cannot be fully achieved, the venture becomes vulnerable to its competitors and even to its customers. Selective neglect of one element of the business model, even while achieving excellence in others, seems to be a recipe for eventual disaster, as the text box story on page 26 suggests.

The Living Business Model

Most entrepreneurs do not begin with an entire business model, their understanding complete, their plans mature and ready to implement. Rather they shape and refine their business models as insight grows and experience accumulates. Indeed, reality compels such evolution. You will quickly reach the point where the value of further conceptualization diminishes sharply, and new information can be elicited only by trying something.

25

Figure 2.1 Basic Forces Driving the Business Model

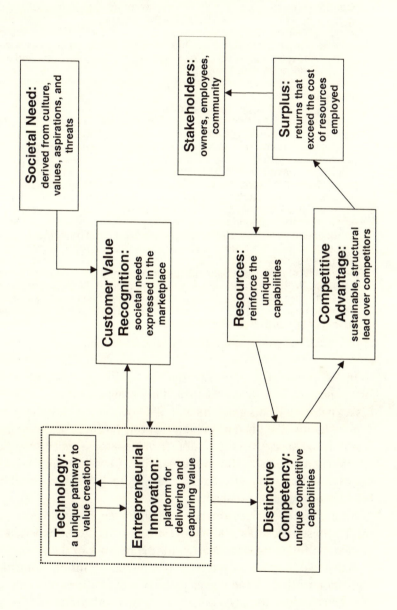

Stan Lapidus, founder of Itran, a supplier of advanced machine vision technology to the auto industry, notes the problems of a business model that emphasizes some components (like technology) but neglects others (like market understanding). Itran raised $15 million in venture capital, became a leading supplier to the auto companies, and enjoyed great technical success. But for all that, the company went on to fail financially, a consequence of misreading the nature of markets in the auto supply business.

First, the market for machine tools of any kind was fragmented, and that was especially true of advanced technologies like machine vision equipment. As a result, every sale was unique, and recurring revenue difficult to come by. This, in turn, required a large sales force, so that the gross profits were good but the net was not—hence leaving insufficient surplus to reinvest in new technologies and products. Itran's chief customer, General Motors, did not have a satisfactory way to understand and measure the value added by Itran, and so the value proposition could not be established. And finally, completing the ruin, recurring cycles of boom and bust in the auto industry would leave its suppliers without business for extended periods. Established companies operating in multiple markets can sometimes endure such cycles, but the entrepreneurial venture can rarely survive—the river runs down but the stream runs dry.

Would a clearer view of the market have helped the company survive? Probably. Would Itran have joined the 1 percent of high-growth companies? That is unknowable. In any case, Itran was acquired by Robotics Visioning Systems in 1995 and ceased to exist. The founders, once friends, no longer speak to one another.

In the case of EnerTech Environmental, for example, Kevin Bolin first conceived a licensing company built around a set of chemical processes patented by his grandfather. It did not become clear until the first demonstration plant had been built that this business model would not work. To be sure, the core customer value—the efficient and benign removal of municipal waste—remained firm. But a licensing model could not capture that value effectively, and EnerTech Environmental had to become an operating company.

Similarly, the business model for Nth Power Technologies evolved from a consultancy to a venture investment company as experience improved the founders' appreciation for the realities of the market. Even with that evolution, however, the founding market insight—that the deregulation of the electric power industry would afford rich and attractive opportunities for new companies—remained constant.

Though your business model will surely evolve with implementation, you have to start somewhere. Most technology entrepreneurs find their business models originate with one of three ideas: a market insight, as in the case of Nth Power; a technology insight, as in the case of EnerTech Environmental; or an organizational insight, the entrepreneurial innovation of Figure 2.1. But whichever insight becomes the point of departure, the enterprise must eventually comprehend all three or it simply will not work.

Market Insight: Necessity as the Mother of Invention

The market insight begins with the realization that a need, either unrecognized or previously thought unreachable, can be met with a tailored application of technology. Conventional technology often works best—consider the automobile in the 1950s. The prevailing wisdom held that an auto manufacturer had to offer a complete line of cars from the inexpensive to the luxurious. An increasingly affluent population would then (presumably) upgrade its car choice as an outward manifestation of new wealth.

Following this thinking, Ford introduced the Edsel in the 1950s to fill out the top end of its line. The new product, however, could not offer sufficient customer value, and by the end of the decade had become a manifest failure. But disaster and triumph are equal imposters, and the demise of the Edsel opened the way for the real market insight of the early 1960s—the "concept car," aimed at a particular lifestyle rather than economic class. Ford combined this design insight with purely conventional technology in the highly successful Mustang, which followed the Edsel to become one of Ford's most profitable ventures. A decade later, the full product-line strategy suffered further damage as Japanese and German automakers entered the U.S. market with only low-priced, fuel-efficient vehicles.

Technology Insight: Invention as the Mother of Necessity

The technology insight is most common among engineers and scientists, the golden moment in which they realize they can do something that nobody else, anywhere in the world, can do. The worldwide expansion of research and development suggests that technology-driven opportunities will only increase in the future. In the United States alone, research and development expenditures reached an estimated $265 billion in 2000, according to the National Science Foundation estimates (U.S. NSF: 2001). This is a bit less than 3 percent of that year's estimated GDP, which is consistent with recent experience.

New knowledge increases the ability of a company or a nation to create even more new knowledge in a cycle of self-reinforcing success. For example, the information technologies—computer hardware, advanced communications, and the software to link them—fuel this progress in fields ranging from space science to genetics and thus appear to drive a new industrial revolution. The United States, however, is not alone in recognizing the economic power of new technology, and research investment increases in like measure overseas. All this implies that technology-based opportunities will be more plentiful in the future—and so will the competition.

Entrepreneurial Innovation: The Midwife to Both

The ways that society conducts business have changed throughout history. Goods were first exchanged through simple barter, later with precious metals representing the actual goods, more recently by paper representing the value of the precious metals, and now by paper essentially representing itself. Each improvement in the method of exchange enabled improved processes for bringing goods and services to customers. Similarly, advances in information technology, especially the Internet, will enable new ways of doing business, and the organization itself—the entrepreneurial innovation of Figure 2.1—will increase its capacity to create customer value.

Dell Computer accomplished this most famously in the 1990s. Michael Dell recognized before his competitors did that the dynamics of the personal computer (PC) market were changing rapidly. At the heart of the matter, a set of standards had emerged that reduced production costs and gave PC customers a much-prized ability to switch among the PC brands. The lower production costs reduced one important barrier to entry. And, IBM's 1980 decision to outsource two key components of the personal computer—the microprocessor and the operating system (see page 65, Chapter 4)—left the new standards in the hands of the industry's suppliers, Intel and Microsoft. Thus, the ability for the PC makers to capture the value created by the PC eroded markedly.

In the market that emerged, a successful business model could be organized around direct channels to market, low-cost but effective customer service, and products built from standard components, yet offering performance enhancement in modular increments for customers who require it. The increasing availability of the public Internet reinforced this model—at no cost to Dell—by enabling more rapid fulfillment of customer orders. Estimates of the advantage conferred by the direct channel alone suggest a 10 percent to 15 percent cost reduction relative to competitors using a distributor/retailer model (Zook and Allen 2001: 47). The lower cost structure combined with greater customer value to give Dell higher profit margins than its competitors. And so, an entrepreneurial start-up successfully challenged the established industry giants with standard technology and an innovative business model.

Less celebrated but equally effective, entrepreneurs have responded to the financial carnage in the telecom industry to build value where others had built ruin. Throughout 2002 and into 2003, telecommunication companies around the world laid off employees and wrote off losses to pay the debts incurred in overbuilding their global networks. But the new, perhaps wiser, generation of entrepreneurs has taken the opposite approach—rather than owning global networks, they lease connections from traditional operators and weave them into a virtual network. In that way, the virtual network operators (VNOs) can tailor the connections to the geographic footprint of their customers, often large, multinational corporations. This provides two ancillary services: the VNOs isolate their customers from the risk of a single carrier going broke; and they can consolidate billing, relationships with telecom operators and regulators, procurement, and a host of nuisance activities. By serving as independent brokers of telecom services, the VNOs can ensure the best price for their customers and the latest technology on the wire. Thus, an innovative business model employs the same technology to beat the old business model at its own game—telecom services.

Other entrepreneurs, however, have suffered through a lengthy evolution of organizationally inspired business models. Consider the extended trial-and-error of the third-party business-to-business (B2B) marketplace, once among the most-hyped elements of electronic commerce. The generic business model for B2B began with the observation that any business can benefit from more effective purchasing of supplies and services—not much original there. However, the organization of purchasing as a third-party marketplace through an Internet portal was thought to add efficiencies having great value for traditional industries, especially in highly fragmented markets. It would, in effect, replace traditional supplier-customer relationships with an auction market. But, alas, there are many more ideas that ought to work than ideas that ever really do.

In the beginning (if that phrase can be used to describe events as recent as 1999–2000), several elements of the marketplace seemed to converge in favor of the third-party B2B model. Venture investment funds, historically undercapitalized, were flush with money from unions, pension funds, and the like. They supported the initial B2B exchanges, which capital markets often rewarded by eliminating profitability as a criterion for the initial public offering. At the same time, trendy business publications touted the new economy and the economic power of networks, which would set the new rules by which the competitive game would be played. And "old-economy" CEOs felt pressure to show their investors and their boards that they too were in the hunt for the new sources of value.

In fairness, this kind of third-party exchange probably did add some value. It was just not enough to sustain the B2B model as an independent business. In industrial supply markets, where margins were thin to begin with, most third-party B2Bs could not capture enough value to sustain themselves. Thus, an apparently promising business model failed for reasons that could not be seen a priori, but rather had to be learned in the school of hard knocks, where the tuition is quite expensive.

In their place, some industrial purchasers continued to use electronic data interchange (EDI), a generic software system that allows buyers and suppliers to exchange data, invoices, and payments directly, without the expense of a third party making the market for such transactions. EDI, however, must be wired individually for each customer-supplier pair, a costly, labor-intensive operation that lacks the flexibility of an open marketplace.

Others have set up captive B2B networks. For example, Covisint, an on-line exchange established in December 2000 as a joint venture among automakers, seeks to establish an auction market for suppliers to the partnership—chiefly DaimlerChrysler, Ford, General Motors, Nissan, Peugeot, and Renault. The Covisint system, however, proved unpopular with auto company suppliers, who recognize its potential to cut their margins more deeply than their costs. Further, the operation of Covisint has not been inexpensive for the auto companies, and the future of this business model seems clouded as of mid-2003.

Indeed, the Covisint model might be a further step, but not the end product, in the evolution of Internet-enabled business models. That claim might fall to a concept with an unpretentious name—Web services—but far-reaching consequences. Web services promises to tear down the Tower of Babel accumulated through years of isolated enterprise systems and enable unprecedented interoperability among information systems.

The Web services architecture, constructed on the Internet, would improve supply chain efficiencies by connecting the application software (reservations, inventory, billing, and the like) of any customer and supplier. These application systems cannot link well with one another because they vary widely in vintage and run on machines of widely disparate power. The Web services model would enable widespread interaction among all suppliers and customers without the overhead burden occasioned by the makers of third-party markets. Once the necessary standards and protocols are put in place, businesses will be able to connect their operations with suppliers and customers, cutting transaction costs and improving customer service. Ultimately, companies will be able to buy their information technologies as services provided over the Internet rather than owning and maintaining proprietary hardware and software.

Will the Web services concept overpromise and underdeliver, as so many other systems have in the past? Or will it become a powerful enabler of entrepreneurial innovation throughout all industrial supply chains? Those questions are now unanswerable. I can only observe that the basic business of entrepreneurs is not to guess the future but to build it. We can all look forward to learning what gets built.

Technology and the Business Model

In too many cases, the skills and interests of technologists lure them into an obsessive focus on their technology, leaving the remainder of the business model in relative disrepair. Yet a well-designed business model creates value in harmony with the design of the product or service. The basic elements of value creation and value capture reinforce one another to build for the enterprise a sustainable competitive advantage.

Consider, for example, the case of the electric-drive fuel-cell vehicle, now promoted by the federal government as a solution for two significant national concerns: carbon emissions from the burning of fossil fuels and the dependence on oil from the Persian Gulf. But the promise of the electric-drive vehicle is not new. Over 100 years ago, electric-drive vehicles also competed to relieve an environmental and health problem that threatened the growth of big cities: the excreta accumulating from the prime mover of the day, the horse. The outcome of that race would not depend exclusively on the relative merits of the competing technologies, but also on the relative strength of the competing business models.

A Horse Race

The problem was solved—or, at least, replaced with others—by gasoline-powered rather than electric vehicles. In part, this was due to the inherent limitations of the competing technologies, electric and steam. But reinforcing this difficulty, one of the most promising and capable proponents of the electric auto, the Electric Vehicle Company (EVC), wrapped the technology in a business model that proved ineffective in delivering customer value.

Historian David Kirsch notes that the EVC, "wary of entrusting the operation of their experimental electric vehicles to untrained and unsupervised drivers, opted to establish a limited cab service instead of directly selling or leasing the vehicles" (Kirsch 2000: 30). The company chose a vertically integrated business model in which the electric technology was bundled into a comprehensive service package. City dwellers seeking transportation could opt for a variety of conveyances ranging from electric cabs to electric trolleys. As Kirsch describes the EVC business model, "The stand-alone . . . automobile would be owned by [the] corporate entity, operated by its paid drivers, housed and maintained by the same experts who looked after the [electric] streetcars, and, most importantly, powered by electricity at the streetcar company's own generating station" (Kirsch 2000: 30).

In retrospect, this integrated service model proved too cumbersome relative to the value conferred on customers. By the early 1900s, consumer preferences had shifted decisively in favor of the competing model: the privately owned, independently operated, always available touring car, capable of excursions to the countryside as well as urban transportation. In this market, the limited range afforded by batteries contrasted with the growing availability of gasoline, initially offered in packages at general stores. The production economies becoming available through the mass-produced Model T completed the ruin, and by the 1920s the internal combustion engine had become king of the road.

Epilogue and Redemption

One hundred years later, interest in electric-drive vehicles has once again emerged, this time in response to concerns over global climate change and the security of oil supplies. But this time, the technology might prove a better mesh with the dominant business model. Hybrid electric vehicles are now on the market that combine: a conventional gasoline-fueled engine, employed as an electric generator; a more capable battery, serving as an electric "flywheel"; and an electric drive to convey the energy to the wheels. These are beginning to offer performance and cost sufficiently close to the internal combustion engine, but without the external drawbacks. Ultimately, the gasoline-fueled generator would be replaced by a fuel cell for even better economy and environmental performance. If successful, this would align the new electric technology with a central customer value, independent transportation, and so increase its likelihood of market penetration. Sometimes it takes a hundred years for the technology and business model to align well—but when they do, the combination can be formidable.

The Power of Technology: A Chilling Tale

Technology is a powerful creator of opportunity, but also a powerful destroyer. To understand the power of technology to attack a well-established business model, we must analyze the cycles of life and death of a business—that for making ice available when and where needed. This story has been ably summarized by James Utterback of the Massachusetts Institute of Technology (Utterback 1994: 146–57). Here, we interpret it in light of the basic forces driving the success of the business model, shown in Figure 2.1. The story illustrates the power of the self-reinforcing cycle to sustain a business—and the blindness that can result from success.

A nineteenth-century social critic once observed that the rich and the poor get the same amount of ice—the rich get theirs in the summer, and the poor get theirs in the winter. But in colonial America, the uneven distribution of ice was geographic, not social. In New England, reliably cold winters made farming and fishing impossible. In their place, New Englanders held an annual ice harvest in the communal tradition of corn husking, hog butchering, or barn raising. Entire communities would turn out to cut ice from the ponds and store it in ice houses for use over the rest of the year. The ice harvest began as a communitarian, not commercial, enterprise (Jones 1984: 15–20).

The Rise of a Business Model: The Ice Harvesters

By the early nineteenth century, Yankee entrepreneurs recognized that wealthy *seigneurs* in southerly climates would pay well for a cold drink in the summertime. They introduced a series of productivity-enhancing innovations and substituted the processes of business for the rituals of community. These innovations included (Utterback 1994: 148–49):

- For cutting the ice into uniform blocks that facilitated shipment, horse-drawn "ice plows" and mechanized tools were developed. When an unusually warm winter lowered the natural yield of a pond, water was pumped to the surface and allowed to freeze.
- For shipping the ice without undue melting, specialized wagons, vessels, and containers were developed.
- And for maintaining inventory, insulated ice houses were built, capable of preserving ice over a summer even in tropical locations as far removed as Havana.

Taken together, these new technologies turned hand-sawn ice into a commercial and marketable product. The price of ice, though volatile, fell quickly. For example, in Charleston, South Carolina, the price fell from $166 per ton in 1817 to $25 per ton by 1825 (Utterback 1994: 150). This contributed to market expansion, especially in the rapidly growing economy· of the southern United States. New applications for ice were enabled by the falling price: iced drinks, food preservation, medical uses, food transport, home iceboxes, year-round beer brewing, and similar social necessities. Price volatility, however, remained a problem for many customers whose use was discretionary.

A Business Model Illustrated

The ice harvesters had built their business around a model of extraordinary power, as shown in Figure 2.2. They recognized[2] that significant *customer value* could be created if ice could be delivered reliably in climates where it does not naturally occur. To realize that value, they adopted and continually improved a sophisticated harvesting *technology*. An *entrepreneurial innovation*, a highly efficient, integrated logistical system, enabled them to reach the market with their offering. Their *technology* and *entrepreneurial innovation* combined with the demographic and infrastructure advantages that they already enjoyed to build a *distinctive competence*. The result was a structural *competitive advantage*: to compete successfully, a rival would have to duplicate this entire infrastructure at scale and then endure the price wars inevitable in a

Figure 2.2 **Business Model: The Ice Harvesters**

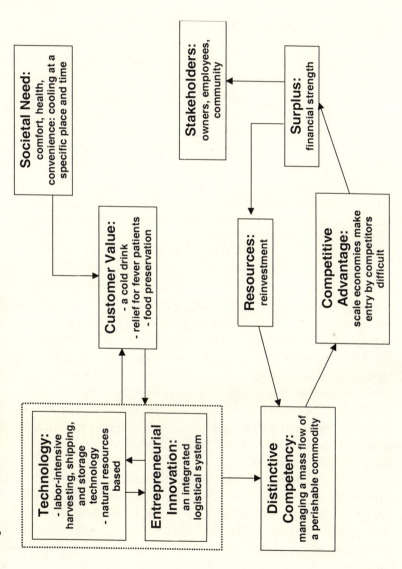

high-fixed-cost, commodity industry. With this structural advantage, the harvesters generated a financial *surplus* to share with stakeholders and to provide *resources* for reinvestment in the business.

No Southern Comfort

Even so, all was not well with the harvesters' customer base in the warmer climates. The problem derived from the seasonal nature of the commodity. Utterback observes that in the North, ice service was reasonably priced and widely available throughout the summer. But in the South, the long logistic system and harsh climate (for ice) raised prices in proportion to the distance the ice had to travel from its source. Exacerbating the difficulty, a poor harvest in New England or a surge in demand, perhaps due to emergencies like a yellow fever outbreak, would cause shortages and price spikes. Thus, the principal market for harvested ice grew increasingly receptive to innovations that would improve this situation.

Manufactured Ice

Scientists had discovered the basic principles of mechanical refrigeration by the mid-eighteenth century, but as is often the case, the supporting technologies—seals against leaks, precision machining, working fluids—were not adequate for commercialization. But by the 1850s, a series of inventions in the United States and Europe had yielded practical designs that incorporated the principal features of refrigeration as it is known today—a compressor, a condenser, an expansion valve, and an evaporator (Anderson 1953: 71–85). The widescale availability of efficient steam power enabled these machines to operate anywhere.

The Civil War delayed commercial introduction, but with peace, manufacturing plants sprang up throughout the southern United States. By 1869, 4 plants, all in the South, were manufacturing ice; a decade later, the number had reached 29; and in another decade, 165. In the coastal cities, the competition between harvested and manufactured ice was about even for a while, but this was little more than a rearguard action by the harvesters. Despite their best efforts, their market share had begun an irreversible decline by the 1890s (Anderson 1953: 86–90).

The Empire Strikes Back

The ice harvesters were not unaware of the manufacturers' intrusion into their profitable southern markets. They responded by reinforcing their well-proven business model (Figure 2.2). The harvesters introduced continual productivity improvements, such as steam-powered circular saws, and the entire logistic system from harvesting to storage to shipment and distribution became increasingly efficient. The New England ice harvesters also enjoyed structural economic advantages in addition to their climate: an ample supply of labor that was not engaged in fishing, farming, or logging during the winter; a well-developed transportation system; and generous supplies of key materials, such as sawdust for insulation. These improvements and the growing demand for ice in a newly prosperous America made the 1886 ice harvest the biggest in history. About 25 million tons were shipped that year, illustrating, as Utterback observes, how a rising market can effectively obscure the challenge to a business model posed by a new technology (Utterback 1994: 155).

All these improvements proved futile. The technology for mechanical ice making also gained rapidly in efficiency and product quality, and by the early twentieth century had spread around the world. By contrast, the investments of the ice harvesters yielded smaller and smaller improvements. Shipments plummeted, and ice-making plants even penetrated the New England ice market.

By radically changing the technology, the manufacturers changed the rules of the competitive game, rendering moot the distinctive competencies and natural advantages of the ice harvesters. They did not attack the harvesters' business model directly. Rather, they made the central competitive skill of the ice harvesters—managing the mass flow of a tricky and highly perishable material throughout the world—irrelevant to delivering customer value. Few of the ice-harvesting companies that had been so prosperous for decades adopted the mechanical refrigeration technology, despite the enormous economic opportunity that it created. Lacking skills in dispersed manufacturing, the opportunity offered by the new technology was unrecognizable to the harvesters. Instead, their companies lost market share and ultimately failed in competition with the superior business model of Figure 2.3. In effect, a radical technological innovation changed the fundamental nature of competition in the ice industry.[3]

38

Figure 2.3 Business Model: The Ice Manufacturers

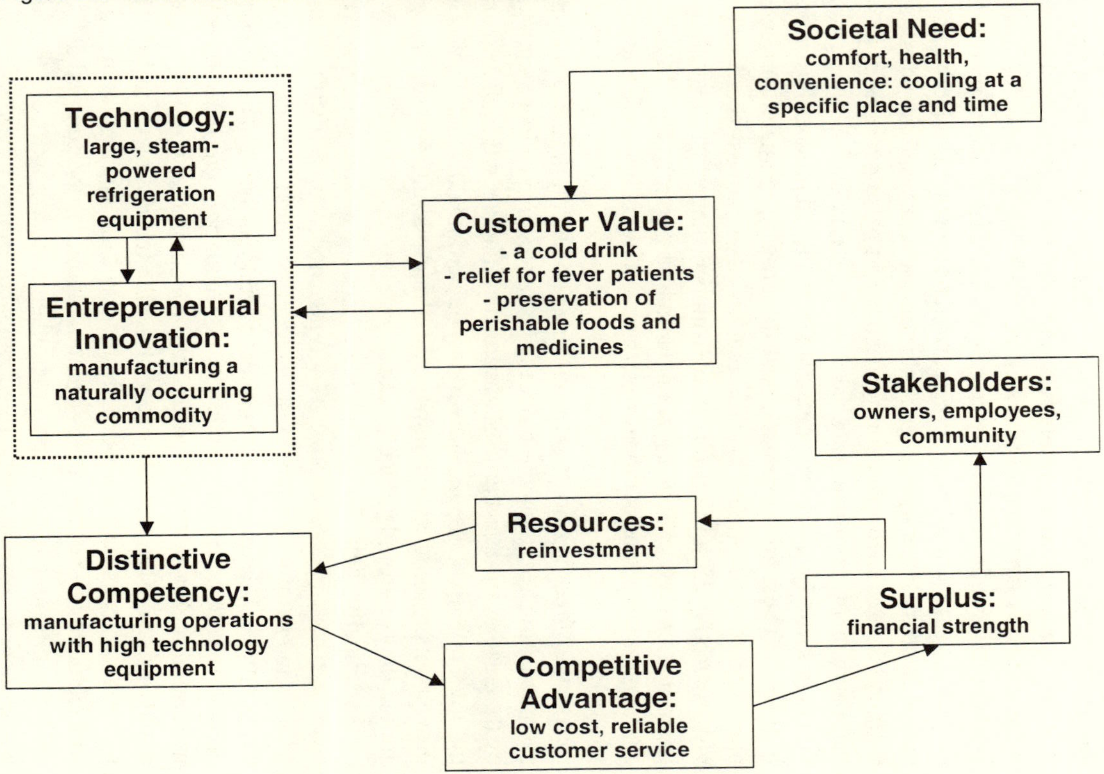

Societal Need:
comfort, health, convenience: cooling at a specific place and time

Customer Value:
- a cold drink
- relief for fever patients
- preservation of perishable foods and medicines

Stakeholders:
owners, employees, community

Surplus:
financial strength

Resources:
reinvestment

Competitive Advantage:
low cost, reliable customer service

Technology:
large, steam-powered refrigeration equipment

Entrepreneurial Innovation:
manufacturing a naturally occurring commodity

Distinctive Competency:
manufacturing operations with high technology equipment

Electric Refrigeration: The Rules Change Again

The ice story has a postscript. Unobserved by either the ice harvesters or the ice manufacturers, a cluster of innovations was emerging that would once again upset the competitive balance. These included the widespread availability of electric energy in the major cities, and the increasing availability of compact and efficient electric motors and refrigeration equipment. These were combined in the electric refrigerator, which allowed an arbitrarily cool space to be "manufactured" on the customers' premises wherever a source of electric energy could be found.

The ice manufacturers could not compete with the additional value in time saved and convenience that on-premises refrigeration equipment provided. By the 1930s, half the nation's homes were equipped with some kind of refrigerator, and market penetration reached 85 percent when manufacture was curtailed by World War II (Anderson 1953: 220–21). Blocks of ice from any source simply became obsolete in every application from home refrigerators to cold storage to refrigerated rail cars. And so the ice manufacturing industry also died, not because it became uncompetitive, but because it became irrelevant to what customers were really seeking—not ice as a product, but rather custom refrigeration services for the home. Nor could the individual companies adapt; the new home refrigeration technology was too far outside their skill set. And so technology had once again changed the rules of the competitive game and rendered a powerful business model obsolete.

The competitive dynamics of this century-long saga of entrepreneurship and change, summarized in Figure 2.4, are at work today as the products and services of the real new economy emerge to displace the old. And if history holds true, this change will occur in ways that are invisible to the current market incumbents.

The Purposeful Search for Opportunity

For some few entrepreneurs, opportunity recognition comes in a flash of insight. But the more common experience suggests that finding the right opportunity results from purposeful search—the systematic application of analytical, conceptual, and perceptual skills to the quest for economic value.

Figure 2.4 The Dynamics of Market Change

Figure 2.4. The Dynamics of Market Change

Business Model Implications of Business Model for…	Ice Harvesters	Ice Manufacturers	Home Refrigeration
Customer Value	Ice as a luxury good - Availability limited - Highly variable price	Ice as a mainstream commodity - Widely available - Affordable, steady price	Refrigeration services
Technology	Advantage derived from natural endowment	Large steam powered refrigeration equipment	Enabling inventions - Electric energy - Compact refrigeration cycles - Electric motors
Competency Required	Integrated international logistics system for highly perishable commodity	Manufacturing and local distribution for highly perishable commodity	Consumer durable goods supplier
Entry Barriers	High - Scale of operation - New England location	Moderate Customer relations	Moderate Brand and market channels

The Insights of Customers

One way to recognize opportunity—or the threat of irrelevance in your own business model—is to observe the behavior of those closest to the need: the customers. Oftentimes inventive customers simply want an improved technology for their own purposes; they do not wish to be in the business of producing it. These customers can be the inventors of improvements to the current technology and even occasionally of breakthrough technologies (von Hippel 1988).

Jones's history of ice notes that a physician from Apalachicola, Florida—Dr. John Gorrie—patented a refrigeration machine in 1851. At first, Gorrie had no wish to be in the ice business, but rather was seeking an air conditioning device to cool the fever of his malaria patients. For the air conditioner to function, however, he needed a reliable and economic source of ice. The ice harvesters could not provide that, and so he set out to make it himself. Gorrie, however, soon recognized the larger value of his invention and turned from customer to entrepreneur. He attempted a commercial ice-making plant in New Orleans, but a series of personal and financial failures caused the venture to collapse. His skills at business could not match his brilliance as an inventor, and John Gorrie died in 1855, a pauper (Jones 1984: 150–51).

The ultimate in customer innovation is open-source software, where customers are encouraged to design applications of value to themselves and submit these designs for inclusion in the standard software package. Yet the practice can be found across a wide spectrum of businesses. Thomke and von Hippel have observed a growing set of industries in which companies use the knowledge of their customers for product innovation. In industries as diverse as plastics and computer chips, suppliers provide their customers with "tool-kits" that enable them to custom design the products they really want (Thomke and von Hippel 2002). In effect, this makes the "customer value recognition" of Figure 2.1 more efficient by reducing the trial-and-error iterations between developer and customer. Customer insight as a pathway to opportunity recognition can favor either incremental innovation, the competitive strength of the market incumbent, or radical innovation, the province of the entrepreneur.

Radical Innovation in Mature Markets

The ice story, and much other evidence, suggests that market incumbents have a distinct advantage in making incremental refinements within the context of their current business models. By contrast, the attack of radical innovation can make these improvements irrelevant, changing the very basis for competition. Eventually some variant of the radical triumphs over the incremental, which should be a great encouragement to entrepreneurs and consumers in every time and place. Were it not so, we would still be using harvested ice—or perhaps none at all.

Effective Search for Opportunity

Peter Drucker notes that an effective search requires deep knowledge of where to look for innovative opportunities and the discipline to pursue that search in a systematic manner (Drucker 1985). I suggest that the point of departure for such a search be your own unique advantage as an entrepreneur—special knowledge of the market, of a field of technology, or of an innovative form of organization. In the case of EnerTech Environmental, for example, the search was technology-driven, a search for confirmation that the concepts and inventions pioneered by Bolin's grandfather actually could be made to work in a commercial operation. In the case of Nth Power Technologies, the search was opportunity-driven, springing from the new economic relations that utility deregulation would bring. But in any case, this purposeful search for opportunity calls for skill in marketing and a deep understanding of technology markets, and to those subjects we must now turn.

3

Marketing the Better Mousetrap

A Technologist's Perspective

> In the field of observation, chance favors
> only the prepared minds.
> —*Louis Pasteur*

Building the better mousetrap is a great intellectual achievement; but to make it a great economic achievement, you have to sell some. The pathway to sales runs through marketing, the management process that clarifies your understanding of customer value and guides you in shaping your enterprise to deliver that value. This chapter offers three perspectives on the marketing process, considerations too often neglected by technology professionals amid the clamor of new enterprise development:

- Understanding your offering the way a customer values it—not as an innovation, but as a package of innovative services;
- Discerning which kinds of customer are likely to yield the first sale and which will comprise the large, mainstream market; and
- Learning what markets are trying to tell you and responding appropriately.

Technology as Service

The journey from technology professional to technology entrepreneur begins with a loss of innocence, a replacement of the technocentric view of the world with one that is more customer-centered. It begins with a view of the technology, not as a tangible object, but as a package of valuable services. Customers have little use for products as objects. They have great use for the services these objects provide. For example, nobody buys a lightbulb for its own sake, but rather for the expectation of illumination on a desk, in a room, or some other useful place. Similarly, computer software can be purchased as a tangible product or conveniently downloaded from the Internet. Either way, its only important features are the services it provides the user.

Try a little self-test in applying this service concept of technology: Imagine how you might offer your product as a package of services rather than as an object. Suppose you are in the lightbulb business. You might then imagine a service that pays the customer's electric bill and guarantees a quantity of light (specified in lumens) and quality of light (color, flicker, and so forth) at desk level in large office buildings—all for a fixed monthly fee. Then, ask yourself whether this service would be strengthened by using a different kind of lightbulb than the one you offer? Or if you are a software developer, you might imagine your software as resident on a remote file server rather than the computer of the user. Could this form of service delivery provide additional value to your customers? If so (or even if not), you will have learned something valuable about your product. And that is the entire point of this thought-experiment—not to design an alternative business, but rather to illuminate the real value that your product holds from the perspective of your customers.

The Dimensions of Performance

To understand the markets for technology, we must begin with the customer's perspective of the offering as a package of services. These services form the basic elements of value that buyers are seeking: speed, convenience, economy, prestige, and so forth. For each of these attributes, more tends to be of greater value than less, and so they can be viewed as performance dimensions along which market rivals compete. Taken together, performance dimensions define for each product or service a "competitive space" as illustrated in Figure 3.1.

Simple products, a haircut or a pencil, tend to compete along one or perhaps two performance dimensions. The pencil, for example, would be characterized chiefly by economy; people don't want to pay very much for something they are always losing, and in any case can be found lying around everywhere.

By contrast, complex technology products—a passenger aircraft, for example—compete along many more dimensions, some of recognizable importance to the market, but others subtle and unrevealed. The builders of the only supersonic transport, the recently retired Concorde, carefully engineered the compromise among competing desiderata such

Figure 3.1 Performance Space
   Simplified performance dimensions for an aircraft—complex
   products typically have more than the three that can be shown
   grapically. These define the performance space within which
   rivals compete.

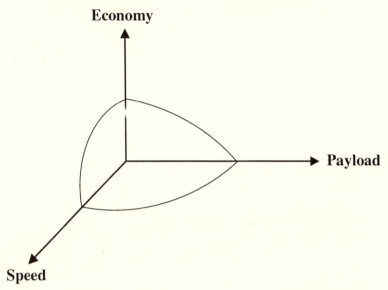

as speed, range, or payload. But to the Concorde's economic performance was added the value of national prestige, often poorly articulated
as "leadership," but apparently prized by the sponsoring nations above
mere economic considerations. The challenge in discerning all the dimensions of customer value is to identify these poorly articulated or
even unspoken components of value and include them in the package
you offer. Consider the following tale.

The Dynamics of Performance

The competitive space of Figure 3.1 changes over time as the performance dimensions themselves evolve, and so tilts the playing field to
the advantage of competitors who understand the dynamics of the marketplace. The principal sources of change in the performance valued by
customers include:

  • *Customer Limitations.* Sometimes customers are unable to use further improvements along some dimensions. Consider the clock speed of

On Products and Services: The Parable of the Nails[1]

For want of a nail, the shoe is lost;
For want of a shoe, the horse is lost;
For want of a horse, the rider is lost.
—*George Herbert, 1640*

Imagine yourself the inventor of a better horseshoe nail back in the days when the most important communications were carried by mounted messenger. The king has just announced a major procurement of horseshoe nails for his dispatch riders, and you determine to bid.

With your superior technology, you can undercut the best price that the competition—a well-established firm called General Nailworks—can offer and still command a handsome margin. So, you submit your bid and sit back to await your contract, no doubt to be brought by dispatch rider. But what comes is not a contract at all. It is the announcement that General Nailworks has won the procurement.

Stunned and confused, you seek solace in dialectic mysticism and a stiff drink (in reverse order of effectiveness). Upon later reflection, however, you understand what you had missed before—that some apparently simple products can compete on dimensions not seen by the casual observer. Your bid assumed that the market would treat horseshoe nails as a commodity, and in that kind of market, the lowest bid should win. For some horseshoe nail customers, that assumption might be valid; but the royal messengers had a special, though unstated, requirement.

Because of the known importance of good horseshoe nails to message, battle, and war, the king in effect bought a two-part package: the nails themselves, and the assurance of uniform quality and timely delivery implied by the size and reputation of General Nailworks. Thus, the winning bid included an implicit and unsolicited service warranty packaged with the product. You bid on the nails, but neither recognized nor countered the implied service offer of General Nailworks.

In fact, your advanced technology worked against you. Horseshoe nail failure had never been much of a problem, and even when horseshoes were lost, it was usually traceable to deferred maintenance, a difficulty in all ages. Thus, most customers thought the old nail design and materials were quite satisfactory. Your advanced technology, unproven in use, actually added an element of risk to the buyer's decision. The king's procurement officer was unlikely to be executed for paying a bit more for the General Nailworks product. But if he chose your untried nails and they failed, any savings would be forgotten and heads would roll.

You now realize that every technology product offers a blend of service attributes. Some are obvious to buyers and sellers alike; others are made explicit by the buyer; and still others remain obscure to the seller and unarticulated by the buyer. Next time you won't be beaten so easily.

the microprocessors used in personal computers, for example. Since the 1980s, chip manufacturers have focused on speed, measured in megahertz or gigahertz, as the most important dimension of microprocessor performance. This attention was well placed, as PC users needed greater speed to operate the increasingly complex software required for business and personal applications. But, little noticed in the computer boom of the late 1990s, user demand for increased clock speed was diminishing. Most PC users no longer required the fastest chip to run common applications, so customer value could be built only by attention to other dimensions of performance: size, cost, and energy efficiency. Or, consider automobiles: increased speed has diminished value, as a host of spoilsports, from insurance companies to the State Police, inhibit drivers from using all that capacity. Finally, think of the whitening agents in household detergents: though further improvement is chemically possible, the current products already advance whiteness beyond the ability of the human eye to detect.

• *Experience.* With use, a product's customers discover which performance dimensions have the greatest value for them, and competition turns to those. The rest are put in the "good-enough" box and forgotten.

• *External Events and Trends.* A host of occurrences, quite apart from the workings of the market, can influence the performance desired by customers. For example, nothing spurs consumer interest in the fuel economy of vehicles like an oil supply disruption in the Middle East. Or, consider the greatly increased participation of women in the labor force that occurred in the 1970s and 1980s. This reduced the discretionary time available to consumers and added convenience as a desideratum for every product or service.

• *Technical Improvements.* New technology, often from apparently unrelated fields, enables better performance along some dimensions. Information technology, for example, has improved the safety and reliability of nuclear power plants in ways not imagined by their designers—indeed, information technology improves the performance of just about anything.

• *Lack of Technical Improvements.* Sometimes a technology reaches the point where further improvements run into physical limits that cannot be overcome—for example, the inherent limits to the speed of sailing ships or to reducing the bulk of electronic systems that use vacuum tubes.

Market Planning: First Sale to Mainstream Market

Nothing builds credibility like sales. Employee morale rises as the payroll becomes supportable—and so does yours. Investors take the company more seriously, and a sale to one customer often begets another. Thus much can be gained from building cash and credibility with sales that occur as early in the venture's growth process as possible. But, as always, there is a catch—these early sales must spring from a well-conceived marketing plan that focuses your scarce resources on the mainstream customers most likely to build your business. To be sure, cash from any sale helps. But failure to focus your marketing efforts can lead your new company away from the larger, more attractive markets that make the gain from entrepreneurship worth its pain. Indeed, the best marketing plans view early sales as having one overriding purpose: to serve as a point of departure for the mainstream markets that will become the ultimate source of sustainable growth for your company. Failing to reach the mainstream leaves you in that shadow-land of companies that neither grow nor die, but rather scratch out a hardscrabble existence and eventually fade into irrelevance.

Analyzing your technology as a service offering with an attendant package of performance dimensions will help create such a plan. But in addition, you must discern which of your potential customers are likely to respond well to innovative technology and which are not. Everything else will flow from that.

Leaders and Laggards

In an attempt to understand why some farmers adopted new agricultural innovations, the U.S. Department of Agriculture developed a model for technology marketing in the 1930s. This model, now a classic in marketing textbooks, sorts potential customers for a new technology into five categories:

- *Innovators.* These customers actively seek change, sometimes for its own sake, and turn first to new-technology solutions. The technology itself is a core interest for them. Alas, they are a distinct minority of your ultimate customer set.
- *Early Adopters.* These customers relate easily to the technology and comprehend its benefits readily. However, they are less interested in the technology for its own sake than for its ability to solve practical problems. More numerous than the innovators, they remain a minority in your customer base.
- *Early Majority.* These customers will be the first to make wide-

scale use of your technology, as they comprise about one-third of the total customer population. They also appreciate technology, but only insofar as its adoption to solve a problem does not cause undue risk. For them, some demonstration that the technology works as advertised is essential to reducing this risk.

- *Late Majority.* Approximately another third of your customers can be considered late adopters. Much less able to handle an innovative technology with skill, they tend to await its becoming an industry standard before adopting. They will also require a lot of support.
- *Laggards.* Laggards tend to focus on price and do not adopt new technology unless it is embedded so deeply in a system that it becomes invisible. Do not bother with these customers—life is too short.

Each generic customer type has unique needs, and hence a unique approach to value. Early adopters, for example, are motivated by their search for a solution, often to a problem that cannot be addressed without innovation, and they are willing to take the risks that attend first-of-a-kind technologies. By contrast, customers in the early majority seek technology with a track record of successful performance, and they respect the opinion of their peers as verification of that performance. These distinctions require that you tailor the package of services your product provides to the customer type you are serving.

Early Sales

Your first sales will come from innovators and early adopters, who should be approached as the visionaries that they are. For example, such persons oftentimes recognize the social dimensions of a product and purchase it for those values, notwithstanding its economics. One such product, solar power, offers a distinct social benefit—environmental improvement—because it can be installed on customers' premises to displace electric power generated by fossil fuels. Even with best practice, the burning of fossil fuels leaves some environmental imprint, and many power plants fall well short of best practice. Thus, the photovoltaic panels that produce electricity directly from sunlight find a ready market among environmentally concerned visionaries and have provided early sales for twenty-five years.

Penetrating mainstream markets, however, has proved to be a greater challenge. The difficulty is cost. Once the solar panels are installed, the sunlight is free—though only intermittently available. But at any reasonable discount rate, the value of electricity savings to the customer cannot overcome capital cost of the installed equipment.[2] And so, these solar panels tend to sprout from the rooftops of *innovators* and *early adopters*, who add the psychic value of pollution forgone to their cost savings; but no analogous value proposition has been found for mainstream markets. As a result, solar power remains confined to boutique applications.

To Swim in the Mainstream

In a path-breaking analysis, Geoffrey Moore calls the transition into mainstream markets the most difficult challenge of high-technology marketing. The difficulty derives from the social structure of the five customer categories. Moore contends that markets cannot be understood entirely in economic terms: the recognizable set of actual or potential customers with similar needs and values. In addition, likeminded market participants often reference each other in making their buying decisions, especially in mainstream markets, where risk tolerance is lower and the opinions of experienced colleagues more highly prized (Moore 2002: 28). For these *early majority* customers, your success with the *innovators* and the *early adopters* holds little relevance—they just do not talk to those people. And so you must plan your entry into the market mainstream to account for this communication gap between your first customers and those who will become your largest market.

The invasion of a mainstream market enjoys all the operating characteristics of the Normandy invasion: you first establish the beachhead, then you stabilize your foothold, and finally you break out to capture the market territory (Moore 2002). Let's follow Moore's reasoning to see where it leads. Most technology companies begin with a "beachhead" in the new market—a niche that is underserved but relevant to the mainstream because its customers are the mainstream customers. In the beginning, this beachhead will command resources entirely out of proportion to the sales that it generates. For that reason, it might well be ignored by a sales-driven business. But for the market-driven business, it builds the customer base within the mainstream market, customers who will later provide the references and credibility essential for the growth of sales.

Your basic offering might have to be revised as you consider how the performance dimensions of your product appear to these customers, and especially what kinds of support services they will require to adopt the technology. But above all, keep your goal in sight—to establish a critical mass of customers in the mainstream market who will serve as references for your offering to other customers in that same market.

To accomplish this, you need to husband your (always scarce) marketing resources and invest them in a few strategic niches in the mainstream market. The first few yards of beachhead will not do and neither will a handful of customers. Your goal is to become the market leader within those critical market niches, because the pragmatists who inhabit the *early majority* and *late majority* territory tend to buy from the market leader. And once established, the word-of-mouth advertising of the satisfied customers will beat any campaign that you could wage.

Some Additional Considerations

Just as the market territory is new to you, so your offering is new to the market territory. In the case of breakthrough products, customers simply might not understand the usefulness of your offering or know how to evaluate its features. Some introductions might be in order, and in the beginning your marketing plan should emphasize education over sales— a notion called concept marketing. You should begin by engaging credible sources, not to promote your specific product but to educate customers into the need for something that functions as it does. You can build the education campaign around books, mention by publicly credible persons, presentations at conferences, and other channels perceived to be less biased than traditional advertising. Once you have helped potential customers understand the need and the various means for satisfying it, you can then provide evidence that your offering does the job best (Waite, Cohen, and Buday 1999).

Price, a second consideration, is more than just a number. An effective pricing strategy not only helps you gain new customers but also prevents you from losing those you have already acquired. Yet advances in technology are making effective pricing more difficult than ever. For example, the Internet tends to shift control of transactions to the customers for many goods and services. Customers can compare prices much more efficiently over the Internet, and can often become price-makers instead of price-takers. As price becomes the determining issue

Consumer Acceptance of a New Technology:
The Return of Broadband

Actually, broadband never went away. Masked by the demise of many broadband providers in the dot-com debacle, customer use of this technology around the world is accelerating. Even as many broadband providers collapsed under the weight of ill-conceived debt, consumer use soared according to recent research by the McKinsey consultancy: 15 percent growth in the Americas from the fourth quarter of 2001 through the second quarter of 2002; 31 percent for the Asia-Pacific region; and 46 percent for Europe. As a result, about 94 million households in the United States are now within reach of a broadband connection, with about 15 million actual subscribers (Beardsley, Doman, and Edin 2003).

This market growth follows the classic pattern of technology adoption. During the launch phase, the market consists of *innovators* and *early adopters*, perhaps 10 percent of all households according to McKinsey. For these customers, the broadband connection solves a special need for home office productivity—or perhaps simply gratifies a yearning to have the most advanced toys. In much of the West, these early markets appear to have been saturated, and the technology is crossing into the mainstream. In the United States, for example, only 13 percent of all households subscribed to this service as of mid-2002. During the expansion phase, another 40 percent of the potential market, the *early majority*, is likely to subscribe. These customers are attracted by the utility and convenience of the broadband connection, less concerned with cool technology, and more sensitive to price. The broadband market will eventually become saturated as *late majority* customers subscribe, perhaps another 40 percent of the market. Some of the smaller Asian markets—South Korea, Hong Kong, and Singapore—might be approaching saturation at present (Beardsley, Doman, and Edin 2003).

This mostly early-stage market presents a striking opportunity for entrepreneurs who can deliver what the mainstream markets are seeking: compelling content. The first customers wanted the connection for its own sake, or to meet some special need. The early dot-coms failed in part because they could not see beyond those early customers and develop business models suited to the mainstream. And so the mainstream customers were slow to appear.

These *early majority* customers will have to be attracted by a package of convenience, price, and content/applications that are worth that price. Just as the first mainstream customers for the personal computer needed a compelling application to complete the value package (the spreadsheet, either through Lotus or VisiCalc), so too will broadband customers. And as the mainstream broadband customers enter the market, the nature of the opportunity will change. The broadband connection will quickly become the commodity, ceding the opportunities for differentiated products to the application and content providers.

in purchasing decisions, the tendency toward commoditization of your product is accelerated.

A recent analysis of entrepreneurial pricing in this dynamic business environment suggested that the most successful companies follow four strategies (Schindehutte and Morris 2001):

- base your price on the value of your offering to the customer rather than your cost to produce;
- be willing to assume the risk of novel pricing strategies, such as offering separate prices for unbundled services;
- use these novel strategies proactively without waiting for competitors to initiate the pricing action; and
- remain flexible in pricing, allowing variances in both offering and price based on market segment and the price elasticities of classes of users.

Successful execution of these strategies requires a deep understanding of the customer and continuous tracking of changes in marketplace dynamics. To gain this understanding, you must view marketing as a learning process, not a selling process—and to this concept we turn next.

Marketing as Learning

Marketing wisdom begins with understanding your offering as a package of services. It ends with understanding the value function of the customer—the package of services that people actually want to use in work and living. You must learn to analyze customers and markets from their own framework and logic, rather than forcing them to respond to your framework and logic. The process for accomplishing this is called organizational learning, and its concepts can help the new venture start-up and established company alike.

Learning in Organizations

Chapter 2 introduced the idea that customer innovation provides one way to recognize an opportunity. And in many cases, your customers actually invent the products for you to sell to them—recall that Dr. John Gorrie invented the first commercially practical refrigeration system, not because he sought a new business opportunity, but rather to cool the fever of his malaria patients. While customer innovation can serve well as the initial market insight, these early conditions change radically and swiftly as the market matures. To build a sustainable enterprise, you must train your organization to discern more subtle market signals and to respond effectively to them—to become a learning organization.

Organizational development professionals distinguish between two kinds of learning (Senge 1990): *adaptive learning* in which the organization seeks new insights within a set of self-imposed boundaries that reflect its assumptions about itself and its business environment; and *generative learning* in which the enterprise questions its internal framework of assumptions about its mission, capabilities, strategy, and value to customers.

In taking the dominant logic as its point of departure, *adaptive learning* is highly focused and efficient. Much market research follows this pattern: surveys of customer response to proposed product features, focus groups that chart reactions to advertisements, and the like. The demonstration plant that EnerTech Environmental built for the Japanese consortium (Chapter 1) is another example—the learning was concentrated around the engineering and market assumptions designed into the plant. Some assumptions were validated and some were not, but the demonstration by itself offered no new hypotheses about the market. Those had to be generated separately.

Though focused and efficient, *adaptive learning* tends to concentrate the solution space within the same framework of assumptions. Thus the actions taken in response to the learning tend to be sequential and incremental. These actions are often constrained to mesh with the current set of core capabilities, which can become "core rigidities" as they inhibit innovation (Leonard-Barton 1992).

By contrast, *generative learning* requires you to develop new ways of understanding the world and the relationship of your new venture to it. Thus it is more likely to suggest breakthrough strategies than *adaptive learning*, as a classic study of motor vehicle manufacturing demonstrates (Stalk 1988). By the late 1980s, manufacturers around the world were seeking a source of competitive advantage beyond the flexible factory paradigm that dominated strategic thinking. Most recognized that effective use of time would become the next decisive competitive advantage, and those who managed well the time required to execute basic business processes would lower their costs, improve quality, and enhance their ability to respond to shortened market cycles. Manufacturers who sought answers outside the range of their habitual assumptions were able to redefine their basic business processes in ways that cut cycle time dramatically. Those who sought answers within the domain of their current systems and processes did succeed in making them more efficient. But they failed to grasp the strategic advantage that other manufacturers found in reducing their response time across the entire manufacturing enterprise.

Each approach to organizational learning offers limitations and advantages. An exclusive focus on *generative learning* can leave you with more possibilities than you can reasonably pursue, all of which seem equally plausible and equally attractive. It leads to the classic "paralysis by analysis." Further, breakthrough strategies can be swiftly imitated, and continuous breakthrough innovation is difficult to sustain. Thus, you must strike a balance among learning styles, selecting the externally focused or the internally focused as appropriate to the situation. You must exercise the kind of judgment that you get paid for.

Managing the Learning Process

New ventures that are launched from a corporate platform can take advantage of the contacts and learning processes of the parent company. But for the independent start-up, systematic contacts with key constituent groups, not involving transactions, must be built. One way to accomplish this is through a board of advisers.

A carefully chosen board of advisers can provide you with the insights into the realities external to your own enterprise and help you find the right balance among learning styles. In most cases, you will have to compensate these persons with a small equity stake in your company. But if you select persons of independence and broad knowledge, that investment will repay itself handsomely.

As a practical matter, the first "organizational learning" will take place inside your own head and the heads of your partners. Thus you must begin by doing your own market research. Consider, for example, the experience of Stan Lapidus, founder of Itran, later of Cytyc, a company offering advanced testing for cervical cancer, and most recently of Exact Sciences, which seeks a leading role in the eradication of common cancers, especially colorectal cancer, through early detection.

The Power of Market Research

In the late 1980s, while the struggle with Itran continued, Stan Lapidus began experimenting in his basement with a new technology for the Pap test, a standard screening method for cervical cancer named for its inventor, Dr. George Papanicolaou. An electrical engineer by training, Lapidus built the technical foundation for what would later become Cytyc from his accustomed discipline. But an entrepreneur by inclination, Lapidus avoided the easy assumptions about market acceptance. Instead, he worked to understand the key elements of customer value in cancer screening, and especially the ways that customers could recognize that value in Cytyc's products. During the first 12 months of operation, he spent $120,000 on market research in contrast with $80,000 on product engineering, a ratio of 1.5 to 1.

The market understanding paid off handsomely. With market research leading the engineering, Lapidus recognized that the real customer problem was not reading the Pap smear slides once they had been taken, but rather the preparation of the slides. Thus Cytyc changed its initial product concept, a machine-vision Pap smear reader, to automated technology for preparing the slides. The product became a striking success. Cytyc attracted about $44 million in venture capital investment, and offered its stock to the public in 1996. More important, the company was a success in the competitive marketplace, and investors rewarded it with a market capitalization of $1.7 billion in late 2003.

Reflecting on that experience, Lapidus now considers the ratio of marketing effort to engineering effort a key performance metric for any new technology venture.[3] In starting his next company, Exact Sciences, in 1995, Lapidus spent 2.3 times as much on market research as on engineering. The point is not that engineering is unimportant—plainly the technology has got to work. Rather, the point is that engineering should be guided by a clear view of the marketplace and of the performance that will create true customer value.

As the enterprise grows, you should build your marketing organization around open-minded people with a capacity to shed assumptions when the evidence of the marketplace requires it. At heart, successful entrepreneurship is a market-driven process, and so we must next turn our attention to understanding the salient characteristics of the technology marketplace.

4

Evolution and Competition
in Technology Markets

> To everything there is a season, and a time
> for every purpose under heaven.
> —*Ecclesiastes, 3.1*

Every innovation, large or small, vital or trivial, lives or dies within a specific context—a context of cultural expectations and constraints, of economic imperatives, of institutional capabilities and limitations, and of technology opportunities. Some of this context is obvious. But much more is subtle and unspoken. All of these external forces shape the marketplace that surrounds the new venture. The most discerning entrepreneurs listen to and understand that market context.

In like manner, many venture investors view market context as a primary driver of entrepreneurial success. Venture capitalist Don Valentine, noted for the consistently high performance of his investments, seeks opportunities in markets that offer possibilities for explosive growth, thereby overcoming the mistakes that will inevitably be made, even by a skilled management team (Katz 1996: 139–40). Or, as Warren Buffett once observed, good jockeys do better on good horses (Buffett and Cunningham 1998: 95).

This chapter concerns market context—the dynamic structure of technology markets, and especially their tendency to evolve in recognizable patterns. Each phase offers distinct opportunities for entrepreneurs as well as special limitations, and the competitive game is played differently in each. You will need to know the rules, especially if you intend to change them. Chapter 5 continues this theme by addressing special characteristics of technology markets that accelerate or retard their evolution: disruptive technologies, the path dependency of technology, the close links between technology and society, and the explosive growth of technological change.

The Technology Market Cycle

Technology markets tend to evolve over time in discernible, but not predictable, patterns. And as the technology game changes, so does the capacity for entrepreneurship, either independently or from a corporate platform, to create and capture economic value. This is because the basis for competition swings from major innovation in the product to increasingly incremental innovation in process technology and finally to nontechnology distinctions in a mature market. This pattern of innovation has been observed in industries as diverse as autos, commercial jet aircraft, glass, and computer chips (Utterback 1994). The three general phases that characterize technology markets, shown in Figure 4.1, draw inspiration from the general model for innovation proposed by the late professor William Abernathy of the Harvard Business School (Abernathy 1978) and later refined by James Utterback (Utterback 1994).

The vertical axis of Figure 4.1 represents the propensity for major innovation. Innovations are considered in two classes: *product innovations*, involving technological change in the product itself, and *process innovations*, advances in the way it is manufactured and delivered. The horizontal axis measures the time over which the market cycle plays out. The labels for each phase reflect the entrepreneur's perspective, and seek to capture the effect of marketplace dynamics on the new enterprise—*A Thousand Flowers*, for the blossoming of many competitors and market offerings; *The Weed Whacker*, for the transition period in which these companies and offerings are pruned; and *The Return of the Suits*, for the more incremental, institutional innovation that characterizes competition in mature businesses. Though far from a law of nature, this model seems at least a central tendency.

Sometimes these phases pass slowly, but more recently they have passed at a dizzying pace. Consider the early days of news delivered by Internet, for example. By the late 1990s, a group of upstart news and Internet-content companies, largely based in the San Francisco area, were posing a serious challenge to the established East Coast news media. On-line 'zines acquired scriptural significance for the new digerati—those who *got* it, who understood not only that the Internet would change everything, but who also understood inerrantly the nature of that change. The *Industry Standard, Upside, Info World, PC World*, and many others were among the technology publications competing on the Internet, and

Figure 4.1 **Phases of Technology-Based Innovation: The Entrepreneur's Perspective**

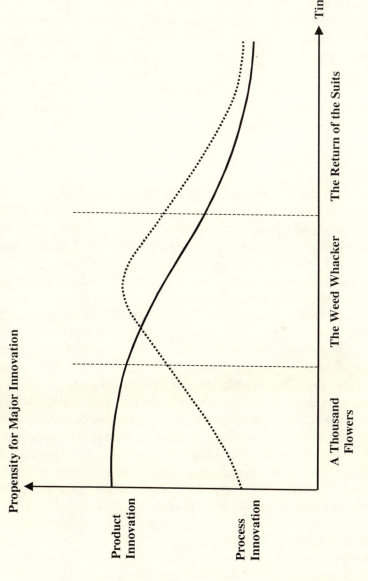

Propensity for Major Innovation

Product Innovation

Process Innovation

A Thousand Flowers

The Weed Whacker

The Return of the Suits

Time

Source: Abernathy 1978: 72.

CNET became the premier Web site for technology news. The content was "new economy," the presentation slick, the innovation frequent.

But consolidation also came on Internet time, and by the end of 2001 was in full swing. The evidence: the *Internet Standard* closed, AOL Time Warner purchased *Business 2.0* and merged it with *eCompany News*, many content-sites closed, and the survivors suffered severe layoffs. Even so, the remaining companies have emerged stronger. As one observer put it, the early Internet "created this spectacular Precambrian explosion of life forms and not all of them would make it. But for every 1000 startups, there are 100 that are still left and doing interesting things" (Lasica 2002). And so the cycles of change proceed.

A Thousand Flowers Blooming

In the first phase of Figure 4.1, the competitive environment exhibits high rates of innovation in a dynamic and uncertain marketplace. This is an entrepreneur's paradise because the most valuable competitive skills are those of the innovator. New companies proliferate, and a thousand ideas bloom, though only a few will survive.

In the first phase, generally chaotic business conditions prevail. Customers cannot articulate clearly their real needs, in large measure because they do not understand them very well themselves. And suppliers are uncertain how well their own technologies will meet that demand, both recognized and latent. The variety of market offerings is high, each one in effect an experiment, usually betting the life of a new company on the outcome. The myth of the company started at the garage workbench is truest in early-stage markets—each offering tends to be produced by skilled artisans using general-purpose technologies and flexible methods. Improving the production process remains important, but of secondary value in creating competitive advantage. The most attractive opportunities for entrepreneurs in such early-stage markets spring from product innovation. The competitive skills most relevant in capturing these opportunities include the following.

Reading the Market

Because potential customers cannot express their needs clearly, you must find them out experimentally. You must learn the art of the cheap market test. In a lecture given at the Massachusetts Institute of Technology in the early 1970s, Amar Bose, founder of Bose Electronics, told of his early market experiments with consumer stereo equipment. To test the value that his advanced technology might have for customers, Bose packaged the speakers in a battered old case, really little more than a packing crate. He took these to a high-end stereo store and asked the sales staff if they would listen and comment on the quality. They agreed, though privately snickering at the poor cabinetry. But when he saw how their faces changed when they heard the sound, Bose knew he had a winning product.

Technology Adaptation

Informed by your best understanding of the market, you must quickly assemble the suite of product characteristics most likely to yield the performance demanded along all dimensions.

Cycle Time

A rapid learning cycle—minimizing the time from an observation about the market until you can act on that observation—is essential. Fighter pilots call this "turning inside" an opponent. For this reason, high-technology industries have tended to cluster in regions like Boston/Cambridge in Massachusetts or Palo Alto in California. These clusters provide companies located there with superior access to relevant information, both about the market and about the technology, thus enabling a more rapid operating cycle from concept to product. Nevertheless, reducing cycle time depends more on skill at knowledge management than on geography. Consider, for example, the innovators of flat-panel displays, which replaced the cathode ray tube for displaying computer data, and thus made notebook computers practical. The most successful of these innovators mobilized knowledge resources from around the world to ensure timely market entry (Murtha, Lenway, and Hart 2001: 132–36).

Effectiveness in Production

Low-cost production is less important here than it will become in the future, because competition tends to focus on segments of the market that are less price sensitive. But effectiveness in terms of timely delivery and performance quality will matter greatly.

Paradise Lost: The Weed Whacker Cometh

The second stage of market maturation is transitional in nature. Customers have discovered the performance dimensions that truly add value for them, and competition comes to focus on those. Cost and reliability grow in importance, leading to the rise of innovation in the production process as a source of competitive advantage. Product innovation remains important, but tends to center around a common paradigm, often called the *dominant design* (Utterback 1994: 23–55). Technological changes to this common design paradigm become less radical. New firms enter the industry, especially at the beginning of the transition, with offerings that imitate and improve upon the dominant design. Competitors who can reach critical scale quickly and thereby achieve production efficiencies move into industry leadership. Those original competitors whose designs proved less than dominant exit.

Product Design

Commercial aircraft demonstrate the influence of a dominant design on the pace and direction of subsequent innovation. The DC-3, an all-metal, low-wing passenger plane was introduced in 1936 by the Douglas Aircraft Corporation. It combined features pioneered in earlier passenger aircraft built by Boeing, Lockheed, Ford, and Douglas itself, and its market success sprang from the skill with which these features were integrated into a design of comprehensive quality. The DC-3 paradigm so dominated innovation in the industry that all succeeding aircraft through the Lockheed Constellation could be considered improvements on this basic design. Two decades would pass before the next major innovation in commercial aircraft, the turbine-powered transports first introduced in the United Kingdom and more successfully in the United States with Boeing's model 707 (Miller and Sawers 1970: 98–127).

Business Design

The concept of dominant design applies to more than product technology. Innovation in the way that a product or service is delivered—the *entrepreneurial innovation* of Chapter 2—can yield competitive advantages that are analogous to a dominant product design. Consider retail sales, for example.

Harvard professor Clayton Christensen points out that retail selling through the Internet is really the fourth in a series of game-changing innovations. When the downtown department stores became prominent in the 1870s, they established a paradigm that remained in place for two decades, bringing high-quality, affordable consumer goods to the urban public. The next major innovation, the mail-order catalog, took advantage of a public infrastructure, the U.S. Postal Service, and brought equivalent retail services to rural America. Two subsequent waves of innovation followed: the discount department stores, such as Wal-Mart, in the 1960s; and the on-line retailers of the late 1990s, also building upon a public infrastructure, the Internet (Christensen 2001: 106–7). Each wave of retail innovation introduced a new source of competitive advantage that allowed entrepreneurs entry into established markets. Once in place, these dominant business models could be sustained for decades.

Or, consider Federal Express, which invented the hub and spoke model for overnight package delivery. The superiority of moving all packages to a single center for subsequent redistribution rather than sending them point to point soon became apparent to all shippers. Federal Express's competitors either adopted this model or dropped out of the business.

At the same time that a dominant design standardizes the product (or service), the way that it is made (or that the value is delivered) becomes rationalized. Economies in production then rise to become an important source of competitive advantage.

Production Economies

In Chapter 2, we observed that the competitive victory of the gasoline-powered vehicles over the electrics could be explained, in part, by the weak business model of the Electric Vehicle Company. This says nothing, however, of the victory of internal combustion over steam.

Like the gasoline engine, steam offered the independent mobility of a stand-alone touring car, but with a compelling set of advantages. Historian Robert Pool notes in his analysis of the competition between these products that steam engines were simple, smooth, and quiet—and powerful, setting the world land speed record of 127 miles per hour in 1906 (Pool 1997: 153). To be sure, steam power had drawbacks too. Starting was slow, and required ten to thirty minutes to build up adequate steam. Until automated controls became available in the 1920s, the boiler required constant attention from the driver and was a maintenance challenge at all times. Every 30 to 100 miles the early boilers needed refilling with water—usually available from the public watering troughs provided for another competing prime mover, the horse (Fox 1998: 38).

By contrast, gasoline-fueled vehicles were difficult and dangerous to start, more complex, and required greater skill of the operator. Thus, the marketplace competition looked about even from a product perspective. Pool offers the most persuasive explanation for the triumph of the internal combustion engine—that its developers were simply better businessmen (Pool 1997: 154).

In particular one entrepreneur, Henry Ford, recognized before his competitors that the automobile market had matured. Ford's core idea was that competitive advantage could best be secured through cost competition rather than further refinement of the auto itself. This idea was intensely controversial, and implemented only after much internal strife and expulsion of a group of dissident stockholder-managers (Abernathy and Wayne 1974: 113).

Ford consolidated its product line around the standard Model T, built modern plants, and introduced assembly-line concepts. Scale economies were achieved in purchasing, and the division of labor increased—as did worker turnover. With increasing production, learning-curve economies lowered the price of the Model T from over $24,000 (in 1999 dollars) to $14,500 two years later (also in 1999 dollars). As a result of this single-minded pursuit of production efficiency, Ford sales rose to over 55 percent of the U.S. auto market by 1921 (Abernathy and Wayne 1974: 110–14).

This remarkable economic performance had less to do with the technical virtues of the Model T and more to do with the strategic genius of Henry Ford: recognition that the marketplace was entering a new phase of competition and the courage to introduce the needed changes.

Combining Technologies

Finally, apparently disparate technologies can combine to tip a market decisively toward maturity. Consider the case of the personal computer. When IBM introduced its personal computer (PC) on August 12, 1981, that machine irrevocably changed the basis of competition for all involved in the computer industry—computer makers, software companies, microprocessor makers, and especially customers, whose work lives and personal possibilities were radically altered.

The IBM PC was not the first personal computer to reach the market, nor was it the highest performing. Apple would claim those distinctions. It was, however, the first to combine enough of the features that customers found useful with the business imprimatur of IBM—its large-scale production capability and its reputation for quality and customer service.

The success of the PC depended critically on two antecedent innovations: a microprocessor sufficiently powerful to run useful applications, yet cheap enough to be sold to individuals through retail computer stores; and software application packages with functions that customers found valuable rather than merely amusing—principally word processing (typing, as it was called in those primitive times) and spreadsheets. The role of the chip is plain. Without a 16-bit processor like the Intel 8088, the IBM PC simply could not have mustered the needed computing power. Yet with an 8-bit data bus—which governs the rate that data can be sent and received—the chip was not attractive enough to draw attention from IBM's mid-range computers, which cost much more but in truth performed only slightly better (Cringely 1992: 131).

Yet the role of the application software in establishing the PC mattered even more because customers value the service that a product provides, not the object itself. That service was spreadsheet calculation. The software that delivered the service was VisiCalc, an application powerful enough to induce people to buy the computer just for access to that program (Freiberger and Swaine 2000: 288). For many business users, this program quickly became essential and moved the personal computer from a hobbyist's toy to an engine of productivity.

Despite Apple's initial lead as the first to offer VisiCalc, the company made a strategic error by refusing to license its internally developed hardware and software to others (Shapiro and Varian 1999: 248). By contrast, IBM chose a different strategy and reaped a different, though not entirely salutary, set of consequences.

IBM chose an open-architecture approach that allowed other companies to design and make components that would operate with IBM's PC. The major components were outsourced—the microprocessor, much of the application software, and most important, the operating system. The operating system, the software that gives instructions to the computer's processor, was procured from a start-up company called Microsoft, which also secured the right to license to other companies. This licensing ability would later ramify in unexpected ways.

In the early 1980s, however, there were no other companies, and IBM's advantage in large-scale production soon dominated the market. IBM produced 13,000 of the new machines between their introduction in August 1981 and the end of that year, and the company would sell over half a million over the next two years (Freiberger and Swaine 2000: 349). As production accelerated, programmers found incentive to write application software for IBM's MS-DOS operating system. Lotus Development Corporation, for example, aimed its new Lotus 1–2–3 database application toward the IBM system. This made the PC more valuable to users, and the larger market attracted even more software writers— the classic virtuous cycle.

IBM's success, however, soon attracted imitators, who could also license the MS-DOS operating system and thereby offer their customers access to the same application software as IBM, and the term "IBM-clone" came into the language. At the same time, the original technology companies that had pioneered the personal computer revolution began to drop out of the marketplace, unable to play by the new rules of the game. When the weed whacker had finished its work, none of these original contenders other than Apple were left in bloom. The ultimate winner, however, was Microsoft, as its MS-DOS became the standard for the entire industry outside the narrow niche occupied by Apple. In effect, Microsoft would sell ammunition to all combatants in the increasingly fierce PC wars to come.

Competitive Skills in the Transition

Early-stage technology markets can be viewed as a search for a dominant paradigm, which like the DC-3, the Internet retailer, or the IBM PC becomes (for a time) the market leader. Once competition begins to settle around this new standard, a new set of competitive skills is needed.

Strategic Recognition

Nobody will post signs that the nature of the competitive game is about to change. Therefore, you must discern on your own that the market will reward a shift from fundamental product innovation to competition around some emerging industry-wide standard. Niche markets that are related to the mainstream can offer clues, as we will find in Chapter 5. You should watch these closely.

Crossing the Gap

Chapter 2 noted how the characteristics of your customers change when you enter mainstream markets. To cross the gap between early adopters and mainstream customers, you must use these niche markets to build credibility and a set of satisfied customers who will serve as reference for those to come.

Scale-up

If your recognition is accurate, then you must be able to reach critical scale quickly and effectively. Otherwise, someone else will. Licensing your technology for others to manufacture can sometimes serve well if you are truly production constrained. To be sure, your competitors gain access to your technology, but you will have a profit margin advantage through royalty payments (see Chapter 8).

Process Innovation

As the locus of competitive action shifts toward the production process, you must continue to lower your cost of production. Here, nothing works as well as continuous improvement—simply paying attention to the numerous small innovations that generate "learning curve" economies and that can accumulate into a structural cost advantage.

Product Innovation

Improvements in the product are not irrelevant, though they tend to become increasingly incremental. Thus you must develop an institutional capacity for continuous, incremental product improvement, rather than fundamental innovation.

Return of the Suits

The transitional market intervenes, sometimes only briefly, between the amorphous, early-stage competition and the mature market. If the early phase is an entrepreneurial paradise, the last can be an entrepreneurial desert—occasional oases of opportunity exist, but they are scattered among arid tracts of business-as-usual. Institutional rigidities and procedures govern action, and the suits are firmly in charge. Innovation itself becomes institutional in character.

Products once considered high technology take on the economic characteristics of commodities, and substantive product innovation drops as shown in Figure 4.1. Customers often cannot make use of, and hence value, further improvements in performance. Even in cases where further performance would have value, fundamental physical barriers often inhibit the needed improvements. Thus, advances in performance tend to be incremental, sometimes achievable only after large investments and extended time. In such cases, product differentiation can best be achieved by a solid brand name or by bundling the product with a package of services. Purchasing decisions tend to be based on price or on intangible differentiators, such as appearance, prestige, or the ever-popular appeal to the opposite sex if all else fails. Major innovation in the production process also slows, and static economies of scale rise in importance.

Pressures Toward Incremental Innovation

Three characteristics of the mature phase of the technology cycle lead to this galloping incrementalism. First, a mature market emphasizes skills in execution, not innovation, and so successful organizations require relatively mechanistic structure and cultures. This culture clashes with the relatively fluid culture required for radical innovation. Because these differ so greatly, corporate acquisitions attempting to graft new technology onto a mature organization often find success elusive. The cultures do not mesh well, and so the knowledge and skills of the innovator cannot be absorbed readily—which is why so many entrepreneurs who have sold their companies to mainstream firms find their new working environment intolerable and leave.

A second reality compounds this difficulty—simply injecting new technology into an established business model creates conditions in which the technology itself is unlikely to perform to full capacity. The ice harvesters, for example, also used steam-powered refrigeration—but only to help make their warehouses more efficient, and not to enable a more competitive business model.

And third, companies competing in mature markets often find that radical innovations create second-order consequences that ripple through complex, integrated systems. Consider the automobile, for example. The consequences of an incremental innovation, say, a sequential turn indicator, would be quite limited—in this case to the vehicle lighting system. But a radical innovation, like a fuel-cell power plant, propagates consequences throughout the vehicle system—controls, power train, fuel system, and so forth. This provides an incentive to constrain the scope of the innovation to minimize the "collateral damage," as the rippling effects of change might be termed. For significant innovations, it raises the hurdle rate for change. A component change in an integrated system must demonstrate enough value to overcome the cost and risk associated with these ripple effects. None of this is to argue that major innovations cannot happen, but rather to note that their cost is higher in an integrated system.

Schumpeter's Revenge

In maturity, an industry consolidates down to a few large players, often with global reach. In principle, this state of affairs could continue indefinitely. Yet the field is ripe for overthrow, the "creative destruction" of Joseph Schumpeter on a massive scale through creation of another paradigm-breaking technology and business model. When this happens, the technology market cycle restarts.

Wireless telecommunications markets offer a contemporary example of the conflict between the imperatives of a mature industry and the opportunities that new technologies are beginning to make possible. Recent years have witnessed a trend toward consolidation of the wireless telecom companies. In part, this springs from the debt burden undertaken to finance the build-out of their wireless networks, especially the large number of base-stations needed for effective area coverage. The consolidated companies can spread this debt burden over a larger customer base, while benefiting from network and scale economies. In all likelihood, only a handful of global wireless operators will remain independent as the consolidation unfolds over the next five years or so. At the same time, however, a pattern that challenges this mature business environment seems to be emerging from several scattered threads.

First, customer demand is building for services that reach beyond simple voice transmission—especially for broadband Internet access independent of the users' location. Second, new wireless technologies are emerging that could provide this service but not as simple improvements on the current wireless network, usually termed the 2G (second generation) network in telecom parlance. Emerging technologies such as ultra-wideband transmission or "ad hoc" networking would make the installed 2G architecture irrelevant—not a pleasant prospect for those still paying off the debt from building it. And third, a host of new, entrepreneurial companies are being formed to capture the value resident in these new technical capabilities. How these entrepreneurial ventures will overthrow the incumbents in the now-mature telecom market remains to be seen, but history suggests that the real questions concern "when" and not "whether."

Competitive Strategies

Pending such overthrow, the entrepreneurial art in a mature market differs in important ways. For entrepreneurs, the most effective competitive strategies do not attack the industry incumbents directly, but rather seek to make them irrelevant to customer value. Technologies that change the nature of the competitive game and disrupt the mature marketplace find the greatest traction, and the skills to use them are those of the early technology cycle. By contrast companies that merely offer "better mousetraps" often fare poorly against mainstream incumbents who tend to dominate the established market channels.

For established players, the competitive strategies that seem most effective in the mature phase of the technology cycle emphasize incremental innovation, nontechnology differentiation, low cost, and service. You should understand these in case you find yourself competing with them. Incumbent strategies include the following.

Incremental Innovation

Continuous, incremental improvements, especially to the production process, can lead to an overwhelming cumulative advantage. Many mature businesses demonstrate considerable skill at this. Recent studies of innovation in mature firms observe that patent activity does not diminish during the mature phase of the life cycle (McGahan and Silverman 2001). Though much of this patenting is likely to be defensive (see Chapter 8), it might nevertheless build a foundation for incremental improvement and corporate entrepreneurship.

Product Positioning

In the absence of technological distinctions, market incumbents often seek advantage by positioning their products to appeal to identified categories of users. One brand of motor oil, for example, is sold to men (presumably real) who change their own oil, while another to those who appreciate auto racing—yet the underlying product is an indistinguishable commodity. Shaving creams are sold in similar fashion.

Economies of Scale

Bigger can be better, yielding advantages in supply chain management as well as production. And when a large company introduces an innovation, it gains immediate attention in the marketplace, as did IBM with its PC.

Creative Service

In mature products, changes in the kind of performance that customers value and the market shift toward late adopters can require competitors to shift from a product-oriented business model to one that is service-oriented.

In some cases, the service can be derived from the mature product—enterprise software, for example. Consider *salesforce.com*, the provider of software for customer relations management (CRM), founded in 1999 and one of the few dot-coms to prosper through the market shakeout of 2000–2001. The company is built around the idea that customer value can be increased with software that is rented rather than purchased—in effect, a service business. The rental would be accomplished over the Internet using the Web services concepts discussed in Chapter 2. The analogy would be customers at Amazon, who receive shopping and purchasing services through the Web without having to install any special software. Customer value would be derived from rapid installation, easy adaptation to the users' needs, no maintenance issues, and easy upgrades. Offsetting these would be customer concerns with reliability and with entrusting their data to an outside service supplier. Thus, the domain of applicability for rental software remains unclear, but the essential point remains—in a mature product, new value can sometimes be created by offering the product as a service.

In other cases, the service can be built around the core product and technology skills, not with the intent to sell more product, but rather as the primary revenue generator. Consider, for example, the story of the computer maker, Compaq, and its last attempts at both product and service innovation prior to the merger with Hewlett-Packard.

Business Model Innovation: Compaq's Move into Services

By early 2001, the personal computer market was showing the classic signs of maturity: stagnant market growth, intense price competition, and commodity treatment by consumers. With profits under pressure and market share falling, Compaq Computer responded to an apparent realization that market conditions were unlikely to improve. In June 2001, Compaq announced a strategic innovation, a massive restructuring to deemphasize computer hardware and focus instead on industry-specific packages of computers, software, and services. Compaq also announced it would end production of its proprietary Alpha chip and instead use Intel's newly released Itanium processor (McWilliams 2001).

This announcement marked a departure from the previous strategy, which had sought to distinguish Compaq products through superior technology and performance. To build this strategy of technological differentiation, Compaq had bought Digital Equipment Company in 1998, also acquiring Digital's advanced Alpha chip. Integration of the purchase proved difficult, however, and Compaq reported a loss of $2.74 billion in that fiscal year. In 1999, Compaq announced that Microsoft's Windows software would not run on future Compaq servers using the Alpha chip—in effect, betting that the improved hardware would offer customers such attractive features that they would not miss the de facto standard that Microsoft Windows had become.

The bet was not and indeed could not be won, as the network economies (discussed in Chapter 5) afforded by the software gave customers more value than the superior hardware. In its 2001 strategy announcement, Compaq in effect admitted that proprietary hardware is unlikely to confer competitive advantage in the mature personal computer market, and that competition has shifted to customer-specific packages of hardware and services. The move had the additional effect, whether intended or not, of preparing Compaq for its subsequent merger with Hewlett-Packard. The combined company will emphasize delivery of computing services rather than the machines themselves. This economic bet stands in sharp contrast with that of Dell, which continues to sell machines through its direct-order business model without a major service emphasis.

Concluding Thoughts About Market Cycles

The market-cycle framework can help you understand the varying nature of opportunity in technology markets, provided that you do not interpret it too literally. It will serve you well as a tool for understanding, but poorly as a tool for predicting. Consider the case of the artificial heart, which illustrates the fitful nature of innovation in a technology market that has been "emerging" for seventy years—and which shows that the world is never so tidily arranged as the sweeping curves of Figure 4.1 might suggest. Indeed, this is fortunate because if it were so, the value of entrepreneurial insight would surely diminish.

The Beat Goes On: Innovation and the Artificial Heart

The concept of the artificial heart can be traced back to the 1930s when animal heart bypasses were first being performed. These experiments required some form of ventricular assistance, which in turn gave hope for mechanical hearts in humans. In 1953, Dr. John Gibbon demonstrated that an external heart-lung device could replace the human heart function for brief periods during surgery. That success raised hope that a practical, implantable device could replace a failing human heart for extended periods, perhaps indefinitely. Innovation with artificial heart technology began in earnest, and a variety of design concepts were soon employed in animal experiments.

Despite the accelerated innovation, actual progress proved elusive. Tests of the early designs in animals yielded results that were only marginally satisfactory, especially from the animals' point of view, and survival times on the artificial heart were measured in hours. The chief problem was the pressure of the early pumps, which crushed the blood cells that passed through them, making the artificial heart an engine of destruction rather than salvation.

The problem of cell crushing was solved only to reveal other unresolved issues such as rejection by the host body, fit within the chest cavity, wear on the membranes used in the implanted heart, and so forth— a typical path of progress in the early days of any technology (Foster 1986: 90–96). Thus, the best performance those devices could muster advanced slowly and fitfully.

By the late 1970s, however, Dr. Robert Jarvik had designed and tested a series of improvements that extended the life of the device and meshed better with the needs of the living organism in which it would be implanted. Building upon these improvements, subsequent research efforts began to yield meaningful extensions of the lives of patients. The most famous of these, the Jarvik-7, was implanted in Seattle dentist Barney Clark in 1982. Clark survived for 112 days in wretched circumstances before succumbing to pneumonia.

Twenty years of incremental improvements followed the Clark implant, mostly based on the fundamental Jarvik-7, which became the dominant design of its era. But all the variants of this dominant design shared a common flaw—their need for a large, external power source. This required an opening to the body, and hence a channel for infection. No amount of incremental improvement could overcome this basic flaw of the artificial heart, and as a result the technology became marginal in the fight against heart disease.

Competing technologies entered the market, including heart transplants from other humans and a variety of devices that regulate the heart and improve its pumping efficiency without replacing it. Heart transplants, once state of the art, have become routinely successful. The American Heart Association claims one-year survival rates of 86 percent and five-year survival of 70 percent. And so, artificial hearts became relegated to standby devices used for patients awaiting a transplanted human heart.

Nevertheless, the situation remained unsatisfactory. Each year, heart failure contributes to the deaths of some 700,000 persons in the United States, and as many as 100,000 of these could benefit from a total heart replacement (Abiomed 2004). Despite this need, the availability of suitable donors limits the possibilities for heart transplants to about 2,000 patients per year.

Figure 4.2 offers a qualitative view of the performance of this always-emerging technology as a series of S-curves. The vertical axis measures progress, and the horizontal measures cumulative research effort. To date, the technology has remained trapped in the early-market phase of its life cycle, with each innovation improving performance but none offering enough value to enter mainstream medical markets.

Recent developments, however, suggest that artificial heart technology might at last be able to achieve the explosive growth so long promised. A series of minor improvements have been made in pumps and materials. Improved control mechanisms allow the heart to respond effectively to changes in blood oxygen requirements caused by exertion. The cumulative effect of these incremental improvements has been great. But most important, energy can now be transmitted to receivers implanted inside the body without a permanent penetration of the skin. If these devices prove effective in the clinical trials now in progress, a new era could be opened for the many patients currently unable to find a transplant donor. After seventy years of fitful development, this always

Figure 4.2   **The Artificial Heart**
Early trial and error followed by rapid improvement

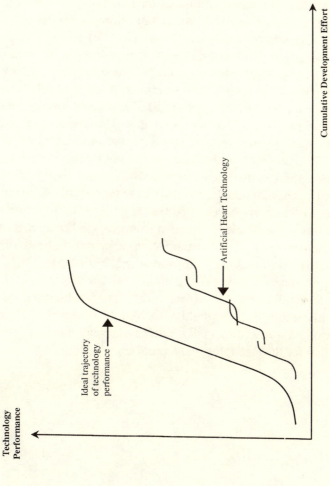

Source: Foster 1986, 97.

promising, never quite delivering innovation might yet emerge to offer bright hope for extending human life.

The Real and the Ideal

Bookies and purchasers of mutual funds know well that the real often diverges sharply from the ideal. The development of the artificial heart demonstrates in broad outline the principles of an early-stage innovation. But rather than advancing in the smooth upward sweep of Figure 4.1, the technology progressed in fits and starts, overcoming one obstacle only to be confronted by another. A high payoff often appears within reach, but the pathway to realization remains unclear until a dominant design, like the Jarvik-7, puts the right elements in place. Then progress accelerates, only to encounter yet more obstacles as did the Jarvik design. None of this was predictable by the competitors in this turbulent market, by the investors, or by outside observers.

And just as individual technologies are unpredictable, so are changes in the evolutionary phases of technology markets. To be sure, isolated indicators of an incipient transition from one kind of market to another can often be observed—for example, the approaching limits of a mature technology in improving performance or lowering cost.

But in general, predictions about the life cycle of most technologies have not demonstrated notable accuracy. The world, it seems, is rarely as neatly arranged as we would wish. Neither, however, is it as irrational as we might fear, and so, understanding the conditions of competition is essential for the technology entrepreneur.

5

Technology and the Fight
for Competitive Advantage

> The race is not always to the swift, nor the battle
> to the strong, but that's the way to bet.
> —*Damon Runyon*

Chapter 4 addressed the general tendencies of markets to shift the basis of competition as the technologies that serve them mature. Sometimes these changes proceed gradually, sometimes abruptly, their rate and direction influenced by four forces:

- *Disruptive technologies*, which have the capacity to change the rules of the competitive game;
- The *path dependence* of technology, which is why so many better mousetraps remain unsold;
- *Societal preferences*: the close interweaving between a society and the kinds of technology that it finds acceptable—a brake for technologies such as nuclear power and perhaps genetically engineered foods, an accelerator for others such as the Internet or perhaps renewable energy; and
- The *acceleration of technological change*, which opens new opportunities for entrepreneurs who can master the fast-paced business cycles that follow.

Disruptive Technology

Technological innovations can be grouped into two general kinds: those that are *sustaining* and those that are *disruptive*. The term *sustaining* applies to technologies that advance performance along dimensions already recognized and accepted by customers. These tend to be incremental improvements: first, the two-blade disposable razor replaces the single blade, and later three blades become the cutting edge of shaving technology. These sustaining innovations need not be trivial advances, however—consider the improvements in commercial aircraft brought about by the introduction of composite materials. Yet these very significant improvements were all made along established performance dimensions, chiefly strength and weight. The cumulative effect of these incremental improvements can be quite spectacular, as demonstrated by the improvements in processor speed for computers.

In contrast, *disruptive* technologies introduce performance dimensions quite distinct from what the mainstream customers have come to value, yet frequently offering inferior performance along the accustomed dimensions. Because of their inferior mainstream performance, these technologies initially gain traction only in niche markets. With continued use and improvement, however, disruptive technologies gain adequacy along the original dimensions and then enter the mainstream markets. Their entry can cause competition to shift to the new dimensions of performance in cases where customers do not greatly value improvements in the old. This disrupts the market—hence the term *disruptive technology*—a process often fatal to incumbent products and companies. You must understand how this happens, whether you are the disruptor or the disruptee.

Memories Are Made of This: Competition in Computer Disk Drives

Harvard professor Clayton Christensen illustrates one way that a disruptive technology can work with the experience of the makers of computer disk drives (Christensen 1999: 123–28). As shown in Figure 5.1, the performance dimension of interest when the 14-inch, rigid disk drives were introduced in the early 1970s was memory capacity, most commonly measured in megabytes (MB). In the early days, the memory capacity required of disks selling in the mainframe marketplace approximately matched what the suppliers were able to deliver. But the disk-drive makers were clever innovators, and were soon able to deliver drives with performance that exceeded what most computer manufacturers were willing to install in their mainframe machines, as the figure shows.

Christensen notes that around 1978 an entirely different set of disk-drive suppliers began competing for the minicomputer market. The 14-inch drives were too large and costly for the minicomputers, and so smaller 8-inch drives had to be used. With only 20 MB of memory, their

Figure 5.1 **A Case of Disruptive Technology**

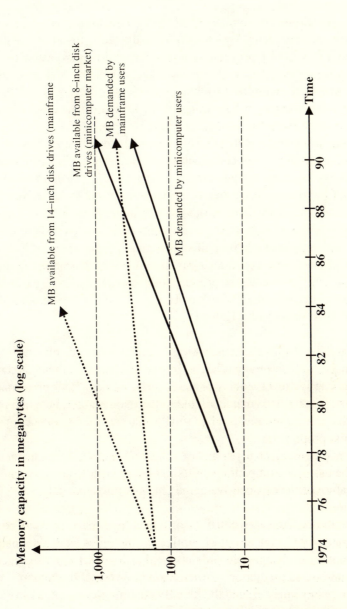

Source: Adapted from Exhibit 1, Christensen 1999: 16.

performance was far inferior to the 14-inch drives. Still, they resolved the serious issue of size for the minicomputer makers, and so thrived in that niche.

Like the 14-inch drive makers, the 8-inch suppliers improved the performance of their technology well beyond the requirements of the minicomputer market. Within a few years the 8-inch drives were able to meet the memory requirements of the mainframe makers, and so came to compete directly with the 14-inch drives. Since differences in memory capacity were no longer a meaningful discriminator, the basis for competition shifted to other product attributes.

Christensen suggests that these other attributes centered around reliability. The 8-inch drives contained fewer parts, were less susceptible to breakdown, and caused fewer storage errors. As the basis for competition shifted to these performance dimensions, the 14-inch drives were swept from the mainframe marketplace (Christensen 1999: 126).

These findings seem most true in technology markets where the demand side matures even though substantial opportunities for technical improvement remain on the supply side. Christensen observes game-changing discontinuities in product markets ranging from excavation equipment to executive education. These lead to three general propositions (Christensen 1999: 129–34):

- Suppliers to advanced technology markets tend to extend the performance of their products beyond the requirements of their customers.
- Disruptive technologies begin in niche markets with performance that is inferior to that available in the main market, but soon overtake the requirements of the main market, a consequence of the first proposition.
- Once equivalent performance is established in the main market, the basis for competition shifts to other product attributes, and the nature of the competitive game changes fundamentally.

Like the evolutionary behavior of technology markets sketched out in Chapter 4, the concept of disruptive technologies explains a pattern of competitive change, but predicts neither its onset nor its outcome. Explanation and prediction, however, are the work of bystanders—professors, policy analysts, and the like. By contrast, your work as an entrepreneur is to create the future, to risk your time, energy, and personal resources in pursuit of what can be, of what ought to be. Disruption, not stasis, creates the future, and opportunities abound as emerging markets collide with mature ones. Yet the disruption need not always follow the patterns observed by Christensen. The auto industry, that poster child of maturity, and home entertainment offer contrasting examples.

On the Road to Revolution: Disruptive Transitions in Autos?

Innovation in the auto business has never been easy. Consider the unfortunate engineer Frank Kulick, who suggested to Henry Ford that larger valves might improve the power obtained from the Model T's engine. To fire him properly for this impertinence, Ford's security chief threw him from a moving car outside the plant's gate, and then rushed inside to lock him out. Kulick was never again allowed inside a Ford plant (Halberstam 1986: 83–87).

In the gentler times since World War II, two waves of innovation have swept through the auto industry. The first was the high-compression engine, which raised power-to-weight ratios from around 3.5 gross horsepower per 100 pounds in 1949 to 7 horsepower per 100 pounds by the late 1950s. These improvements provided power for the faster road performance demanded by consumers and for the power-hungry (and profitable) devices like air conditioning pushed by the automakers.

Microprocessor-based electronic components became the second wave of innovation, which began in the 1970s. A series of federal regulations for environmental protection, fuel economy, and safety drove the first introduction of microprocessors because the old mechanical systems—carburetors, mechanical distributors, and so forth—could not deliver the mandated performance (Ealey and Mercer 1999: 6–17). In that case, there were no issues of niche markets, early adopters, or mainstream customers; the entire market adopted the new technology by regulatory fiat. But once the microprocessor components had been installed for regulatory purposes, their extension to market-driven features, such as cruise control, audio systems, and climate control, followed swiftly because they offered consumers value along the accustomed dimensions of performance.

In neither case, however, did the basic configuration of the automobile or its closely linked systems—roads, tires, fuels, manufacturing, repair, and so forth—have to change to accommodate the new innovations. Could the auto industry now be ripe for the kind of far-reaching change that opens new opportunities for entrepreneurs? Many observers think so, and cite three areas of potentially major innovation: telematics, manufacturing, and electric-drive vehicles.

Telematics

The "telematic" concept considers the automobile an information site, a rolling Internet node, offering entertainment and office services (presumably for passengers, not the driver) as well as pertinent traffic and weather information. Yet telematics promises to reach beyond the vehicles themselves into the larger telecommunications and transportation infrastructures, and thus offers broader scope for entrepreneurship than the previous waves of innovation. Just as the Internet opened new channels for a variety of innovative services, so might the fully wired vehicle. Such services might include real-time monitoring of key vehicle parameters to detect incipient maintenance problems, antitheft systems, special content for on-board entertainment, and automatic driving and control systems. These new services are not integral to the vehicle, unlike previous waves of auto innovation. Thus the auto transportation market might well open to an entirely new set of competitors who add value to the basic platform along new dimensions of performance without disrupting the old.

Manufacturing: Driving Change in Auto Production

Automobile manufacturing, a global enterprise that entered the twenty-first century with production capacity exceeding demand by 25 to 30 percent, could become another area for disruptive change. As the older plants are being retired to align production capacity with demand, sweeping structural changes might become possible. For example, the basic production system might be reconfigured to track customer demand more effectively. The Internet suggests the basic business model. Auto customers increasingly seek to use the Internet to create the same kind of order-to-delivery cycle found in many other products—Dell computers, for example. Making this possible requires much more than building an order-taking Web site. Instead it would require a reorganization of the entire automotive value chain. While the ultimate shape of this new value chain can only be guessed, several elements appear likely:

• The new manufacturing plants are likely to be much smaller than those in place now. For example, Volkswagen's home plant in Saxony, Germany, can turn out 750,000 vehicles per year. Plants like this will be replaced by those one-third to one-tenth that size.

- The new plants will be flexible enough to switch from one model to another overnight. They will employ highly flexible automation and draw on the labor of fewer, more highly skilled workers.
- The automobiles themselves will be increasingly modular with major components capable of being assembled in several ways to create variety in the product. Ford, for example, already plans to employ the same platform—the chassis and other under-the-skin parts—for ten different vehicles.
- And finally, much more of the work will be done by specialty suppliers under contract to the owner of the brand. Some of this is already happening. For example, the Porsche Boxter is assembled by Valmet, a Finnish engineering firm.

Electric Drive: A Powerful Concept

The third and perhaps most potentially disruptive technology in the auto industry concerns the power train—replacing the standard spark ignition engine with an electric generator, most likely a fuel cell, and the transmission with direct electric drive at each wheel.

Vehicles with these electric power trains might further enable modular assembly because of their flexible geometry. Unlike the spark engine, which requires a large mass of engine up front and a bulky drive train to connect with the rear wheels, the basic chassis of an electric vehicle—the fuel cells, electric motors, steering, and suspension—can be arrayed in any sensible geometry. The concept presented by General Motors at the 2002 Detroit auto show, for example, looked rather like a giant skateboard. Its chassis was 15 centimeters thick, though as long and wide as a conventional auto. Alternative vehicle bodies could be manufactured and sold separately from this chassis. They would mount to the chassis through standard mechanical and electrical connectors.

At present, electric-drive cars are inferior in performance to the standard vehicles now on the road in the United States. Thus, these power train technologies would probably follow the classic niche model of innovation, appearing first in small markets where they solve some special problem. For fleet use in, say, Bangkok or Mexico City, they would be valued for their ability to cut the noxious pollution that has become a public health problem in those communities. If we were to observe such vehicles penetrating niche markets in the developing world, might we not anticipate them in the United States sooner rather than later?

Alternatively, the first use of fuel-cell electric generators might occur on a small scale—as long-lived batteries for computers or portable electronic equipment, a niche where the fuel cell could solve a special problem for a motivated customer, the U.S. Army. The army is seeking small-scale, portable power sources for its soldiers, in part to relieve the large logistics burden that battery supply has become and in part to lighten the soldiers' load in combat operations. But rather than engaging its customary research, development, and procurement process, the army has taken an entirely new approach with the hope of reducing its own cycle time for innovation. The army has engaged a venture capital firm, OnPoint Technologies, to invest in early-stage companies with relevant technical solutions. If microfuel-cell technology is up to the challenge, the experience gained from serving this high-value niche would translate directly to other small-scale devices like handheld computers and mobile phones, and from there move into the automotive markets. All of these innovations are likely to stimulate an industrial structure quite distinct from that in place today. Thus even an industry as mature as automobiles holds prospects of opportunity for the vigilant—and the lucky—entrepreneur.

Technology and the Video Industry: Farewell to All That

Sometimes, a disruptive technology casts its shadow over a host of ancillary businesses, and the home entertainment industry offers a case in point. Video-on-demand has long been the couch potato's dream—home access to the accumulated library of the film industry at any time and at an affordable price. The obstacle has been technological. A typical movie running about 120 minutes commands about 5 gigabytes. Even with a DSL or cable modem connection, the download time becomes prohibitive, rather like filling your swimming pool with an eyedropper. And in any case, only 13 percent of U.S. households had a broadband connection as of late 2002, despite rapid growth among the early adopter community. Would more subscribers sign up if video-on-demand were a reality? Many think so.

Enter the technological solution—advanced codec, compression/ decompression algorithms. These are essentially sets of equations that reduce the number of bits required to produce an image, and that do so in ways not noticeable by the viewer. By late 2002, the most widely used codec, MPEG-2, could compress content to lower the required transmission rate to 2 megabits per second for relatively still movie scenes, and 80 megabits per second for rapid action. This served some markets—DVDs, satellite television, and digital cable—but was still beyond reach of standard home connections, even digital subscriber lines and cable. This mainstream market awaits emerging systems like MPEG-4 with a required transmission speed as low as 40 kilobits per second. Although such advanced codecs simply extend performance along dimensions generally recognized as desirable, their disruption of established business models will be profound.

This is because the new technology can be packaged into boxes that fit on top of the family television set, which is where people prefer to watch movies, rather than the computer screen. Such boxes could be manufactured by anyone willing to pay the fee to license the technology and would enable access to the entire Internet. And this would gore an entire herd of incumbent oxen.

The first would be the cable-TV operators, who now stand between the viewers and the content providers and allow access only to the content they select. These worthies would be bypassed by the new compression technology. In addition, this set-top box would eventually replace the highly profitable VCR and with it the (also profitable) video store. Its disruptive reach might even extend to the multiplex cinema, as the convenience and cost-efficiency of home viewing trumps the economics of the shopping-mall theater.

We should derive two larger lessons from the cases of the auto industry and home entertainment. The first is that disruption of established markets can take a variety of forms, and that both market incumbents and the attacking entrepreneurs must remain alert to the rich variety of possibilities. Second, and perhaps most important, the established technology is not the chief victim of the disruption, but rather the established business models of the incumbent competitors.

Path Dependence, Lock-In, and Network Economies

In a better world, efficient markets would sort out the superior technologies, and these would advance in the marketplace. Simple observation, however, tells us that this does not always happen. To the contrary, a technology can sometimes secure a locked-in position in an early-stage market that cannot be dislodged by later entrants even with demonstrably superior performance.

This lock-in begins when a competing technology gains some small advantage, often through a series of small, even random, events. Brian Arthur of the Santa Fe Institute suggests a conceptual example. Imagine a very large urn filled with an equal number of red balls and white balls, thoroughly mixed. Then draw a ball at random from the urn. If it is red, return it to the urn and add one more red ball. If white, then return the white ball and add a white. Repeating this process will eventually bias the system and lead to a predominance of one color or the other (Arthur, Ermoliev, and Kaniovski 1987: 297).

In like manner, coincidence or just plain luck in the early days of a technology ramifies for decades. Consider the beginnings of the personal computer, for example. When IBM chose the Intel 8088 microprocessor in 1980 for its new personal computer, the project team found that the 16-bit chip could not use the operating systems designed for 8-bit processors. To move the PC to market quickly, IBM sought its operating system from an outside supplier. The supposed market leader, a company called Digital Research, was approached, but appeared to have little interest in the opportunity.

The IBM team then interviewed a young, unknown entrepreneur named Bill Gates. Microsoft, Gates's newly founded company, had acquired an incomplete operating system from a local software house that could be made to run on the Intel 8088, and thus became a contender; but the selection of Microsoft was by no means assured. Robert Pool describes the way IBM chose Microsoft to provide what would later be called MS-DOS, the Microsoft Disk Operating System. "Gates did everything he could to convince IBM that Microsoft would be the right choice, but the ultimate selection of Microsoft came down at least in part to a personal connection: IBM Chairman John Opel had served on the Board of the United Way with Gates' mother and thought it would be nice to do business with Mary Gates' boy's company" (Pool 1997: 20). And so the selection that was to make MS-DOS the industry standard and Microsoft one of the richest companies in the world would turn, in part, on an accident of personal history.

It takes more than mere idiosyncrasy, however, for an early advantage to become entrenched. In addition, technologies that secure a structural advantage over their rivals generally seem able to establish network externalities, the reinforcing effect of large numbers of users on the propensity of additional users to employ the same technology. The more users such a system has, the more valuable the system becomes to those users. And so more are attracted to the system in a virtuous cycle. Communications technologies, such as telephones, e-mail, and fax machines, offer classic examples of the scale effects of networks. Consider the fax machine: if only a few persons have one, the usefulness of each machine is small. At that point, a significantly improved fax machine that is not compatible with the installed base might have some chance of market acceptance. But once fax machines become ubiquitous, then they are highly useful, and the incentive to own a machine that is compatible with the established network overwhelms any noncompatible machine, no matter how superior.

These network externalities appear in many forms. Consider Apple computers, for example. Each "Mac" user gains when the market for these computers expands. This encourages software writers to develop more programs for the Mac, builds demand for help services, and enables easier exchange of files. But the classic case of network externalities was the struggle between competing systems for viewing videocassette recorders.

The War of the Formats: VHS vs. Betamax in Home Video

Once, two technologies struggled for a market. Each was backed by powerful corporations. Each had its competitive advantages, though in truth, the differences were not striking. But in the end, one prevailed, driving the other entirely from the marketplace. A great deal of mythology has grown up around this struggle, but the real story of how it happened illustrates the subtle, yet powerful, effects of network externalities.

The competition for home video entertainment began in the late 1960s as a classical early-stage market. Consumer preferences were poorly understood, and industry pundits assumed that few customers would want to record television programs themselves, but rather simply to play prerecorded material—a direct extrapolation from the audio record model. A variety of dissimilar technologies competed for the home video market, and disc players modeled after high-fidelity audio equipment seemed to have an early advantage. Fortunes were made, and then quickly lost as an overhyped industry failed to meet the expectations its publicists had created.

Sony took direct aim at the consumer market in 1975 when it rolled out its Betamax system in Japan and the United States. For a year, the Betamax was the only VCR in a hot market. Despite this first-mover advantage, however, three strategic failures cost Betamax the market.

First, the initial versions of Betamax could play only one-hour tapes, a compromise required to meet the ambitious rollout schedule. This was too short for the Betamax to play an entire movie, and so users were required to interrupt the show in the middle and change tapes. This annoyance militated against the otherwise superior technical performance of the Betamax. By contrast, Matsushita introduced its VHS format in 1976 with machines able to play a two-hour tape and began to gain market share.

Second, Sony was unable to persuade enough other manufacturers to adopt the Betamax standard. It had lobbied Japan's powerful Ministry of Internal Trade and Industry (MITI) to force its principal rivals, JVC and Matsushita, to join, but without success. By contrast, Matsushita secured a marketing agreement with RCA and so was able to license its VHS format more widely than Sony. Soon, half a dozen other brand-name manufacturers were offering VHS products.

And third, the VHS makers became the price leaders while Sony became the innovator, offering a stream of technological improvements including three-hour tapes. This strategic choice mattered greatly, though for reasons that were entirely invisible at the time. Faced with a choice between two popular but incompatible systems, most consumers chose to own neither. Instead they rented, and by 1980 "out of an estimated 100,000 homes with VCRs, 70% were rented" (*Business Week* 1982). And because the rental shops preferred the cheaper machines, they tended to invest in the VHS format. By contrast, owners tended to prefer the Betamax.

These small differences began to accumulate. As more video stores (and, increasingly, home users) purchased machines requiring the VHS format, the providers of entertainment had greater incentives to offer their products in that format. And as a greater selection of movies became available in VHS, purchasers of videocassette recorders had greater incentives to prefer a VHS machine. These network effects meant that VHS ownership became more valuable as more people became owners— a self-reinforcing cycle. By 1988, when Sony announced it would abandon the Betamax design and make only VHS machines, the company's market share stood at 5 percent.

The comfortable competitive world that emerged from the Format Wars is about to be shattered once again by a disruptive technology, the recordable digital video disc (DVD). At the time of this writing, five distinct format standards are competing for a share of this market. The lessons of the VCR have not been lost on the competitors, and the struggle for leadership will surely center around establishing the industry standard and the attendant network economies.

The Power of Lock-In

Market analysts and entrepreneurs alike frequently overestimate the power of network economies. Professor Stan Liebowitz of the University of Texas distinguishes between two degrees of networked lock-in (Liebowitz 2002). The weak form occurs when customers incur costs beyond the purchase price when they switch to the new product. These costs might include the time spent learning how to use it, or a poor interface with products that they already own. The strongest indictment of weak lock-in rises like smoke from the rubble of the "new economy" companies that built business models around achieving dominant market share, essentially asking the investors to subsidize use by the customers. And when these companies attempted to charge the full cost of their services, their customers fled to other providers whose investors still had some cash to spend.

Weak lock-in contrasts with the strong form, which occurs when a new product is incompatible with the choice of *other* customers. In that case, the entire network of users of the standard technology are out of reach of the new product. It must offer enough value to become the new standard very quickly or it will be trapped within a small community of early adopters and eventually fade from the economic scene. Thus, if you seek to capture customers through network economies, you must carefully distinguish between these forms.

Technology and Social Systems

We humans are tool-using creatures. We choose our tools within a societal context; and, in turn, that societal context shapes the tools we choose. Thus, any social system, be it a private company, government agency, military organization, or an entire culture, is irrevocably linked with its tools—its technology base. This means that you cannot change the technology of any social system without also affecting its culture. And organizations resist cultural change, instinctively and usually effectively, because it disrupts well-established patterns of interaction among people.

As a consequence, simply proving that your innovation offers superior performance is not enough. You must also recognize the social resistance to change and account for it in your plans. Entrepreneurs, technologists, and customers rarely enjoy the exclusive ability to shape the configuration and performance of any technology. Like it or not, politicians, government regulators, lawyers, courts, psychologists, ethicists, and an entire cottage industry of activists for one cause or another all influence the success of a new technology.

Even innovations that offer relief from much human misery often run a gauntlet of social protest. In the early days of the artificial heart (Chapter 4), ethicists questioned the morality of human implants, which too often merely prolonged the misery of patients already doomed. Much truth could be found for this claim, but the protest never gained traction in the courts or in the opinion of the public. In contrast, genetically modified foods, which could not only relieve hunger in much of the world but also serve as a delivery platform for medicines that do not survive well in harsh climates, face well-organized and effective opponents. It is entirely irrelevant whether this opposition would be considered rational by technology proponents or whether it is simply the work of neo-Luddites, grown bored with daytime television. It is further irrelevant whether honest concerns or self-interest motivate all this protestation. The fact remains that societal expectations can be as profound an influence on a technology as can the marketplace. You must learn to work with that fact, and consider carefully the societal needs component of the business model presented in Chapter 2 (Figure 2.1).

Part of the difficulty is that societal expectations are conveyed through multiple channels, often carrying contradictory messages. For example, the federal government has been a proponent of nuclear power for fifty years, and has done much to advance that technology, both through research and through laws like the Price-Anderson Act, which limits the liability for nuclear accidents. At the same time, a series of court decisions and effective intervention in local licensing hearings has done much to limit use of nuclear technology to power plants ordered in the 1970s and before.

Or consider energy conservation, a policy desideratum in the United

States at every level of government for the past thirty years. Experience shows that price is the most potent incentive for energy conservation, and that consumers respond with energy-saving behaviors and the purchase of energy-efficient equipment. Yet price signals that reflect the true cost of energy compete with a second and overriding public objective, low prices for consumers. Thus a host of pricing policies blunt the economic signals that would encourage and enable the desired conservation. Sometimes the best you can do is to recognize the contradictions and idiosyncrasies of our society, adapt where you can, and fight where you must.

The Acceleration of Technological Change

One of the most remarkable observations about the pace of technological change concerns its nonlinearity—the *rate* of long-term improvement along performance dimensions of interest tends to increase exponentially. Consider information technology, for example. Ray Kurzweil, a successful entrepreneur and artificial intelligence pioneer, has analyzed the rate of improvement in processing performance, measured in millions of instructions per second (MIPS), from 1900 to the present. He observes that the phenomenon known as Moore's law is really the fifth such expression of exponential growth in computing performance in the twentieth century. The previous paradigms went unnoticed because the early stages of exponential growth appear linear to the casual observer. These paradigms included: (1) electromechanical, such as the calculators that performed the first computations for the U.S. Census in 1890; (2) relay-based machines, such as the computer that cracked the Nazi "enigma" code; (3) vacuum-tube computers, such as the CBS machine that predicted the election of Eisenhower; (4) transistor-based computers, like the ones used in the early space program; and (5) integrated circuits, to which Moore's law applies (Kurzweil 2001).

But Kurzweil also observes the most important characteristic of this century of performance growth: the *rate* of improvement, not just the improvement, is exponential. When one plots the curve of performance, measured in MIPS, over time and uses a logarithmic scale on the vertical axis, one does not see a linear trace, but rather the curve shown in Figure 5.2. On a log scale, this means the rate of change is exponential. The better the technology gets, the faster it gets better. Thus a linear

Figure 5.2 **Exponential Growth of Computing**

Millions of instructions per second per $1000 investment (MIPS)

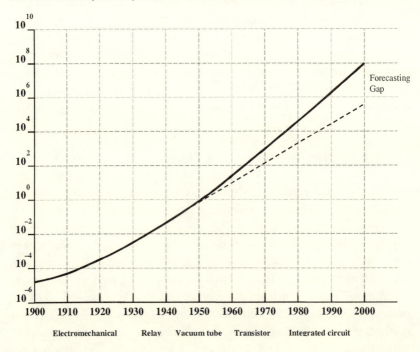

Source: Adapted from Kurzweil 2001.

forecast made in, say, 1950 (the dashed line in Figure 5.2) could err by as much as an order of magnitude by 1970 and two orders of magnitude by 1990. Similar performance growth can be shown in other technologies as well, especially the biomedical. If Kurzweil is right, human civilization stands on the brink of a literal explosion in technological capabilities.

The implications for entrepreneurs are profound, because an explosion of technology implies an explosion of opportunity—and competitive threat. For one thing, the time that any product can enjoy dominance in the marketplace is likely to be sharply curtailed. Indeed, much evidence suggests this is already occurring. Professor V.K. Narayanan notes three expressions of this phenomenon:

- Shortened product life cycles from introduction to commoditization, which makes constant innovation the surest way to sustain the enterprise;
- Shortened development times, the interval required to turn a technical possibility into a marketable product; and
- A decreasing payback period, which gives entrepreneurs less time to recoup the costs sunk into a particular product (Narayanan 2001: 47–49).

Two conflicting forces work here. On the one hand, the shortening of product life cycles combined with the fragmentation of markets into a proliferation of niches would seem to favor the entrepreneur, the attacker of established companies. Entrepreneurs are better able to execute a strategy of fast market entry and exploitation, followed by a rapid redeployment to the next opportunity and so would seem to enjoy a structural competitive advantage.

On the other hand, the general quickening of the pace of business could motivate the established companies to narrow the decision cycle advantage now enjoyed by entrepreneurial firms. If these large and well-funded rivals can adapt their business processes to take advantage of the information technologies becoming available, they might be able to combine scale economies with information economies. Web services, discussed in Chapter 2, provide one means for accomplishing this. In addition, companies like General Electric are installing integrated information systems for internal management. In effect, these are vastly expanded versions of the simple spreadsheet. They enable management decisions to be made in real time by providing information that is updated as events occur. The good news: This new imperative offers a large market for start-ups with relevant technology, and many new ventures, TIBCO Software, for example,[1] have sprung up to enable the integration of internal legacy systems. The bad news: The standard for timely and decisive action is about to be raised.

As advanced computing power becomes ubiquitous, it will combine with essentially infinite bandwidth to move the intelligence thus created anywhere at any time. This implies a world in which commodity-like products and services diminish sharply in value. In such a world, everything from the fit of clothing to the design of medicines can be tailored precisely to the individual customer. Convergence of hitherto distinct technologies to create value will be common, even as the digitization of information (a television show, a Bach fugue, a telephone call) has erased the distinctions among once-differentiated media: television, radio, and the telephone. All this upsetting of entrenched interests should energize those with the heart and mind of the entrepreneur. The attacker will have the advantage in these markets, and that is you.

6

A Tale of Two Entrepreneurs

The Journey Continued Through Heights and Valleys

> If you can meet with Triumph and Disaster
> And treat those two imposters just the same . . .
> —*Rudyard Kipling*

Nearly four years had passed since Kevin Bolin and Maurice Gunderson parted company in Little Rock—years of triumph, disaster, and just plain hard work. Though their experience diverged sharply over those years, both Bolin and Gunderson had learned important lessons. These are the subject of this chapter.

EnerTech Environmental
739 Trabert Avenue
Atlanta, Georgia
Spring 2002

It is easy to miss Trabert Avenue if you aren't paying attention. It's also easy to miss it if you are. A cul-de-sac tucked between the city reservoir and an auto body shop in Atlanta's industrial district, Trabert Avenue offers ideal quarters for a start-up company. The plain functionality of the building and offices tells the visitor that invested funds are being used to build the company, not furnish a palace. From his modest office Kevin Bolin, EnerTech's founder, reflected on the emotional roller coaster that he and his team had ridden for the past three years.

A Financial Hat Trick: Three Kinds of Capital

Bolin realized that several aspects of the EnerTech business model would pose an uncommon financing challenge. For one thing, EnerTech did not mesh well with the standard expectation for venture capital in the dot-com era: exponential growth for three to five years followed by some monetization event to return the investors' money at a fivefold increase. To achieve this, professional venture capital seeks companies with products or services that are totally "residual." In the words of Maurice Gunderson of Nth Power Technologies, such companies do the work once and sell the product/service a million times.

The EnerTech model is the reverse. Instead of making a large number of small items, EnerTech would construct only a few, each carrying a $30 million price tag. Typical of infrastructure facilities, these plants would have an operating life around thirty years, and once built, would generate a stream of earnings throughout the life of the project. Thus EnerTech offered long-term cash flows and growth through multiplying the number of such projects. Mainstream venture investors had no difficulty recognizing the value in such an offering, but most seemed able to find enough deals that fit their preferred model without incurring the risks of a start-up. They had little interest in unproven ventures.

Bolin knew that he had to secure three kinds of capital to ensure the growth of EnerTech. First, he needed technology development funds to build a process demonstration plant and to perfect the company's patent position. Venture capital firms are characteristically reluctant to support this, even for companies putatively conforming to their preferred growth model. Second, he needed project financing for the large-scale waste-to-fuel plants he hoped to build—again, not what most venture investors are able to do. And third, EnerTech needed working capital so the company itself could grow and realize the promised earnings. This financial hat trick occupied much of Kevin Bolin's thinking as his company approached the new century.

First Money In

The first external equity capital had come in early 1999 from an "angel" investor, a high-net-worth individual who put up $1 million in exchange for about 40 percent ownership of EnerTech. (See Chapter 7 for a complete discussion of the various stages of equity investment.) This person had built significant wealth in the electronics industry and now sought to help environmentally beneficial technologies move into the economic mainstream. The investment gave EnerTech sufficient working capital for a year, and enabled Bolin and his team to focus on developing the organization, the technology, and a portfolio of projects.

Team Building

The next significant addition to the EnerTech team was Cliff Gould, who became General Counsel in early 1999. A native New Yorker, Gould was educated in the South: Duke University, class of 1983, and Emory University Law School, 1986. As he began to practice corporate law for a large Atlanta partnership, Gould had one of those rare epiphanies that prove decisive for the rest of one's life—he realized that what he liked about corporate law was not the legalities but constructing the business deal. He soon started his own law firm doing just that.

Gould's introduction to EnerTech was something of an accident—as with much of the new venture experience, chance seems to triumph over intent. Gould's wife Colleen had shared a locker with Bolin's wife Laurel-Ann in law school. The families became friends, and when Gould started his own practice, EnerTech became a client. With the infusion of equity capital in 1999, EnerTech could afford Gould's skills on a full-time basis. These skills would be greatly needed, as each waste-to-energy plant seemed to demand its own deal structure.

Technology Building

By early 1999, the EnerTech technology had evolved away from the basic patent positions carefully built by Norman Dickinson over many years. Seeking to reassert technology as a distinctive competency of EnerTech, Bolin and his team drew together an omnibus application for a process patent. Their claims would be as broad as possible—every possible process configuration, every possible feedstock, and every possible use of the fuel product (see Chapter 8). By May 2002, EnerTech had filed in the United States and nineteen other countries at a total cost of around $200,000.

At the same time, the experience gained with the Mitsubishi plant in Japan was depreciating rapidly in relevance. It was becoming clear to the management team that a process demonstration plant built in the United States and available for the inquiries of potential funders and partners would be essential. A proper process demonstration unit (PDU) would cost about $400,000, plainly beyond the checkbook of a start-up company; but a Phase II Small Business Innovation Research (SBIR) grant from the National Science Foundation arrived in time for construction to begin in nearby Conyers, Georgia. In retrospect, Bolin felt that the 1999 decision to build the PDU was one of the best in the history of EnerTech.

These accomplishments—building the management team, developing the technology, and constructing the PDU—were relatively controllable by EnerTech. Much less controllable were the actual deals to construct the first working waste-to-energy plant, because they involved a wide range of outside stakeholders, each with interests that would only coincidentally align with EnerTech's and that frequently conflicted directly.

Mine Hill

The first opportunity for a commercial-scale plant arose in early 1999 in the town of Mine Hill, New Jersey, a small community in the north-central part of the state. After nearly two years of patient negotiating, Bolin had convinced the local authorities that the project would be good for the community. EnerTech received a 440-ton-per-day permit to process sludge, the largest such permit ever granted in that part of the state.

Bolin knew EnerTech had gained something of considerable value, if only a means could be found to finance the construction project. Then, fortune smiled twice. First, the state of New Jersey offered to issue tax-exempt bonds to finance the project. And second, in March 1999, the U.S. Department of Energy offered a $5 million grant to offset construction costs. Much of the grant could be used by EnerTech for working capital—provided that project milestones were met.

But the smiles turned dark in December 1999, as an untested assumption collided with a basic characteristic of EnerTech's SlurryCarb technology. Sludge—technically, and more politely, called biosolids—inherently contains about 80 percent water. To make the boiler fuel, most of the water must be removed. That water has to go somewhere, and in most cases that "somewhere" is the local wastewater treatment plant. In the case of Mine Hill, the wastewater treatment plant had reached its capacity and could accommodate no more. The town's earlier assertions that ample treatment capacity existed had not been examined and now proved untrue. And so, the project died, and EnerTech's investment in design, permitting, and local goodwill became worthless.

Letting sunk costs go always presents a difficult choice, made even harder by the emotional investment required of the entrepreneurial team even to reach a point where there was something to be lost. Mine Hill, however, was not to be the last time the EnerTech team would make this choice.

On a Roll Again

Travelers flying in to Newark International Airport are familiar with the scene from the cabin window: an expanse of flat land, a gray to brown ambiance, a haze in the air, and miles of bridges, harbor facilities, and heavy industry. This was also the scene of EnerTech's next project, one that would set the roller coaster skyrocketing upward once again.

Even while the Mine Hill plant was moving forward, Chuck Carter had been laying the groundwork for the next project. The site chosen was spectacular—at least from the perspective of sludge processing. Its location near the Newark Airport served as home to a sole proprietorship that was already processing sludge. To dispose of the material, however, this company had to truck it into Pennsylvania and there spread it on the land, a costly and time-consuming process. In place of that, paying EnerTech to take the sludge would be far cheaper, and would provide EnerTech with profit margins sufficient to support the entire venture without charging for the fuel at all. The Newark site offered several other advantages: a nearby customer for the fuel, a cement kiln; easy environmental permitting due to its proximity to a large power plant and municipal waste incinerator; and no houses for miles. Most important, wastewater treatment capacity, the fatal limitation of the Mine Hill project, was ample—EnerTech checked thoroughly this time.

At the same time, the U.S. Department of Energy decided to allow the $5 million originally intended for Mine Hill to be used for the Newark project under the same terms and conditions, noting the strong public interest in promoting this environmental technology. This support reduced the financial risk of the project to potential investors, but did nothing for the technical risk inherent in first-of-a-kind technology applied to large-scale plants. Bolin needed a way to convince potential bondholders that the technology would actually work.

In mid-1999, EnerTech turned to a unique product, system performance insurance, then offered by Hartford Steam Boiler (HSB) to reduce the investors' technical risk. The HSB engineers would perform an extensive technical analysis of a prospective customer's process technology—at the customer's expense, of course. If it passed, then HSB would write a positive report and forward it to the underwriters to prepare the policy. The coverage gave potential investors reasonable assurance that an independent third party would stand by the technology with dollars and not merely with words.

The technical due diligence that HSB required eventually cost EnerTech around $300,000 and made extensive use of the process demonstration unit in Conyers, Georgia. Without that facility, proof of performance would have been impossible. With it, EnerTech's engineering team was able to convince HSB, who issued the policy in late 1999. This recognition gave an enormous boost to the credibility of EnerTech and to the morale of the EnerTech team.

At the same time, an unforeseen opportunity arose in Shreveport, Louisiana. The city was facing a crisis with its sewage sludge that required a $40 million investment. All-up costs of disposal were estimated at $500 per dry ton, while Bolin figured EnerTech could do the job for less than $300 per ton and still turn a handsome profit. Early discussions expanded the project to an eco-energy industrial park, which would include a 500 MW combined cycle electric generator. The total size of the project ranged from $500 million to $700 million, depending on the size of the generator. EnerTech's staff was eight joyously overworked people.

Thus, by early 2000, EnerTech was on a roll. The company had secured system performance insurance, built an operating PDU to show investors, and put two large projects into the pipeline. All this, however, was rapidly consuming the $1 million in venture capital investment. It was time to seek new money.

In Pursuit of Venture Finance

One central fact governs the life of an entrepreneur: Too many things must be done within a time that is grossly inadequate to accomplish them. Chief among the "too many" for Kevin Bolin was the pursuit of working capital. Sufficient working capital buys time for the enterprise to work out complex deals like the Mine Hill project, and to recover if they fail. The million-dollar equity infusion, together with the government funds, might have provided sufficient working capital for more than a year, but the new opportunities were consuming funds faster than planned. In early 2000, the hunt for venture capital began again.

EnerTech hoped to raise between $5 million and $7.5 million for three purposes: to build working capital for operations; to provide an equity infusion into the Newark project, thus giving EnerTech a larger ownership share and further aligning the interests of the company with those of the other investors in the plant; and to serve as a cash reserve. After eight months of negotiation by Cliff Gould and some additional work required to satisfy the investing firm's need to understand the business, EnerTech signed term sheets for $2.7 million. This was not as much as had been hoped and the terms were customarily onerous—but at least it provided the means to get the first plant built.

Sludge Happens

In 2001, the emotional (and, worse, the financial) roller coaster took a plunge. In February of that year, the management of the venture capital fund that had signed the term sheets was replaced. The new group decided to start the due diligence investigation all over again. The agony did not last long, however—in March, the new management decided not to fund EnerTech at all, despite the signed term sheets.

At the same time, the Shreveport project died. Though Bolin and Carter had taken care to establish local contacts, they were outmaneuvered politically. The contract for sludge disposal went to a friend of the mayor of Shreveport. All was not lost, however, as EnerTech's work on the eco-energy park had secured for the company proprietary rights in the project. The participating utility bought EnerTech's interest for $500,000, a sum far less than EnerTech had invested in it, but far more than they had expected.

Meantime, the Newark project was advancing approximately as planned. To structure the project financing, EnerTech engaged a boutique investment banking firm that specialized in such deals. The investment bankers attracted the attention of some of the big players in the sludge industry, which in turn suggested to Bolin the possibility of a strategic partnership in place of the lost venture financing. In April 2001, shortly after the collapse of the venture funding, Bolin and Gould began making inquiries of potential partners.

The permitting for the Newark plant went smoothly except in the local zoning board. There, the $30 million project joined the queue with swimming pools, decks, and backyard patios. Further, the local rules required that a majority of members, not the majority of a quorum, approve any application, so habitual absentees from the zoning board meetings added to the delays. All of this might have been tolerated as the fumblings of a local prefecture—but then serious opposition arose. A local landowner wanted to develop the area into a truck terminal, and EnerTech's partner, the sludge processor, was in the way. The EnerTech project would ensure the survival of the sludge processing company, and so was vigorously contested.

EnerTech's opponents managed to slow the zoning board's already glacial pace so that the hearings stretched through the spring and summer of 2001. During this time, expenditures mounted for lawyers, consultants, and other expert witnesses. The vote was finally taken in October 2001—astoundingly, EnerTech lost by a four to three decision. Bolin admits to shedding more than a few tears on the courthouse steps.

While the zoning process unfolded, the newly formed venture finance arm of Hartford Steam Boiler took its own engineers seriously and began to consider EnerTech as a candidate for investment. In October, however, a large insurance and financial services company, AIG, purchased HSB. The new owner immediately made two changes. First, the new owners closed the venture capital group, thus ending that possibility for investment. And second, AIG notified EnerTech that they would no longer offer system performance insurance. Despite a signed contract, EnerTech's policy was cancelled, the larger company saying, in effect, "come sue us." As is true with many start-up companies, EnerTech had neither the time nor the resources for another protracted legal battle. Thus, 2001 ended as it had begun. At least the year was consistent.

A Day at the Beach

The events of 2001 had taken a severe toll on the EnerTech management team. They had worked hard only to see success snatched from them by unmerciful and idiosyncratic disasters. The way forward was unclear and morale was low. To work on both problems, Bolin, ever the frugal entrepreneur, took advantage of an airline special—roundtrips for $79—to organize a management retreat in Florida. The respite was therapeutic and the strategic conversation revealing. Despite the catastrophic events of the past year, EnerTech had actually achieved quite a bit, and its situation remained encouraging, albeit not with the ebullience of old.

First, the technology had been validated by three independent companies—Mitsubishi, builder of the demonstration in Japan; AMEC, an engineering firm retained earlier to design the full-scale plant; and the now-defunct Hartford Steam Boiler. In addition, the PDU continued to perform well, and gave visitors tangible evidence of the capabilities of the technology. The chief impairment to this otherwise hopeful outlook was the loss of that extraordinary and capable engineer, Heinz Ropers.

His precise and thoughtful character simply did not mesh well with the cycles of triumph and disaster typical of a start-up technology company, and he left for another opportunity.

Second, the business climate began to turn favorable. Communities across the United States were realizing that the practice of spreading sludge over land was becoming costly and impractical. They were searching for a cost-effective alternative. Catching the following wind, the indefatigable Charles Carter had developed three significant opportunities by early 2002: Ontario, Canada; a city in the Midwestern United States; and a regional sanitation authority in California.

Third, in addition to the nascent projects elsewhere, a New Jersey court overturned the zoning board's appeal and directed that EnerTech be granted the variance. Dilatory tactics continued to impede progress, but the legalities became much more favorable.

And fourth, EnerTech began 2002 with enough working capital to last the entire year at current burn rates, the consequence of additional SBIR grants and prudent husbanding of the resources available. That amount, however, would not give any project the kind of balance sheet it would need to attract additional investors. Thus, Bolin and the EnerTech team accelerated their hunt for strategic partners, the large players in the waste industry, to join EnerTech in turning sludge into money.

As he reflected on these events in the spring of 2002, Kevin Bolin began to feel renewed hope that the "Dead End" sign at the head of Trabert Avenue referred to the street only and not to the future of EnerTech.

Nth Power Technologies
50 California Street
San Francisco, California
Spring 2002

Nth Power Technologies moved into its new quarters in San Francisco's financial district in February 2001, but the suite had already acquired the plain, functional look that follows busy and intense people with little time for pretty. The portfolio of investment companies had grown enormously since the closing of its first fund in 1997. More portfolio companies required more associates, who eventually required more space.

Fourteen companies had received investment through this first fund. Of these, ten were still active, and several showed promise of significant growth. A second fund had been started in late 1999. This time, fund-raising was relatively straightforward, a consequence of the growing reputation of the Nth Power team and financial markets that generally favored venture capital investment. The second fund closed in September 2000 at over $120 million. A third fund, however, reflected the difficult market for new venture finance that followed the implosion of technology stocks in 2000–2001. This closed in early 2002 at around $75 million. Reviewing the progress of these venture funds, Maurice Gunderson and Nancy Floyd, the founding partners of Nth Power, reflected on their experience and its meaning for those daring enough to start new businesses with technology.

Many Are Called, but Few Are Chosen

Imagine the universe of all business ideas to be the size of a rather large beach ball. Then imagine further that within this beach ball is the set of all business models that will actually work. This would be about the size of a baseball, and would include barber shops, consultancies, and insurance companies. Then imagine within that baseball a small marble. This represents the kind of high-growth enterprise that Nth Power and like-minded venture funds are seeking: companies with a cure for the common cold or a way to generate electricity without producing carbon dioxide.

The 500 business plans that Nth Power receives each year break down into these categories. From this large "deal flow," Nth Power seeks to discover the few start-up companies with the capacity for exponential growth and a return of five times the invested capital—the marble in the beach ball. Nth Power will invest in 5 to 10 of the 500 aspirants. How they sort out the candidates is worth knowing.

All the Diligence That Is Due

That odd phrase "due diligence," now a term of art in the venture capital community, derives from the legal and fiduciary requirements that the law places upon fund managers—in effect, to exert themselves sufficiently to discover the deep truth about candidate investments. Though not inerrant, the due diligence process remains the most effective way for a free society to allocate resources in the new-growth sectors of its economy. Nth Power typifies the way that the better venture investors perform their due diligence.

Most of the 500 business plans are screened out at the beginning of the process because they should never have been sent in the first place. Many come from mass mailings of business plans—the spray and pray approach—and are not even closely related to the Nth power investment thesis. For example, Nth Power once received a business plan for a combination funeral parlor and Internet chat room. It was buried without discussion. Other entrepreneurs simply ignore the criteria that Nth Power and similar venture firms post on their Web sites. No business plan that ignores these criteria is likely to become a candidate for investment.

The business plans that do get serious attention tend to be recommended by persons known to (and respected by) the Nth Power principals. Indeed, any venture capital firm responds better to recommendations than to the unexpected business plan.[1] And once you have serious attention, the process advances through several layers.

First, and most important, the investors have to get comfortable with your business story—what we have called the business model in Chapter 2. Technical due diligence does not play a major role at Nth Power. If the principals do not understand the technology, you will not get funded. Period. Beyond that, you must show the investors the full business model set out in Chapter 2. Nth Power emphasizes several key elements of that model:[2]

- A resourceful management team that knows the technology, but can think, speak, and act in market and profit terms;
- A realistic market strategy that projects rapid growth while thoroughly accounting for the competitive environments; and
- Defensible strategies that maintain marketplace leadership.

You should not include significant funds for technology development among your capital needs. The ideal business will have progressed beyond the proof-of-concept, R&D, and "seed" funding stages and will be ready to introduce commercial products. Finally, you should pay special attention to the timing of market development. Gunderson observes that most entrepreneurs get the size of the market about right, but they miss its timing. They wax overly optimistic about how fast the market will develop, how soon mainstream customers will buy, and how long the sales cycle will take. Alas, everything takes longer than it would in a better world.

The most common flaws with the management team all derive from lack of experience, especially in:

- High-growth operations: managing exponential growth is itself an art form.
- Sales: in many technology companies, nobody on the management team has ever sold anything.
- Competition: the too-common assertion that you compete with another technology instead of a company betrays a flawed understanding of competition—technologies don't compete, businesses do.

For all these specifics, the heart of the due diligence process is simple: the investors must be able to figure out realistically what can be accomplished by *your* management team with *your* technology pursuing *your* defined opportunity. Once the Nth Power team becomes comfortable that your company can match its claims with enough achievement to fit the venture capital model, then the next layer of due diligence can begin—a structured review of the proposed management team.

This review is highly personal in nature, in essence a thorough background investigation of each member of the management team. It includes legal background, credit checks, criminal history, and so forth. Potential investors take this very seriously, and with good reason—Nth Power once found a member of a management team who had been convicted of insurance fraud, and the rest of the team was unaware. Most venture investors subcontract this investigation to outside firms.

The final layer of due diligence is legal. The investors' lawyers use elaborate checklists to verify corporate structure, employment contracts, noncompete agreements with other companies, board meeting minutes, and the like.

The Value and the Price

The most successful venture investors spring from the entrepreneurial mindset rather than the financial, because at this early stage in the life of a company the real issues center around entrepreneurship. Thus the valuation process at Nth Power tends to be judgmental first and quantitative second. As the decision to invest matures, the Nth Power principals seek a sharper appreciation of the true value of the prospective company—not what it is as presented, but what it can become.

The Valuation Process

Maurice Gunderson contrasted the valuation process for an existing business with that for a start-up. Imagine yourself purchasing an ongoing enterprise, say a corner drugstore that has been in business for ten years or so. To place a value on this purchase, you have an operating history, which you can subject to the standard tools of financial analysis: discounted cash flow and the like. You expect that in your hands it will do at least as well as it has in the past, and so you are able to know, within a reasonable uncertainty, the right price to pay.

In contrast, an entrepreneurial technology company is about the future. The interesting questions do not concern where it has been but where it is going: how much this company *can* be worth, and how many financing steps will be needed to get it there. Any quantitative analyses must be performed on these projections of this future, and naturally beg the question of why anyone should believe the projections in the first place. Thus, the real issue is the credibility of the projections and not the sophistication of the mathematical tricks performed with them.

Income Statement vs. Balance Sheet

Gunderson advanced a second perspective on valuation. Equity value can be approached either through the income statement or the balance sheet—both of which you will need in your business plan. From the income statement perspective, the new company looks like a disaster. It plans to lose millions of dollars over the next several years and asks investors to support the anticipated loss. A discounted cash-flow analysis of this is not a pretty sight.

In contrast, the story that you must tell concerns the balance sheet, especially growth in owner equity. In the standard venture capital model, the value for investors resides entirely in equity growth, which is their reward for a protracted period of illiquidity and high risk. You must convince investors that owner equity will indeed increase through your team executing your business model. The strength of that story will determine your valuation.

A Structural Advantage

In new venture valuation, Gunderson and Floyd saw two structural advantages in the Nth Power business model. First, as a specialty investment firm, they could know more about the energy business than their more generalized rivals. Thus, they would understand the market context for the technology and its range of value within that context. And second, as successful entrepreneurs themselves, they could comprehend entrepreneurial skills in ways that mere financial analysts could not. These structural advantages in the inherently judgmental valuation process meant that Nth Power's assessment of value was likely to prove more accurate than the valuation of competing investors, and also more accurate than that of the entrepreneurs seeking funds.

For that reason, Gunderson and Floyd avoided extensive bargaining with prospective companies over the appropriate valuation. If an entrepreneur held fast to a valuation that exceeded that of Nth Power by a significant amount, this intransigence was taken as a symptom of poor judgment that would later show up in other areas. More important though, marked differences in valuation would undermine the complete and unreserved alignment of interest between investor and entrepreneur. Without this alignment, no new enterprise is likely to succeed. Even if an unrealistic valuation could be negotiated down, the process might well leave the entrepreneur feeling cheated. As Nancy Floyd noted, life is just too short to take on a resentful business partner, and so Nth Power would simply pass on a deal rather than attempt to negotiate away a large difference.

The Dark Side of Venture Capital: How Companies Fail

Once Nth Power becomes involved with a company, it maintains that engagement with vigor, actively counseling the management team, often participating in decision making as a member of the board of directors, and leading the subsequent rounds of investment. Indeed, the insights so painfully acquired by Gunderson and Floyd over many years can become one of the principal resources for their portfolio companies. Despite this, some companies still fail, and you should understand why.

Companies are a bit like families: the successful ones tend to follow similar patterns, but those that fail seem to find unique ways to do so. Even so, some generalizations can be made. Gunderson and Floyd have found technology failures rare— though this might simply be the consequence of a business model that does not buy into technological uncertainties. Instead of technology, they point to market timing as one of the principal causes of failure. The anticipated market just does not appear before the company runs out of money and the investors run out of patience. The equity story works well in the beginning, but in the end the cash must actually flow.

Gunderson reflected on a second principal cause—management failure, especially that of the CEO or the founding entrepreneur. In Nth Power's experience, the CEO has been replaced in about 75 percent of the portfolio companies. Some companies experienced CEO changes several times. Simple burnout causes much of the problem. The job of CEO of a start-up company is one of the hardest that can be found. Enormous pressure from investors combines with too many things to do in too little time. Some CEOs just break under the stress.

In other cases, the founder must be replaced because some personal flaw interferes with the needed performance. For example, an incapacity to respond to advice (called "coachability" in athletes) can turn the desirable character traits of strong will and perseverance into a liability. Clearly the worst flaw, however, is dishonesty. You must never conceal bad news from your board or from your investors, as one Nth Power CEO attempted. That person was gone within forty-eight hours of discovery.

Vision Delayed: Vision Denied?

A five-minute conversation with Maurice Gunderson reveals the accuracy of his self-assessment: he is an entrepreneur first and a financier second—a distant second. And as an entrepreneur, he shares the vision and optimism so characteristic of the entrepreneurial mind. But by the spring of 2002, other observers of the Nth Power portfolio might have been forgiven for holding a less sanguine view.[3]

By that time, the three portfolio companies that had become publicly traded—Capstone Turbines, a producer of low-emission combustion turbines for small-scale electric generation; Proton Energy Systems, a developer of fuel-cell electric generators using proton exchange membrane technology; and Evergreen Solar, a maker of photovoltaic modules for generating electricity at remote sites—were struggling in the stock market. The stock of Evergreen Solar, for example, had traded at over $20 per share shortly after its initial public offering (IPO) in November 2001. But by the spring of 2002, Evergreen's shares traded for less than a dollar. The public markets treated the others to similar punishment: the price of Capstone Turbine stock fell from over $80 per share in late 2000 to under $1 per share; and Proton Energy fell from around $30 per share to trade in the $2 range.

Three external factors contributed to the sharply diminished equity of the Nth Power companies. The first was the general decline in public equity markets. From late 2000, when Capstone Turbine made its IPO through the second quarter of 2002, the Standard & Poor's 500 Index lost nearly 30 percent of its value. Not only does this provide a stout headwind for companies already public, but it also forecloses the exit strategies so favored by the venture capital community—the initial stock offering or the private sale, which depend upon the strength of the public markets. While these remain weak, exit can be unavailable and venture capitalists can find themselves trapped in illiquid investments.

The second external influence on the Nth Power companies was California's disastrous experiment with the deregulation of its electric sector. In 1996, the governor signed into law a complex and poorly structured scheme, essentially deregulating the wholesale electric market through an unwieldy administrative mechanism, but retaining price controls over retail electric sales. The state followed up with a series of unfortunate policy and regulatory decisions to complete the ruin. Throughout 2000 and 2001, wholesale prices for electric energy soared and California suffered highly publicized shortages. Buying at the high deregulated price and selling at the low regulated price soon drained the financial assets of the investor-owned electric utilities. One, PG&E, declared bankruptcy, and none were able to purchase further electricity because they had neither money nor credit. At that point, the state intervened to become the sole electricity purchaser for California, spending about $10 billion for electric energy, which it then resold to the utilities at the regulated price for about $3 billion. The crisis faded by late 2001 as demand fell and new power plants came on-line. But by then, the nationally publicized crisis had effectively stifled the progress that many states had been making toward deregulation—and with it, postponed the rich opportunities envisioned for entrepreneurial ventures in deregulated markets.

The third event—federal policy action to promote alternative energy sources and a more competitive business environment in the electric sector—did not happen at all. The U.S. Congress discussed proposals like mandated efficiency standards for automobiles or requirements that a specified fraction of utility generation (usually around 10 percent) use renewable resources. But no action was taken. At the same time, the long-running struggle between federal and state regulators over control of the deregulation process went unresolved. Energy investors and putative customers for new energy technology became reluctant to commit to the new products and services offered pending the outcome of these political events.

As Maurice Gunderson considered these events, he concluded that the original vision that inspired Nth Power remained valid despite its delayed realization. The California experience with poorly implemented deregulation would temporarily mask the successes in other states. But the genie would not go back in the bottle, and eventually a more decentralized, more competitive electric infrastructure would emerge. And federal and state authorities would eventually agree, even if a public crisis were required to force the agreement. Thus, he knew that entrepreneurial businesses would eventually fill a vital economic role in the energy infrastructure—but when? Start-up companies with negative cash flow and limited reserves often lack the capacity to wait out a delayed market. For them, opportunity delayed becomes opportunity denied. And like all entrepreneurs, patience became for Maurice Gunderson a virtue imposed by necessity, not one chosen out of personal preference.

A Reflection

The experiences of EnerTech and Nth Power commend several lessons to our attention. First, you must take care not to confuse a need with a market. Even the most pressing societal needs do not necessarily translate promptly or well into the marketplace, often for reasons that are invisible to the entrepreneur. For example, the trustworthy and trusting Kevin Bolin had no way to uncover the indifference and venality of the local officials in charge of sewage without attempting a deal. Yet carelessness and ancillary considerations led these officials to deny the public the benefit of more effective sludge disposal.

Similarly, no amount of a priori analysis would have led Nth Power to anticipate the delayed course of electric deregulation. When public policies make an incomplete transition to effective markets, entrepreneurs can become trapped in apparently valid business models that they cannot implement. There is no cure for this; you simply must remain alert to the possibility and find ways to work with it.

Delays in market formation cause start-up companies to spend their precious cash for mere survival rather than progress. Indeed, this mis-match in time scale becomes a salient issue for the start-up company in introducing new products. By contrast, new product development from the platform of an established company can sometimes allow greater patience when drawing support from ongoing cash flow.

Important as cash is to the new enterprise, the chief contribution of a good venture investor reaches beyond mere money. The best venture capitalists provide their companies a web of contacts and the benefit of their experience—intellectual riches outside the reach of simple cash.

7

New Venture Finance

An Entrepreneur's Perspective

> An ox for a penny? And if you haven't a penny . . . ?
> —*Yiddish proverb*

And if you haven't enough pennies to ensure timely growth for your new enterprise, then you must secure the needed capital from others. Building your growth around advanced technology offers at once a financial challenge and a unique opportunity. The challenge rises from the reluctance of many venture capitalists to invest in the early stages of technology development, which are required in order to demonstrate the feasibility of an advanced concept.[1] Most often, you must look elsewhere for the resources needed to prove your technology.

The opportunity rises from the market. Advanced technology, once exclusively yours and captured in a product, attracts new venture investors by providing the kind of sustainable competitive advantage discussed in Chapter 2. As a result, start-up companies with technology-based products or services typically absorb the great majority of venture capital placements because they offer the growth opportunities these investors are seeking.

This chapter offers an entrepreneur's perspective of new venture finance—not to make you a specialist, but rather to help you ask the right questions in building a street-smart financial strategy. We begin with that most fundamental of all financial concepts: cash.

Cash in the New Enterprise

Cash flow to the new venture is like blood flow to the body: good substitutes just aren't out there. At the beginning, cash flow comes from the drawdown of funds invested by the founders. This first cash serves to move the fledgling enterprise far enough toward maturity that knowledgeable investors will see it as a good bet. Indeed, the new enterprise will probably require several rounds of professional funding to develop fully the technology, the offering, the market, and the organization. Eventually, if enough goes well, cash from operations will begin to supplement invested capital and the company will achieve a positive cash flow. The simple scenario below illustrates the dynamics of this inexorable need for cash.

A Cash Flow Scenario

Figure 7.1 illustrates a simplified pattern of cash flow in a start-up venture. The horizontal axis measures the life of the company from its inception to the time at which revenues become significant. The vertical axis measures cash, positive or negative. The "Net Cash Position" line shows the financial resources immediately available to meet operating needs. In this scenario, the company begins with a positive cash position, the capital put in by the founders.

Operating expenses draw down cash rapidly, and at t_1 a new infusion of capital resets net cash back to a more salubrious position. This too is drawn down, but with success, revenues increase and outlays abate. By t_2, the company's cash reserves are increasing, and by t_3 it has turned cash flow positive. Further investment rounds might be needed for rapid growth, but not for mere survival. This sketch, of course, heroically oversimplifies reality—the cash life of real companies is much more interesting (to the observer) and harrowing (to the company) than this rather plain illustration. Instead, it seeks to illuminate the strategic character of cash flow and the requirements it imposes for controlling the outflow and timing the new rounds of investment.

Measuring Cash Flow

To keep your net cash position positive, whether through new investment, borrowing, deferred payments, or even revenues, you must think ahead to the next round of funding, the achievements that will make your company attractive to these investors, and the cash that these achievements will either require or generate. The financial tool that allows you to do this is called the "pro forma." A good pro forma models the hypothetical flows of revenue and cost through the company and the accretion or dispersion of its wealth. Its use requires facility with three basic tools: a cash flow projection, an income statement, and a balance sheet.

Figure 7.1 Illustrative Cash Flow

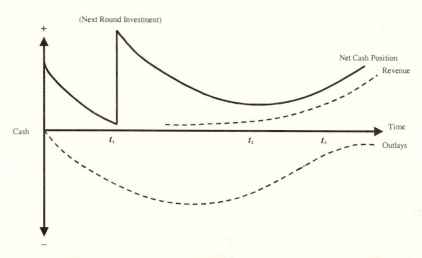

A pro forma should be considered a projection of the feasible, an analysis of the financial implications of a future that is both desirable and achievable. The desirable part will come naturally; to convince potential investors of the achievable, you will need a thorough and plausible explanation of the assumptions that underlie your projections.

Equally important, you must be able to answer the inevitable "what if" questions, posed not only by investors but by yourself at three o'clock on a wakeful morning. You can accomplish this without undue aggravation by linking these basic statements into an *integrated financial model* of your company. This will allow you to trace the implications of a change in assumptions for cash flow and the other parameters of interest. Numerous off-the-shelf software programs are available, or you can easily build your own with any capable spreadsheet program.

However it is built, your pro forma is more of a framework than a blueprint. Circumstances will change, and a good model alerts you to the financial implications of such changes. Such a tool will prove invaluable in the dynamic business environment of the start-up company. Used as a scenario tool to test alternative futures, a financial model can help exorcise your venture of several evils. The first is the evil of ignorance, of blundering into the future, as ill-prepared for good fortune as for bad. The second, deriving from the first, is the evil of desperation. One does not wish to appear before potential investors with three weeks of cash left in the bank. This is as much fun as a root canal, but rather more expensive. And finally, good financial planning can avoid the worst evil of all, wasting the only resource that is truly not renewable: your time.

Financial Strategy for Entrepreneurs

You will find it helpful to take the long view of financial strategy. Think first about the connection between financing and operations. To make the new venture most attractive to potential investors, each round of funding should be identified with a set of milestones, which once achieved will significantly advance the company. Investors appreciate knowing what they are buying and how to measure your progress.

In addition, the special burden of the technology company is to find the means to develop the technology. And beyond that, you must secure funding for product, market, and organizational development. The key to success will be to consider all the options available and to tailor the package best suited to your company, technology, and market.

A Strategy for Finance: The Right Tool for the Job

A complete and balanced financial strategy would blend four distinct kinds of instruments:

- *Founders' Capital*: The first financial commitment, sometimes called "bootstrap" capital, must made by the founders themselves.
- *Development Financing*: A variety of instruments can provide resources to advance the technology to a maturity suitable for equity investors. Often the amount required exceeds the resources available from bootstrap capital.
- *Angel Investment*: Also called "seed capital," this first outside equity investment is usually provided by wealthy individuals who combine other motivations with a desire for investment success. In addition, some professionally managed funds provide angel investment.
- *Classic Venture Capital*: These professionally managed funds seek equity or equity-equivalent investments in high-growth companies that offer a realistic prospect of liquidity within an acceptable time, typically about five to seven years.

Now consider the strategy of financing from the investors' point of view. The technology companies that they will consider for funding generally fall into two categories (Wetzel 1997: 186):

- *Middle Market Ventures*. These offer the equity investor a reasonable prospect of achieving annual revenues from $10 million to $50 million within 5 years. An Initial Public Offering (IPO), the first time common equity is offered for sale to the public, is the most desirable pathway to investor liquidity. But only 10 to 15 percent of venture-backed companies achieve an IPO. For the remainder, the investors' reward is most likely to be achieved through a private sale, perhaps to a strategic partner.
- *High Growth Ventures*. Less than 1 percent of all start-ups, these offer credible revenue projections in excess of $50 million after 5 years. They typically fuel that growth with several rounds of venture capital funding and typically seek liquidity through an IPO. A private sale is a fall-back strategy.

Table 7.1 relates the essential features of the four generic financial instruments to these archetypal enterprises. Of course, the real world never organizes itself so neatly, but the point of the table is that a variety of financing strategies are possible. For each individual enterprise, financial wisdom begins with weaving these elements into a coherent, balanced strategy to ensure that the cash needed for growth will be there on time and affordably. Precious time and energy must not be wasted in futile pursuit of financial instruments ill suited to the task.

Bootstrap Financing: The First Skin in the Game

The first skin in the game must be yours. Otherwise, other investors are likely to find your commitment to the enterprise suspect. The problem derives from an asymmetry of information between the entrepreneur and the investor. The entrepreneur will always know more about the true prospects for the enterprise than the investors will ever be able to know—indeed, were it otherwise, the entrepreneur would not be doing his or her job (Gompers and Lerner 2000: 128–37). Investors, however, cannot be expected to commit their funds to an enterprise if the persons who know most about it do not commit theirs. These investors

Table 7.1

Elements of Financial Strategy

Financial strategy	Middle market	High growth
Bootstrap	Essential for credibility	Essential for credibility
Development finance	Essential for bringing technology to investment grade	Possibly helpful for technology development
Angel investment	Helpful, both for capital and mentorship	An interim step toward venture capital
Venture capital	Helpful, though possibly unnecessary	Necessary for IPO

will consider participation *with* you; they will not consider participation *instead of* you.

Entrepreneurs use a variety of instruments to make this commitment. The most common (and least painful) are personal savings; loans secured by property, such as one's home; and personal debt. As the company matures, extended terms from vendors and customer advances can also become a source of cash, though sometimes at a cost measured in credibility rather than money. Some founders even use credit card debt, and simply shoulder the burden of unpleasant people calling at all hours demanding payment. All of this, of course, brings with it great personal risk. You really could lose it all, a the case of Heartware International shows.

Heartware International: An Entrepreneur's Commitment

Mr. Gerald Seery founded this company in October of 1988 to market an advanced medical technology. He kept his day job as director of international marketing and sales for a small medical device company for 6 months before resigning to devote full time to *Heartware*. The initial capitalization included $185,000 from Mr. Seery and his wife, taken from their savings, personal debt, and a home equity loan. Shortly afterward, four relatives invested $85,000. In addition, Mr. Seery's wife prepared the business plan and served as chief financial officer. Her full-time salary at an established company supported the family.

Sadly, this company became insolvent two years later, after failing to raise the needed capital. The entire investment was lost, as was compensation for the time devoted to the enterprise by Mr. Seery and his wife.

From the teaching case, *Heartware International* (Oviatt, McDougall, Shrader, and Simon 2000).

The real issues, however, reach beyond founders' capital to the ways that cash flow can be sustained. For the ongoing funding that will redeem your own investment, you must plan for later-stage financing well before you need it. Even with a clouded view of the future, this beats relying on vague expectations of future financing.

Development Finance

Professional equity investors tend to decline opportunities to fund the research needed for demonstrating the feasibility of an emerging technology. This is true even (perhaps especially) when that research is central to the success of the enterprise. From the investors' perspective, an unproven technology adds an unaccustomed risk to the more easily understood market and business risks. But even more fundamentally, equity investors seek to own a portion of a company, not an option on a technological capability. The strength of that company, and hence of their interest, rests on the strength of the entire business model of Chapter 2. If any part of a complete model is not in place, you will fail to get investors' attention. They simply have too many opportunities that are complete to devote time to those that are not. And even when some technology development is included in the financing package, venture investors prefer that it be small, often using rules of thumb like that employed by Maurice Gunderson at Nth Power: $1 for technology development, $3 for product development, and $9 for market development.

Thus street-smart technologists will consider the special sources of support that are designed to promote technology development: public funding from both the federal and state governments, and alliances with established companies.

Public Technology Investment: The Federal Government

A rich variety of federal programs seek to promote specific technologies in the public interest, one of the links between technology markets and contemporary society discussed in Chapter 5. The favored fields frequently change, however, and programs come and go. Thus, you should always search the Internet thoroughly for opportunities in your own technologies of interest. Four kinds of federal programs, however, have endured long enough to warrant mention on the printed page.

The first of these is the Small Business Innovation Research (SBIR) program. Under a law enacted in 1982, federal agencies that fund extramural R&D must set aside 2.5 percent of these monies for research by small, high-technology businesses. At recent budget levels, the amount set aside exceeds $2 billion per year. The SBIR provides grants that enable small companies to move a technology from concept to commercial readiness. Program administration is left to the individual agencies with R&D budgets, such as the Department of Defense, which operates its SBIR program through its Defense Advanced Research Projects Agency (DARPA). At DARPA, for example, typical awards for concept development are around $100,000, while those for later-stage commercial development can be as much as $750,000 for two years. The technologies funded must relate in a meaningful way to the mission of the sponsoring agency. The support is a grant: the government does not take an equity position nor does it become a creditor.

Follow-up studies have shown that companies receiving SBIR funds enjoy substantially greater sales growth than matching companies that did not receive these funds. For example, sales for the average company receiving an SBIR award grew by $4.1 million from 1985 to 1995, an average increase of 98 percent. By contrast, the mean sales growth for the matching firms was only $1.1 million, a 27 percent increase (Lerner 2000: 977–79). The best of the SBIR companies, however, outperform these averages by a wide margin. For example, the Ballistic Missile Defense Office, the branch of the Department of Defense in charge of what was once called the "star-wars" defense, invested about $1.5 billion in SBIR awards beginning in 1983. By 2003, the market capitalization of the top twenty-five companies receiving awards exceeded $5 billion, a remarkable performance considering the fall in value of the NASDAQ that began in 2001.

Current eligibility requirements for the SBIR program can be found at the Web site for the U.S. Small Business Administration or any of the participating federal agencies. The specifics of the program change with the political winds, and you should investigate the requirements rather than assume them.

The second major federal program assisting technology development is the Advanced Technology Program (ATP). Unlike the SBIR, private opportunity rather than government needs drives the technology agenda. Also unlike SBIR, firms of any size may participate, though the ATP does require some cost sharing, which varies upward with size. The program is highly competitive: since 1990, over 6,000 proposals have been submitted seeking about $13 billion in funding. Of these, 709 projects were awarded about $4.1 billion in funding.

The value of an ATP award, however, goes beyond money. The program design builds the social networks of participating firms by encouraging them to relax their boundaries and share knowledge with other members of the joint venture. Participants thus gain access to complementary knowledge and business resources of their R&D partners and collaborator firms. The ATP is managed by the National Institute of Standards and Technology (NIST), and specific eligibility requirements can be found at the NIST Web site.

The third major federal instrument, the Cooperative Research and Development Agreement (CRADA), is less a source of technology development funds than a way to leverage funds you already have. The CRADA allows private firms of any size to form a research partnership with one of the national laboratories. In general, the intellectual property created by these partnerships can be retained by your company, but details differ among federal laboratories. These details bear close scrutiny, preferably before you begin.

Finally, numerous federal agencies operate special technology development programs in pursuit of their own missions. For example, technologies relevant to homeland security are now greatly favored, and the Central Intelligence Agency has funded a semiautonomous venture capital company to invest in new enterprises with relevant capabilities. Similarly, the U.S. Army has recently begun a program for field-portable energy devices.[2] Other agencies simply offer grant programs. In January 2001, for example, the Department of Energy announced a grant program to develop energy-efficient technology for industrial processes. Up to $40,000 can be awarded for concept development and $200,000 for scale-up.

The federal government also offers to support research alliances through Small Business Technology Transfer (STTR) grants. The STTR, an impecunious cousin to the SBIR, funds cooperative R&D projects between a small (under 100 employees) for-profit company and a not-for-profit research institution, like a university. The requirements are similar to the SBIR, and your project must mesh with the needs of the federal agency that funds it.

Public Technology Development: State Support

The urge to give out money resides at all levels of government, and many states provide investment capital to new ventures that originate within their borders. This can provide an initial boost in regions lacking a highly developed venture capital industry. In addition, state financing offers one distinct advantage—the requirement for residency as a precondition for funding will eliminate many competitors, especially in states where private funds are scarce to begin with. On the other hand, any dearth of professional venture capital is likely to make second-round financing more difficult in such states. Some examples illustrate the range of possibilities.

The normally impecunious state of Missouri has begun a state-sponsored seed capital fund with an initial capitalization of $20 million for first money into the venture. The fund takes a small equity position, but can participate in succeeding rounds of funding only if it was a first-round investor.

Another kind of state program lets technology companies operating in preferred fields—biotechnology, for example—package their operating losses and sell them for tax purposes to other companies operating in the state. The technology company gets an infusion of cash, and the purchasing company gets state tax relief. A program of this kind is operating in New Jersey and being considered in Maryland.

And finally, the Ben Franklin Technology Partnership (BFTP) provides a guarantee of up to 25 percent of any loss experienced by qualified private investors—the "angel investors" discussed in the following section—in seed investments made in technology companies located in southeastern Pennsylvania. The BFTP seeks to reinforce the community of first-stage investors in the region, eventually leveraging as much as $10 million into the area.

The most complete catalog of such programs is maintained by the National Association of Seed and Venture Funds, which can be accessed on the Internet (www.nasvf.org). Or, consult the department of commerce in your own state.

GeneTrace:
A Study in Public Technology Funding

The poster child for technology development with public monies was GeneTrace. This systems biology start-up was spun off from SRI International in 1994. Its mission was to discover new drug leads and drug targets using a fully automated DNA sequencing process significantly faster than conventional methods. From the beginning, the company made imaginative use of several financing strategies to develop its technology and create new products from basic science.

GeneTrace began with an ATP grant, awarded in January of 1995, of nearly $2 million, matched by about $700,000 in nonfederal monies. From that time through the end of 1999, GeneTrace won seven additional grants from SBIR and individual agency programs. The total awards discernible from public records was about $5.8 million.

Its private leverage was no less remarkable. In March 1998, GeneTrace and Monsanto announced a broad collaboration in plant and animal genomics research. Under this agreement, Monsanto invested $17.2 million and gained a seat on the board. Monsanto gained exclusive access to license the technology worldwide. A similar research agreement was struck with Berlex Laboratories for an undisclosed amount.

Alliances for Technology Development

Resources for technology development can also be obtained through alliances with established corporations. This is most often done in technologies where the basic science is evolving rapidly and no company, however large, can afford the R&D necessary to keep pace. In those circumstances, a large firm might find it advantageous to support technology development in areas that complement its own in-house research. The terms of exchange usually call for an exclusive license for the larger firm to practice the technology, though equity participation can also be involved. This is a common practice in the life sciences.

A Cautionary Note

If you anticipate seeking venture capital at some time in the future, you should note that professional investors sometimes regard government support with suspicion. They are concerned that the skills required for success in obtaining grants distract from the market orientation required for a successful company. Whether this is really true or merely a tribal superstition of the venture capital community is beside the point—if that is the investors' concern, then you must be prepared to deal with it. Prospective venture funders will also examine corporate alliances to see whether too large a share of future markets has been traded away.

Finally, you should be aware that the decision cycle of the large company is much longer than your own. Not only must approval for action be obtained through successive layers of management, but internal politics can also lead to delays. Small companies have died while two departments of a large corporation quarreled over who would sponsor the partnership. As an entrepreneur, you have surprisingly little leverage over such events—an imperfect world, indeed.

GeneTrace Systems: The Sequel

Every great company begins with a dream, and so did GeneTrace. As the National Institute of Standards and Technology gushed in a September 1997 press release, "The goal is among the most sought-after in science: to design a fully automated process for deciphering the genetic code that is rapid, reliable, and inexpensive." This was to reduce the cost of genetic screening and testing by two to three orders of magnitude. But despite the worthiness of the dream, despite GeneTrace's demonstrated prowess at raising research monies, the company ultimately failed. And in that failure lies a cautionary tale.

In addition to its research grants, GeneTrace had acquired funding from angel investors. The company also had offers from two venture capital groups when the Monsanto opportunity appeared. Monsanto offered GeneTrace a valuation higher than the venture investors by $10 million, largely because Monsanto wanted the company to focus on developing its own product line without the distractions that might be brought by other owners. Unwilling to match this price, the other investors dropped out.

The Monsanto partnership left GeneTrace in an awkward position. Its largest owner was also its principal customer, and so other potential investors found the situation thoroughly unattractive. Thus, if Monsanto did not wish to continue, further resources would be very difficult to raise. And by 1999 Monsanto did not wish to continue, largely because the technology had run into inherent limits that precluded commercial feasibility in the markets that Monsanto sought. Further, Monsanto approached the GeneTrace investment as if it were buying a technology deliverable rather than a stake in an enterprise. When the deliverable proved impossible, Monsanto lost interest in the enterprise. (At the same time, Monsanto shut down the research unit to which GeneTrace had been attached, partly in response to mounting social protests against genetic foods[3] and partly distracted by the Pharmacia-Upjohn merger.)

A new president, brought in shortly before the Monsanto deal, tried to adapt the gene expression platform to other markets.
(continued)

But GeneTrace's software was not adequate for the task. Atto sell the company failed. GeneTrace ran out of cash in late 2001 and closed its doors forever.

Two cautions should be drawn from this brief tale. First, the ability to secure government research grants does not always translate well into product development skills. When the purpose of the enterprise changes markedly, so must the talent base of its leadership. And second, be wary of partnership with an owner/client who has a product-development agenda rather than a company-development agenda. As GeneTrace's last president said, "GeneTrace became a one-trick pony—and the pony died."

First Money In: Where Angels Tread

A new technology company seeking to finance growth can rarely move directly from founders' capital to professionally managed venture capital. Most commonly, some intermediate, maturing step is needed: project finance can be one kind of intermediate step, and private placement by wealthy individuals is another. Often called "angel" investors,[4] these individuals provide the first outside equity into the new venture, also termed "seed capital."

During the frothy days of the first "new economy," the ranks of private, seed-capital investors swelled to an estimated 400,000 by mid-2000, up from 250,000 just three years earlier. Much of the influx came from newly rich entrepreneurs who had cashed out of their own companies only a few years before (Sechler 2000). But by early 2001, it became clear that the party was over and the hangover just beginning. During the dismal twelve months preceding the first quarter of 2001, all venture capital funds lost 18 percent of their value, seed stage funds 21 percent, and the NASDAQ 36 percent. The net worth of many potential angel investors plunged, and the survivors might logically choose to sustain the ventures in which they are already invested rather than seek new ones.

Those angel investors who remain in the game, however, can take some comfort from evidence that the long-term returns to first-stage capital appear superior to the returns from venture capital in general or from the NASDAQ. An analysis by Henry Wong of Artemis Ventures shows that the twenty-year performance of seed stage funds proved superior to venture capital funds in general, the Standard and Poor's 500, and the NASDAQ (Wong 2001). Further, indirect evidence suggests that by the middle of 2003, the angel investment market might be turning around. After reaching an eight-year low in the first quarter of 2003, first-time financing by professional venture capital firms rose by 12 percent in the second quarter, according to The MoneyTree™ Survey by PricewaterhouseCoopers, Thomson Venture Economics, and the National Venture Capital Association. This implies better fortune for the angel investors whose companies are awaiting next-round financing.

Motivation

Like their venture capital counterparts, angel investors seek equity participation in the growth of the company and as much protection from loss as possible. They have worked hard for their money and do not treat casually the opportunity to lose it. But in addition, angel investors are animated by considerations that reach beyond the purely financial. These nonfinancial motivations include:

- *A Desire to "Give Back."* Many of the best angel investors are themselves successful entrepreneurs. They wish to nurture the opportunity-driven society that has done so much for them.
- *Technology Interest.* Some have an interest in promoting specific technologies, especially those conveying significant societal benefit, such as medical or environmental technologies. Others see angel investing as an opportunity to stay current with markets and technologies of their own special interests.
- *Association.* Angel investors value the opportunity to network with like-minded people and to participate in the thrill of the start-up without committing to all of its agonies.

These motivations are good news for technology entrepreneurs, giving them a special entrée into the angel community. However, this community is not organized as formally as other capital markets, and access depends as much on circumstance as on merit. The keys to the kingdom are your contacts.

Contacting an Angel

It is sometimes said that a wise man knows everything, but a shrewd man knows everybody. This kind of shrewdness is essential in finding seed capital. Making contact with angel investors is not as difficult as reaching one of their heavenly counterparts, but it can seem so.

Local investor associations offer the most systematic way to enter the seed funding network. Seed investors tend to place their capital close to home. This allows closer contact with the funded companies for more effective mentoring. Angel investors increasingly band together to identify and screen venture opportunities. Most communities with meaningful entrepreneurial resources have associations of angel investors, and these can serve as an initial point of contact. Associations often sponsor dinners, special workshops, or other gatherings at which entrepreneurs can present their ventures to the seed investor community. Many of these associations cooperate with public support groups, such as incubators or other sources of entrepreneur assistance. Some target special populations, such as women entrepreneurs.

The most effective contact, however, is a direct referral by a person known to (and respected by) the private investor. Boards of advisers can be quite helpful here, and members should be selected, in part, for their ability to reach potential investors.

Finally, we note that many angels confine their investment to industries or technologies with which they are familiar. If your market or technology is outside an angel's chosen sphere, it is usually a waste of time even to attempt contact.

Preparing for a Visitation

A recent survey of angel investors illuminates their expectations. Most invest in technology-based businesses. The companies receiving these funds typically have two or three employees, a business plan, a prototype that actually works and in which a proprietary position can be achieved and protected, and a potential customer (Roberts, Stevenson, and Morse 2000). Excellence in any of these parameters would, of course, make your company stand out from the crowd.

It is not enough, however, to *be* investment-worthy; you also must *appear* investment-worthy. Accomplishing this requires preparation of three tools for presenting your company. The first is sometimes called the elevator speech: by chance you meet an important investor in an elevator. On the way to the fifth floor (hopefully not starting from the fourth), he or she asks you how things are going. What do you say to capture this opportunity?

The second is a two-page summary of the company. Many seed and venture capital investors will not read a business plan until they have perused this summary, which tells them whether further investigation is likely to be rewarded. Your summary need not sell the company, but rather persuade the potential investor to read the entire business plan.

The third tool is the presentation. In many cases, investor associations whose attention you have gained will ask you to present your plan to the group. You are unlikely to have more than twenty minutes to make your case—possibly less. And as in the two-page summary, you must give investors the information they are looking for. They will not dig it out for you. Success here gets you to a serious reading of the business plan. Fail, and the game ends, at least for that investor group. You can consider the case made when the combination of presentation tools and business plan persuades an investor of the following:

- *Quality of the Market Opportunity.* The market opportunity is so compelling that nobody (even you) could fail to create significant returns for the owners within five to ten years.
- *Quality of the Business Model.* The proposed new venture and its embedded technology offer a plausible platform for creating wealth and capturing a meaningful share of it.
- *Quality of the Management Team.* This team has what it takes—energy, commitment, experience, integrity, and coachability—to implement the business model and to invent solutions to the challenges that will inevitably arise.

What You Must Give

The specific terms of exchange are similar for venture capital investors, and we discuss them fully under that rubric. For the present, it suffices to note the basic nature of the exchange: the founders of the venture trade some, eventually most, of their ownership for the opportunity to grow faster than internally generated capital would allow.

From a personal perspective, many entrepreneurs find this exchange difficult—a bit like indenturing your child in order to buy baby food. It requires the company founder to adopt a rationalist frame of mind in contrast with the emotional commitments that are essential for the success of start-up companies. It requires the entrepreneur to cede control of the beloved venture to strangers in order to see it grow. Some entrepreneurs,

---

Guidelines for Presentations

Joe Ollivier, a member of the Utah Angels Venture Group, has set out ten guidelines for these presentations. We summarize them here (Ollivier 2000):

1. Explain the value proposition and competitive niche as though the investors were the customers to whom you are selling the idea.
2. Set out the kind of deal you are seeking—for example, 20 percent of the company for $500,000. Where did you get the 20 percent figure, and why is it right?
3. Explain how the company is presently valued. How did you ascertain that value?
4. Show the current capital structure. Who owns the shares and what did they do to earn them? What warrants or options are outstanding?
5. Describe the use of the funds. Why do you need investors? These investors? When will you complete the first CPA audit of your financials?
6. Present a chronological marketing plan. Explain in detail how you are going to generate sales. Be prepared to explain your overall revenue model in detail.
7. Describe the current management team and why these people are going to be successful.
8. Describe your outside directors and advisers. Why are these the right people, and what do they contribute?
9. Do not blandly assert that the exit strategy will be an IPO or sale. Provide some details about how you expect to accomplish this.
10. Provide the current financials, no matter how ugly they are. This includes an income statement and balance sheet for the next three years. Cash flow projections should look forward one year. Be prepared to answer detailed "what if" questions, the reason you need the pro formas discussed earlier.

---

consciously or otherwise, prefer control to growth and are unable to cross this divide. But for those who are willing to risk the thing they love to a stewardship shared with others, the rewards reach beyond mere money.

What You Should Expect

Mere money is never enough. The ultimate success of the venture will depend as much on the quality of thought that can be brought to bear. Their willingness to mentor the young company thus makes angel investors of uncommon value. Their specialization by technology or industry niche brings knowledge that cannot be otherwise gained. Further, their contacts can help with every aspect of the company from sales to technology to next-round financing.

The close mentoring relationship between entrepreneur and angel investor puts special demands on the individuals involved. Both have an interest in ensuring that the personal chemistry works before agreeing to any investment.

Professional Venture Capital

Most discussions of entrepreneurial finance are dominated by the venture capital model—professionally managed funds that seek equity or equity-equivalent investments in high-growth companies that offer a realistic prospect of liquidity within an acceptable time, typically about five to seven years. Professional venture capital offers one liquidity strategy for the angel investors and the surest pathway toward a publicly traded company.

A Market Perspective

At the most aggregate level, new venture finance is governed by the basic forces of capital supply and capital demand. The supply of capital seeking new venture investment grew enormously during the late 1990s, providing entrepreneurs with a following wind of increasing force. In all of 1995, about $6.2 billion was invested in 1,262 ventures, according to data taken by The MoneyTree™ Survey of PricewaterhouseCoopers, Thomson Venture Economics, and the National Venture Capital Association.[5] In contrast, the first quarter of 2000 alone, the high tide for venture capital in the United States, saw new venture placements had risen to $28.6 billion invested in 2,164 deals.

This rate of increase simply could not be sustained in an economy growing at 3 percent or so per year, and indeed it was not. By the first quarter of 2001, the quarterly rate of investment had plunged to $12.9 billion invested in 1,312 deals. The decline appears to have leveled after reaching a low of $4 billion in 647 deals during the first quarter of 2003. Falling profitability explains much of this decline. The apparently easy profits of the late 1990s had built expectations on the part of venture fund investors that could not be sustained. Most recently, the three-year returns to all private equity funds have been negative, and the most recent investors have lost about 40 percent of their paid-in value. Early-stage and venture capital investors have suffered disproportionately with 2002 losses ranging from 28 percent for early-stage investors to 23 percent for balanced funds.

This will improve, of course. But in the meantime, the precipitous drop in the supply of new funds is making capital markets much more competitive for entrepreneurs seeking venture investment. And so some knowledge of the central tendencies of the industry will surely be helpful.

A Brief Demography of Venture Capital

The economic demography of the industry strongly influences the prospects for entrepreneurs seeking professional venture capital. Three characteristics stand out: (a) a sharply defined model of the ideal investment, which channels attention toward technology fields where the venture capital model is thought to work best; (b) concentration in a few geographic areas; and (c) the phase of the economic cycle.

With regard to the first, professional investors seek the 1 percent of all start-ups that can be considered high-growth ventures as defined previously. These companies are not distributed randomly throughout the economy, but tend to cluster in sectors where there is great societal need or where advanced technology is creating special opportunities. In 1980, for example, about 20 percent of venture investments were in energy. But as oil prices fell throughout the mid-1980s, this sector was replaced by others offering greater opportunity for growth.

Beginning in the 1990s, the hot sectors were related to information technology. According to The MoneyTree™ Survey, communications and networking alone accounted for $22.5 billion of the $87.5 billion invested in 2000. Including software ($15.7 billion), information services ($8.9 billion), semiconductors ($2.9 billion), and electronics and computer hardware ($1.8 billion) brings the total for the information technologies in 2000 to $51.8 billion.

In contrast, the life sciences, a sector with extraordinary technological potential but often requiring a significant up-front investment in the science, gathered slightly over $7.9 billion in 2000, about 9 percent of that year's total. According to The MoneyTree™ Survey, this was allocated as follows: biopharmaceuticals, $3.2 billion; medical software and information services, $2.2 billion; medical devices and equipment, $2.0 billion; and healthcare services, $0.5 billion. Looking ahead, however, investor emphasis might well shift to the life sciences as progress in genetic sciences moves the action from science to applications, and indeed by the second quarter of 2003, the life sciences accounted for about 25 percent of the total investment.

Because investment is specific to the sector favored by circumstance or opportunity at the time, and because these sectors tend to cluster geographically, we should expect venture investment to cluster as well. Even so, the geographic concentration of venture investment is striking. The Silicon Valley area has always led the nation by a wide margin; but in 2000 that area captured 35 percent of all U.S. venture investment, according to The MoneyTree™ data. By contrast, the runner-up, New England, captured 12 percent, the New York area, 8 percent, and the Southeast, around 6 percent. By the second quarter of 2003, nothing had changed, and the traditional leaders remained solidly in front. Thus companies located in the favored regions have an inherent advantage over those that are not, even if all else is equal.

Finally, please note the importance of timing in new venture finance. The venture capital industry depends upon a robust stock market both to enable liquidity events through the IPO and to provide wealthy investors for their own funds (Black and Gilson 1998: 247–77). In turn, angel investors are encouraged by a robust venture capital industry because it improves the likelihood that the successive rounds of investment will be available. Thus economic downturns ramify throughout all venture finance.

These realities are of central concern to entrepreneurs. Even an excellent management team with an excellent business concept faces a diminished likelihood of funding if it seeks capital outside these demographic parameters. That is not fair, but it is the way the world works. And you need to know it.

The Term Sheet: It's Not Just About Price

Most entrepreneurs dream of the day they will sit down across the table with a venture investor to negotiate the terms of a deal. But like the dog chasing the car, it is best to know what you will do with it once you catch it. Some of the considerations follow.

The "term sheet" is the document that sets the basic parameters for the deal between you and the investor. It is usually a simple document, and its purpose is to explain the basic framework of the agreement— expensive lawyers will follow this with specific implementing language and papers.

Part of the deal is, of course, the price: how much of the company you will have to give up to obtain the funds you need. But you should not focus all your attention on the price, but rather consider it in the context of all the other deal points. You should bear in mind that the basic purpose of the term sheet, rightly considered, is to align formally the interests of the signers. And so wisdom begins with each party understanding what the other needs, where the tension lies, and where common cause can be made.

First, what *you* need: the money is obvious, but this is only a commodity. In addition, you need the best business advice you can get and contacts with persons who can advance the venture. All this has one purpose: to make the enterprise succeed. You pay for this by surrendering some ownership (equity) and embracing the risk that comes with shared governance of the thing you have built.

Those who would invest in your company have needs too: the return on the money is obvious, but in addition the venture investors and those who have entrusted them with their money require some protection from loss. Some of typical loss-minimizing provisions are discussed below. But in the end, the investors' interests are best served, perhaps only served, if the enterprise succeeds. The investors pay for these gains with a loss of liquidity for five to seven years and a heightened risk of loss of principal.

The common interest is therefore plain, the success of the company defined by an event that allows the investors to extract their capital—either sale of the company or an initial public offering (IPO). Note, however, a subtle point that escapes many entrepreneurs. With outside investors comes a slight but growing distinction between the founders and the company. In the beginning, the founders could rightly join with Louis XIV in proclaiming, *l'état, c'est moi*. But as the company grows, so do the legitimate claims of other stakeholders, not only investors but employees and customers. Personal resources become organizational resources, and you must become accustomed to the role of steward rather than king.

Finally, expect the investors to negotiate terms that could separate you ingloriously from the company you have founded, should you later become an obstacle to its growth. I have not found systematic data here, but in the experience of many venture capital investors, the founders are removed from leading their enterprises before its IPO in over half of the cases.

In general, the founders interests will center more around control and operations, while the investors have stronger concerns about financial matters. Thus, a properly negotiated term sheet can leave management with the necessary freedom to operate while investors are heavily consulted in financial matters.

Key Term Sheet Provisions

The term sheet can include several key provisions that in effect assign these rights of ownership and control under anticipated conditions. For some investors, especially angel investors, the term sheet is a relatively brief, informal document. But it becomes progressively more formal with successive rounds of financing, eventually becoming the kind of turgid legal document most of us would like to avoid. Since you cannot avoid it, you should learn to recognize the key provisions that will determine the financial future of your enterprise. (You should also negotiate this with the help of an attorney who has experience in such matters.)

The first of these key provisions is the *liquidation preference*, which assigns to each class of shares the manner in which it will be liquidated in the event of a sale or IPO. Most investors will insist on preferred stock (or debt, often the choice of angel investors) to afford some protection in the event that the performance of the enterprise falls short. And they will want the preferred stock (or debt) convertible into common equity at their option in order to participate fully in the performance that everyone expects. Some later-stage investors will negotiate for the right to receive both the face value of their preferred stock and conversion to common equity at the time of sale or liquidation. This is called "participating convertible preferred stock." These investors, however, should expect to pay more for these additional preferences.

A second key provision concerns *vesting*. The concept is that a founder does not take full ownership of some portion of his or her stock until a specified time of service or operational milestone is reached. The intent is to ensure the continued interest of the entrepreneur in the success of the company. As a founder, you will also want to provide a vesting schedule for your key employees.

Antidilution rights, a third key provision, refer to the effects of later rounds of financing in diluting the ownership share of the first investors. These can be especially contentious in the event of a "down round," a round of financing in which the price per share is less than that paid in previous rounds. The issue is really one of balance. On the one hand, it is reasonable to expect protection of an owner's stake in the company. But on the other hand, ironclad antidilution rights can make the venture less attractive for future investors, thus limiting the capital it needs to grow.

Control provisions including voting rights are often points of discussion and a fourth key provision. Under normal conditions, a venture capital firm might ask for a seat on the board or a right of veto over certain actions, like a merger or company sale. Milestones are likely to be set out, both for receiving disbursements from the investor and as a control mechanism. You should take care to set these milestones with a firm sense of the achievable. Changes in control and ownership can occur if you miss them, and these will not be favorable to you.

On Value

The basic issue that decides what an investor will pay for a share in the company is its valuation. First, you must distinguish between pre-money and post-money valuation. For example, a start-up seeking $250,000 for 25 percent of the company is implicitly claiming a valuation of $1 million immediately after the investment is made— $250,000 divided by 0.25. Before the investment, pre-money as it is called, the implied value would be $750,000—the $1 million less the additional $250,000. Further, these valuations are always calculated on a fully diluted basis—that is, including all equity, convertible debt, share commitments to founders and key employees, and so forth. But these are merely the mechanics. The real issue is what drives the estimate of value in the first place.

For the first round of funding, the seed capital, the valuation process can be relatively informal. Much of it rests with the investor's assessment of your abilities as an entrepreneur and the credibility of your management team. That is why prior success is so highly prized on a management team. Commitments fulfilled in the past imply an ability to do so in the future.

The valuation process becomes more formal with successive rounds of financing. This is because the standard tools of company valuation, especially discounted cash flow, become increasing meaningful as the company matures. These methods are well explained elsewhere, and I can best serve you in this slim volume by referring you to the standard references.[6] Please understand, however, that all such tools derive their analytic power from projections of revenue and profit. Their conclusions track the accuracy of those projections—surely no better, and possibly much worse.

So the valuation issue becomes one of the credibility of the projections. My own discussions with venture funders suggest the following rank high among the credibility builders:

- *The Management/Technology Team.* Those who have "been there and done that" get more credit for street smarts than those who have not.
- *A Hot Technology and/or Business Sector.* The dot-com bubble of 1999–2000 saw extraordinary valuations attributed to ephemeral enterprises simply because they had some connection to the Internet. Companies operating within sectors currently in vogue tend to be compared with peer companies in a self-reinforcing cycle.
- *Sales.* With capital markets focused on economic fundamentals once again, legitimate sales to a real customer go a long way toward validating a business model.

The heart of the matter is to create a convincing case for the potential of your venture—and to recognize that company valuation is a negotiation subject to all the human foibles and idiosyncrasies inherent in the human condition.

The Dynamics of Venture Capital

The structure of the venture capital industry is changing, perhaps fundamentally, in response to the severe correction in technology markets that began in 2000–2001. Two changes—one incipient, the other a speculation—seem most likely to affect the prospects for entrepreneurs seeking venture finance.

In Search of Liquidity

The most immediate consequence is the rise of a secondary market in venture capital fund positions. This allows the limited partners to sell out their positions, usually at a discount, prior to the general liquidations and distributions of the fund. Several implications arise from this, though the ultimate consequences can be foreseen only dimly. For the investors, the secondary market reduces the risks arising from protracted

Cache Flow:
Rags to Riches to Rags to . . .

There are reasons why successful venture capital investors like Gunderson and Floyd consider exuberance the worst of human emotions in evaluating a prospective company. Cache Flow provides many of them. The company began in 1996 to build a business providing quicker access to Internet Web pages. The product (still undeveloped in 1996) was to be an appliance added to customers' computer networks to provide a local cache for frequently used Internet data.

The company soon raised $1 million in seed capital from angel investors in San Francisco and Seattle. Hotly pursued by venture capital companies, Cache Flow sold 25 percent of the company for $2.8 million in October 1996. Founders, selected employees, and the angel investors owned the remaining 75 percent. By the end of 1997, Cache Flow completed product testing, and a second round of financing brought in $6 million for 17 percent of the company. The first-round investors contributed an additional $1.8 million to maintain their 25 percent share. The funds were used for marketing—still no revenues.

By mid-1998 a trickle of revenue began, and investment bankers began to solicit Cache Flow's Board about an IPO. In March 1999, a third round brought $8.7 million for 7 percent of the company. Previous investors put in an additional $5.5 million, but were nevertheless diluted after stock option grants to management. In November 1999, Marc Andressen, cofounder of Netscape, joined the board. Cache Flow offered the public 5 million shares, about 16 percent of the company, at $24 per share. By close of the first trading day, the share price (trading as CFLO) had hit $126, giving the company a market value of $3.9 billion. At the same time, the company's quarterly report showed losses of $6 million on revenues of $2.2 million (McGee 2000).

Though volatile, share price reached a high of $161 in October 2000. The froth began to subside, however, and insiders sold the stock from June 2000 through the end of the year. By January 2001, share price had reached $10 on reported losses of $51 million. By early 2002, the share price had fallen below $1.00 and earnings were still negative. On August 21, 2002, the company changed its name to Blue Coat Systems (now trading on the NASDAQ as BCSI), changed its product line to Internet security systems, and reverse-split the stock 0.2 to 1. Losses continued, but diminished.

From that point on, however, the story becomes happier, for some investors at least. Had you invested $1,000 in Cache Flow shares on August 1, 2002, you would have become the proud owner of about 2,222 shares at the stock price of $0.45. After the split on August 21, you would own about 444 shares. And by August of the following year, those shares would have been worth around $5,300. On the other hand, had you purchased your shares in October 2000, your $1,000 would have secured 6.2 shares. By August 2002, these would be worth $2.80 and by August 2003, $14.81. Timing is everything.

illiquidity. Indeed, the average age of positions in venture capital funds has dropped from more than 7 years prior to 1999 to 3.7 years by the first quarter of 2001 (Pfeiffer 2002). With reduced risk from illiquidity, venture funds should become more attractive to investors, thus increasing the flow of new investment. Thus, the emerging secondary market should be good news for entrepreneurs.

Offsetting this, the partnership agreements of most venture capital funds do not allow such sales absent the consent of the general partner or the other limited partners. The extent to which this will inhibit growth of the secondary market remains unclear. Further, the effect on the commitment of the venture funds to the entrepreneurs remains uncertain. On the one hand, investors with a bailout option might have less commitment to the portfolio companies than they otherwise would. But on the other hand, new investors who have bought in at a considerable discount might be more patient with the portfolio companies than the previous owners were. The net result of these influences cannot be assessed at this time, but the outcome will surely affect the funding of new ventures.

In Search of Income: A Speculation

If the flood of venture capital in the late 1990s led to too much money chasing too few high-quality enterprises, the drought that began in 2001 has surely brought the reverse. Throughout this boom and bust, however, one kind of entrepreneurial venture has been consistently underserved by classic venture capital: the technology company with the potential for strong and consistent revenues, but measured growth.

EnerTech Environmental provides one example. Imagine the financial consequences of setting up a series of waste-to-energy plants around the country. Each project would probably be financed separately, largely with debt capital. EnerTech, and perhaps other partners, would draw a stream of revenues from the plant over its economic lifetime, say thirty years. As the plants accumulated, so would these streams of revenue. None of this, however, provides the pattern of exponential growth sought in the classic venture capital model, and which this chapter describes. Many renewable energy ventures share the same financial characteristics.

This classic model of venture capital was invented after World War II to supplement the traditional lending of banks and similar institutions. Traditional debt capital proved incapable of finding the balance of risk and reward appropriate for the proliferation of new technology-based companies, and a different kind of financial instrument was needed. The now-classic venture capital investment fund answered this need, and it serves this country very well, funding the expansion of American technology beyond the purview of the corporate research labs.

But perhaps the time has also come for another major innovation in venture finance, the income-oriented venture fund. Such an investment vehicle might not be able to offer investors a liquidity event after five to ten years of operation with a reasonable prospect of a return of five to ten times the original capital invested. And so some other means of rewarding investors for sharing the risk of the new venture must be found, perhaps some strong assurance of return of the original capital and a stream of dividends thereafter. This is speculative, to be sure—but some financial innovation is plainly needed, and whatever it becomes might well mark the next great advance in new venture finance.

8

Building Competitive Advantage
from Intellectual Capital

They copied all they could copy, but they couldn't copy my mind,
So I left 'em sweating and stealing, a year and a half behind.
—*Rudyard Kipling,* The Mary Gloster *(1894)*

The chief resource of any enterprise is its intellectual capital—the skills and experience of its management team; their ideas about the business, especially regarding customer value and their inherent competitive advantages in providing that value; and the technological capabilities that underlie the enterprise. This chapter concerns the protection and nurture of those intellectual assets.

Think of technology as capital with a diminishing shelf life. To be sure, it must be protected against theft; but if merely sequestered, its value will depreciate as other innovative approaches, perhaps even some that offer inferior performance, occupy the market. Protecting the core technology remains important, of course; it is just not enough. In addition, you must accomplish two objectives.

First, you must cultivate your formal intellectual property by an aggressive initial filing for patent, copyright, or trademark protection. The initial patent gives you greater credibility in seeking venture investors, and subsequent filings can expand the scope and depth of your formal protection. Extended filings also defer obsolescence, always important in times of rapid technological advance.

Second, you must build "know-how," the informal intellectual capital of the enterprise, the base of experience with your markets and the application of your technology to those markets. Both areas of knowledge, the formal and the informal, must continue to grow. In effect, you must manage your intellectual capital as you would manage any key resource—guarding it where you must; sharing it, where such sharing adds competitive advantage; and continually building it as you learn more about the markets you serve and the technologies that serve them.

Consider the case of EnerTech Environmental. The strong patent position for that company's SlurryCarb Process did not create significant benefit until a demonstration plant had been built. That demonstration allowed EnerTech to develop a form of intellectual capital that complemented its patent base: the experience and know-how gained by the company and its management team. Though informal and difficult to codify, that experience base nevertheless provides a powerful and unique advantage over potential competitors. Note also that the experience gain had to be shared with EnerTech's partners on the project, together with the formal rights to practice the technology in Asia. You will see these terms of trade—intellectual capital for financial capital and the opportunity to gain experience—often as you seek to grow your technology-based enterprise.

Creating and Protecting Intellectual Property

This chapter can offer only a brief introduction to the dynamic and complex legal processes that surround intellectual property; when you come to the real thing, you will need professional legal services. To become a more astute buyer of these services, you might also seek out a specialized and up-to-date text, or even visit the Web site of the United States Patent and Trademark Office (PTO) at www.uspto.gov.

In general, three kinds of protections can be gained for intellectual property: *patents*, which are most relevant to the technology-based enterprise; *copyrights*, which apply to original works of authorship like books, music, or software; and *trademarks*, distinctive representation devices used by a business to identify its own products or services. The same general principles apply to each. But patents tend to be more fundamental to building a competitive advantage from technology, and so we shall focus our thinking on them.

The Patent Process

Most fundamentally, a patent serves as a social contract between an inventor and society. Society, through the federal government, grants you special property rights concerning the use of your invention, provided that it is formally disclosed to the public. This process, invented by the Venetians, seeks to promote trade by advancing public knowledge and discouraging the accumulation of trade secrets.

The proprietary rights conferred by a patent give you several options. You can simply prevent others from using the property for a specified period. Or, you can grant the right of use through a license in exchange for agreed-upon fees and conditions for use. Like any right, it is only as good as your willingness to enforce it, either through negotiation or litigation. And if you fail to enforce your right when you know of an infringement, the law can consider the property abandoned.

There are three kinds of patents: *utility*, *design*, and *plant*. Utility patents are granted for new processes, new machines, or new compositions of matter. These remain in force for twenty years from the date of filing. Design protection for fourteen years can be secured for ornamental designs of an article of manufacture—the styling of an automobile, for example. And plant patents (also twenty years) are granted for asexually reproduced plant varieties. Within these old-fashioned-sounding categories reside the newest of technologies and concepts. Under recent court rulings, business processes are included under process, and human genes are considered patentable as composition of matter.

For any kind of application, you must prove three points to the PTO if you are to qualify for patent protection:

- that your invention is new to knowledgeable practitioners in your field, and not just new to you;
- that it is not obvious to persons with ordinary skill in the technology; and
- that it is useful.

Loose Lips Sink Ships

Protecting your idea should begin well before the patent filing. In technology fields that are advancing rapidly, such as genomics, similar discoveries can be made by competing researchers anywhere in the world. In those cases, patent authorities usually award the patent to the first person to think of the invention. Hence, you might be called upon to prove your precedence, and will need evidence. Laboratory notes, recorded in a bound volume without easily substitutable pages, are powerful evidence. These should be dated and detailed in their description. The signatures of two reliable and independent witnesses also help to support your claim to precedence.

In the United States, you may also disclose your invention publicly and still gain patent protection, provided that you file within one year of the disclosure. In most other countries, however, any public disclosure precludes later patenting. Thus, you should thoughtfully review your business strategy for use of the property prior to any public announcement.

The Sword and the Shield: Tactical Considerations[1]

In many cases, filing an initial patent conveys little value. Put yourself in the place of a competitor and review your invention in light of the ways that you would work around it. If your shield seems a little thin, perhaps additional filings would be needed, both to add value to your base patent and also to protect against circumvention. Patent claims should have the broadest possible applicability.

Conversely, patenting can also serve as your sword. If you are competing against a rival technology, you might review your competitor's patents for ways to improve the basic technology. If this can be done, then you might be able to file supplementary patents surrounding your competitor's basic invention. Such surrounding patents would require the competitor to come to you for a license to practice improvements to his or her own invention. Your tactical advantage can then be traded for a reciprocal right to practice the competitor's invention, thus providing you access to a market that you might otherwise not be able to serve.

One note of caution, however—filing and maintaining patents is expensive, about $15,000 in filing and maintenance cost for a U.S. patent and as much as $50,000 in Europe and Japan. And that excludes legal fees. Thus, a patent-based strategy makes sense only insofar as it supports the strategic intent of the enterprise. In the case of EnerTech Environmental, for example, the broad and growing set of proprietary claims serves that business well. By contrast, the fashion-oriented markets faced by Light Cicles (a story told later in this chapter) seem unlikely to reward much more than the initial patent claim.

International Patents

In these times of global markets, you must also consider filing in other countries. Each country has its own variation of patent protection, some offering little or no value, but others offering much better protection. Enforcement also varies. The difficulty of obtaining patents in some countries reduces the value of the protection sought. The question to ask is where your primary markets are likely to be. There you must file.

The Business Value of Patents

You can also think of a patent as an imperfect call option. It allows the owner to invoke certain, limited rights for the duration of the patent, chiefly to prohibit others from using the patented technology or to require a fee and impose conditions if a license to use is granted. In principle, this call option should increase the value of your company to potential investors. And in practice, it does—the difficulty being that neither you nor your investors have very good ways of quantifying that value.

In some cases, a patent position can become the chief asset of the innovator. Consider, for example, InterDigital Communications, holder of telecommunications patents for technologies to transmit and receive wireless phone calls (trading on the NASDAQ as IDCC). Settlement of its ten-year infringement dispute with cell-phone maker L. M. Ericsson yielded an immediate payment of $58 million in April 2003, and the prospect of strong future earnings as third generation cell-phone technology (3G) gains acceptance.

But in other cases, intellectual property can fail to translate fully into investor value. This seems especially true of business-model patents, as the case of Priceline.com illustrates. Priceline went public in 1999, and part of its value story was the patent it had been granted on the name-your-own-price business model. Priceline continued to broaden and deepen its patent position, and by early 2000 had been granted six more and filed for an additional twenty-five. Investors imagined the start-up moving from one market to another—cars, groceries, real estate, and so forth—with its patented business model keeping competitors away (Weber 2001).

In fact, nothing like that happened. Priceline failed to extend its business model to other markets, and even suffered competition in its native travel market when Expedia offered its own variant of the name-your-own-price scheme. Priceline sued, but the settlement left Expedia still able to offer its services in the travel market. Priceline's stock, once selling for over $150 per share, fell below $2 by late 2002 (prices are prior to adjustment for a 0.16 to 1 reverse split in 2003). Of course, investors still do value patents. But the most savvy of them also recognize that even the strongest patent position cannot guarantee market success. Much better to consider the patent simply one more weapon in the ongoing fight for competitive advantage. The case of an entrepreneurial firm, Light Cicles, is illuminating in that regard.

Frontiers of Change in Intellectual Property

The ownership of knowledge, or more correctly of proprietary rights to a closely defined sector of knowledge, has become a troubled arena of public policy. The corpus of legislation and court rulings that has grown up over the years was built upon an economic and technological structure that is rapidly passing. Advances in technology, especially in the information and life sciences, will require that the established rules be modified to accommodate the new realities. In particular, you should recognize three areas where the rules of the game might change: protecting knowledge products; patenting the business model; and patenting human genes.

Knowledge Products[2]

Consider the book, for example. It is a physical entity that can be used by only one or perhaps two persons at once. If someone has checked it out of the library, everyone else is denied access until it is returned. Hence, even in the presence of public libraries, an incentive remains for multiple users to purchase the book, and the author's rights can be protected relatively well.

Now contrast that with the electronic version, which can be accessed simultaneously by an indefinite number of persons independent of geography. In both cases, the fixed cost to gather the material and write the book is about the same. But the marginal cost to *re*produce the content, low enough for the physical book, is almost zero for the electronic version. All this raises serious questions regarding just compensation for grunge-rock musicians, artists, and, of course, that most worthy group, the authors of textbooks.

Chapter 10 addresses these issues in depth. Here, it suffices to note that copyright violations will become difficult to detect and police in a world driven by advances in digital technology and the Internet. Ubiquitous copiers and software that cuts and pastes with ease reduce the natural barriers that once inhibited copyright infringement. And even

Light Cicles: Enterprise Lost

A somewhat longer taxi route from New York's LaGuardia Airport into the canyons of Manhattan (reserved for times of congestion on the bridges or for midwestern professors at any time) takes you through a neighborhood of modest, well-kept homes. Even in July, the observant passerby might notice a common feature—strings of decorative lights draped from eaves, small porches, and any other convenient overhang. These are the popular icicle lights, and when they were invented, they swept the market as the hottest new holiday decorations in decades.

The Light Cicles story begins, appropriately enough, at Christmastime, 1994, in a rural Indiana town. Two women, a mother and daughter, operating a gift shop and gourmet food store, were seeking to decorate their shop for the holidays in a way that would set it apart. They discovered that way, and with it gained what seemed at the time a major opportunity, an opportunity that would set them on the kind of emotional roller-coaster familiar to Kevin Bolin and Maurice Gunderson.

Juanita Donica had left her job as a postal worker in 1993 to open her gift shop in New Castle, Indiana (population 21,000). Her daughter Dianne Syme,[3] a homemaker with three children, joined her. To decorate their shop for the Christmas holiday, they devised strings of lights that looked like icicles and hung them for display. They soon found, however, that this display attracted more customer attention than the merchandise.

Recognizing the intense customer interest in something that was not for sale, Donica and Syme decided to launch the innovative lights as a product. They hired a welder to fabricate a device, which they called a "Quick-Strip," that would enable purchasers to hang the lights in a way that gave the effect of lighted icicles. Syme's husband, a graphic designer, created an unusual box featuring a house lit with icicle lights against a deep blue background.

The resulting product succeeded beyond the wildest expectations of the Light Cicles founders. In their first commercial season, Christmas of 1996, Donica and Syme saw sales reach $5 million, limited chiefly by their ability to produce the popular lights. The 1997 season was even better. But even in that year, imitation products had gained a significant foothold in the market.

Of course, Light Cicles was not completely unprepared. Recognizing the need to protect a valuable intellectual property, Donica and Syme had hired an attorney and obtained a design patent (fourteen years) on the lights, a trademark on the name Light Cicles, and a copyright on the design of the box. These protections, however, proved porous for several reasons. First, the copyright on the box design was flawed, in effect protecting only the blue color and that imperfectly. Imitators soon paid Syme's designer husband their most sincere compliment. In addition, the patent protected only the Quick-Strip from which the lights were hung. Imitators could simply invent an alternative hanging device, and soon did.

But even if flawed, the intellectual property protection available to Light Cicles should, in principle, have provided some deterrent to market entry. In practice, it did not. Imitators, especially overseas companies,

(continued)

flooded the market after 1998. The Light Circles founders took the most blatant violator, a Taiwanese company, to court, won a cash settlement, and actually collected.[4] But the other violators were so numerous that the founders simply could not pursue the legal remedies that were theoretically available to them. By the 2000 season, the burst of market growth that icicle lights enjoyed had passed. Further pursuit of redress did not seem likely to repay the anticipated legal expenses

Light Cicles fought back, seeking to adapt its business model to the realities of a faddish, seasonal market with easy entry and rapid cycles. Rather than defending their existing products against the flood of offshore imitators, Light Cicles would compete through innovative designs that would be kept strictly secret. Rather than exposing their work in advance at trade shows, the company sought direct relationships with retailers. The core of the business would be the immediate family, and there would be no outside ownership or other employees. Operations and logistics would be carried on under an agreement with a Chicago company, which gained an exclusive license to the entire product line. The new products would have thorough patent protection—Syme hired new counsel after the first fiasco—in order to create a licensable property. In addition, the Chicago firm would provide up-front funding for making early prototypes of the new decorations.

By early 2002, Light Cicles' future looked bright, and CEO Dianne Syme felt confident that the new business model could secure for the founders the rights to their intellectual contributions, even if much of the economic value created would be retained by the partner company. Part of a loaf would still be better than none.

Alas, all this was not to be. The Chicago partner backed away from the deal, claiming the new products would be too expensive to make and that the market would support only bottom-end offerings and not art. The arrangement failed, and with it so did Syme's company, its only remaining value the trademarked name, Light Cicles. Even today, Syme looks at the festive icicle lighting with pride and regret—pride that she invented something of value to so many people, but regret that her company could not find a way to capture that value. But the best entrepreneurs do not spend much time on either emotion, and Syme has already launched a new company with a new set of decorative products. This time, value capture

with legitimate use, price tends to move toward marginal cost in a competitive environment; and with a marginal cost near zero, the ability of copyright holders to recover their investment in content diminishes. The legal protection of knowledge-based intellectual property is an evolving area, which you can anticipate will change significantly over the next several years. In the meantime, a business model that effectively captures the value of a knowledge product will probably protect your interests better than reliance on standard intellectual property law (Davis 2000).

Patenting the Business Model

A second area of controversy springs from a 1988 decision by the United States Court of Appeals for the Federal Circuit. In response to a challenge to a patent for a way of pooling mutual fund assets, the court held that methods of doing business could be patented, provided that the other criteria for intellectual property were met. That ruling, known as the State Street Bank decision, profoundly affects the opportunities for entrepreneurs and innovators, especially in the service industries.

Those taking advantage of this windfall included Amazon, with its patent on one-click ordering systems, E-Data with a patent on selling material downloaded from the Internet, and Priceline, with its version of the reverse auction. Other patents have been granted for technique in scientific experiments, surgical methods, and even haircuts. The new ruling, however, also opens up entrepreneurial opportunities in unexpected markets. In insurance, for example, innovators can now protect novel offerings that were once quickly duplicated by rivals. Recently issued patents protect new insurance offerings for such risks as terrorism, divorce, frivolous lawsuit, and even gambling losses (Chartrand 2003).

Setting aside whether business-model patents are really effective in establishing a competitive position, many legal scholars now assert that these are really no more than trivial adaptations of existing models and fail to meet the standard of a genuinely novel method or concept (*Economist* 2001). Thus the current practice might well change in coming years. In the meantime, you should consider seeking protection for your own business model; if it is raining porridge, you might as well hold your bowl upright.

Gene Patenting

From the perspective of patent law, the genes that each human has carried since conception are man-made chemicals. This is because they must be processed in some way (copied, abbreviated, spliced onto bacteria, or altered in some other form) in order to be identified. Thus, patent law considers genes that are studied in a laboratory not to be products of nature like, say, the elements of the periodic table, but rather processed chemicals. And so they are patentable.

This confluence of opportunity to patent and extraordinary potential for reward has led to an explosion of activity. A mixed set of start-up enterprises, established companies, and universities has devoted enormous energies to securing as many gene patents as possible. As of mid-2000, Incyte Genomics, a start-up that went public in 1993, held the lead with 397 patents. The University of California followed with 253, and Glaxo SmithKline with 248 (Regalado 2000). The anticipated value of these patents was great enough for the market to value the seventy-three publicly traded genomics firms at $96 billion at the end of 2000 (Cook-Deegan and McCormack 2001). Though these valuations surely fell with the technology implosion, they nevertheless provided an incentive for the rush to genomic patenting.

Yet many academic researchers assert that claims made in these patent filings are too often frivolous, an apparent strategy to preempt the field for later applications that cannot be foreseen clearly at present. An over-worked PTO has had difficulty deciding how to evaluate applications against the usefulness criterion. To date, the PTO has tended to favor the applicants, and the backlog of private claims to genetic material is large and growing. However, the standards employed to judge usefulness appear to be tightening. At the same time, a great ethical debate has risen over the patenting of human genes, independent of the rationale that they are just another kind of industrial chemical. As a result, significant changes in the protections allowed for genetic intellectual property might well lie ahead.

Alternatives for Securing Intellectual Property

In addition to patents, copyrights, and trademarks, you should consider two other strategies for protecting intellectual property: simply keeping the core information secret; and making everything public, thus creating an "open-source" marketplace.

The Black Box Strategy

Rather than disclosing your technology through the PTO, you can protect it by creating a trade secret, in effect wrapping the proprietary knowledge in a "black box" from which no information escapes. Trade secrets are enforceable under common law, and offer several advantages:

- *Cost.* It saves the cost of patenting, which can be considerable for the start-up company.

- *Focus.* It saves time and distraction, allowing you to focus on the business rather than legalities. This can be important in the turbulent early phases of a technology market, when rapid performance advances can quickly render patents obsolete.
- *Duration.* A trade secret does not expire in twenty years like a patent, but remains effective as long as you can keep the secret. This can be important in mature markets where the pace of innovation is slow and the products long-lasting.
- *Value Enhancement.* When a patent is put into practice, informal "know-how" is often created and becomes essential for effective use of the patented technology. This tacit knowledge can also be protected as a trade secret and be bundled with a patent to create an even more valuable property in cases where licensing is contemplated.[5]

As a form of common law, trade-secret law has some unique properties. First, the rules of common law are not written in statute, but rather are a combination of the generally accepted rules of society, as these are understood by the courts, and the precedents set by past cases. Second, an innocent duplication of your secret technology is not usually sufficient to convince a court that remedies are required. In addition to proving duplication, you must show that someone used fraudulent or wrongful means to acquire the secret. And finally, you must demonstrate that the secret has value and that you have intentionally maintained it as a trade secret (Foster and Shook 1993: 207–15).

To create an effective trade secret, you should limit access to the knowledge you wish to protect and ensure that those who do have access understand: (a) that it is a valuable trade secret, and (b) that you intend to protect it. Nondisclosure agreements for key employees and for any partners outside your company are essential.

The most famous example of a trade secret is the formula for Coca-Cola, but many other companies follow this practice as well. G.D. Searle, for example, owner of the NutraSweet brand of aspartame, has retained its market dominance long after its patents for the sweetener have expired. The company relies on manufacturing know-how that is kept secret from competitors, and so can produce this branded commodity cheaper than anyone else. Or, consider DuPont, which many years ago developed a process for manufacturing a whitening agent now used in a wide range of products. The company chose to keep this process a trade secret, which still confers competitive advantage forty years after any patents would have expired (Pooley and Bratic 1999).

The disadvantages of trade secrets also deserve mention. Infringements can be more difficult to prosecute because simply observing another party using your technology is not enough—you have to show that the technology was obtained through some wrongful act. Once proven, the courts have considerable latitude to weigh the competing interests and determine what is fair conduct and what remedy is appropriate.

Potential investors might also find a trade secret problematic. If you do not tell them the secret, they have no way of valuing it. Most are reluctant to sign a nondisclosure agreement, and if you simply (and trustingly) tell, it is no longer secret. Thus, prospective investors are likely to place more trust in a documented patent position than in your black box. In most cases, a judicious balance of patents, copyrights, trademarks, and trade secrets will probably serve you best.

The Open-Source Strategy

An alternative to secrecy or protected disclosure is open disclosure. As practiced in the software industry, this is called "open-source," the phrase referring to the source code, the heart of the software system, being made available to anyone. The core presumptions behind an open-source strategy are:

- that the technology is advancing so rapidly that the innovation process in any company inherently lags best practice,
- that enough individuals outside the company are willing to contribute their ideas to advance the field through your company, and
- that the ideas of these volunteers are in fact able to advance the state of the art free from the predations of hackers and assorted vandals.

It is uncertain whether these assumptions can be met in any field besides software, where open-source thinking takes on many aspects of a religious movement. Nor is it clear whether even this movement can sustain the energy needed to survive in the long run. But software is a central technology affecting every business, and open-source appears to work for now. Hence, it merits your consideration.

The business model is simple and elegant. The business becomes steward of the source code for a particular software system by disclosing it and offering it for use without fee. It does, however, ask of its users two things: (a) that they not resell that which they got for free, and (b) that they return ideas for improvement to the originating company. The originating company collects these together with the ideas of other volunteer programmers and packages them in a new, free release of the software.

A business with this strategy would earn income by selling services needed by those using the source code. The model compares with companies offering income tax assistance: the tax code is open to all, though at least as bewildering as any source code. But we all need assistance anyway. Unlike the tax business, the competitive advantage of open-source firms derives from two sources:

- Low-cost, rapid improvements to the code with which it is expert; and
- Experience in the application of this software to customers' unique situations.

Developing a Strategy for Intellectual Capital

Technology-based entrepreneurship derives its advantage from creating a capability that is completely unique. The tools outlined above are key components of a strategy for *protecting* that capability—but you should not confuse them with a strategy for *using* it.

Sequestering a technology will retain for your enterprise all of its value in use. But this strategy also has drawbacks. Most important, it provides a strong incentive for others to invent around the patent, or perhaps even ignore it. As a start-up, you might not have the time and resources to ascertain whether a rival has actually infringed your patent, let alone the resources to prosecute. But if you fail to defend against a known infringement, the courts can rule that you have surrendered the property, and it comes into the public domain.

By contrast, a strategy of liberal licensing can set up rivals in competition against you, albeit at a cost disadvantage equal to the amount of the license fee. But liberal licensing also offers strategic advantages in addition to fee income. For example, it can create the kind of network economies that Matsushita enjoyed when its widescale licensing of the VHS format videocassette and low-cost position made VHS the standard technology over rival Betamax (see Chapter 5).

In sum, there is no single prescription for the degree of control over your intellectual property. The strategic choice becomes a matter of balance, a bit like holding a dove in your hand: hold it too tightly, and you crush it; too loosely, and it flies away.

No Advantage Is Permanent

Finally, you should note the transience of the advantage conferred by intellectual property—if nothing else, the exponential growth in technological capacity noted in Chapter 5 will see to that. In such circumstances, your best defense is always the attack, making continual learning and innovation the foundation of your company. If you can accomplish that, you really will "leave 'em sweating and stealing, a year and a half behind."

9

Corporate Entrepreneurship

Two Perspectives

> Thrift may be the handmaid and nurse of Enterprise.
> But equally she may not. For the engine which
> drives Enterprise is not Thrift but Profit.
> —*John Maynard Keynes,* A Treatise on Money *(1930)*

Established corporations often seek profit from internal entrepreneurship, and some of the most skilled (or fortunate) have actually done well at it, increasing shareholder value markedly through start-up companies. This chapter analyzes the skills and behaviors that support successful corporate entrepreneurship: first from the perspective of the entrepreneur operating inside an established firm, and second in terms of managing the corporate entrepreneurship program to improve value creation for the stockholders.

By "corporate entrepreneurship," I mean the creation of new and distinct enterprises by an established company. New product or new market development by mainstream businesses, though surely innovative and entrepreneurial, falls outside the scope when it is implemented by the industry incumbents and not by a spin-off venture. I further exclude acquisitions unless the acquiring company manages the new enterprise, provides active venture investment (as distinct from passive investment as a limited partner in a venture capital fund), or otherwise directly builds its value.

The Launch Platform: Corporate Advantages

The fundamental principles of entrepreneurship with technology apply whether the new venture is launched from a garage or from the laboratories of a Fortune 500 corporation:

- finding a business model that makes economic sense,
- recognizing the character of the markets you seek to enter,
- securing external investment for growth during the time that your sales will not suffice, and

• recruiting a management team capable of accomplishing all this.

Even with these similarities, a corporate platform for launching the new venture necessarily imposes a more structured internal environment than that experienced by entrepreneurs like Kevin Bolin, founder of EnerTech Environmental. This structure gives corporate entrepreneurs a unique set of advantages—offset by unique challenges. You should understand both to succeed as a corporate entrepreneur.

Support Infrastructure: Administrative Services

A range of infrastructure-like services can be made available to new corporate ventures. These can save your most precious asset, your time, and avert the distraction of setting them up separately. Typically, these include:

• An ongoing research and development operation with expertise likely to be relevant and available;
• Legal work, especially regarding intellectual property, acquisitions, and incorporation;
• Procurement, which allows the start-up to enjoy the scale purchasing advantages of the larger parent;
• Regulatory and environmental management assistance, where those apply; and
• Personnel assistance, perhaps more through help with legal requirements, payroll administration, and benefits rather than through recruiting.

On the other hand, corporations design their service functions around the routines of the large organization. The bureaucrats who staff these functions will have little sympathy with the special needs of the start-up company, and in most cases, you must take these services as they are given or not at all.

Support Infrastructure: Credibility and Contacts

The credibility that derives from a well-reputed parent can give your start-up an edge, especially in markets with strong network economies.[1] Consider, for example, iBiquity Digital Corporation, which began life as a corporate venture of Lucent Technologies, and was built around a proprietary technology that allows digital radio signals to be sent through the airwaves in the same manner as analog AM/FM radio. This technology can improve the quality of sound to make music from any radio station sound as good as that from a home stereo. Further, iBiquity holds promise to integrate wireless data, news, and other entertainment. In such a market, it is plainly advantageous to set the industry standard with one's own technology, just as Microsoft did with MS-DOS. Both iBiquity Digital and its competitors seek to do just that.

Yet iBiquity might begin this race with a distinct advantage, the same kind of advantage enjoyed by Microsoft in the early days of the personal computer—its affiliation with a larger company. The size and reputation of the parent adds to network effects an implication of continuity, which, in turn, assures customers that they will not have to switch systems at some future and inconvenient time. The company was formed in 2000 by the merger of two technology developers of AM and FM digital broadcasting, Lucent Digital Radio and USA Digital Radio, both affiliates spun off from larger companies. Lucent Digital Radio was created in 1998 by Lucent Technologies to develop and commercialize digital technology for wireless applications. And USA Digital Radio was formed in 1991 as a limited partnership between CBS Corporation, Gannett Company, and Westinghouse Electric Corporation. These parent companies continue to own significant shares of iBiquity.[2]

Adding to the network effects, a well-connected parent company can help its start-up ventures in markets where good government relations make a meaningful difference—defense, energy, telecommunications, and health, for example. The size and clout of the parent can secure face time with government officials who would not otherwise be accessible to a start-up. And finally, it can use its connections to persuade busy and distinguished people to serve on the board, some of whom will actually prove useful.

Support Infrastructure: Entrepreneurial Experience

Too often, however, a vital element of corporate support goes missing: advice from experienced entrepreneurs. For the independent venture, such advice can be gained from business incubators and especially from angel and venture capital investors. To replicate this resource, many companies establish internal incubators and advisory relationships with knowledgeable entrepreneurs to provide the experience and skills needed.

The New Ventures Group of Lucent Technologies, for example, seeks outside expertise in ways that mesh with the distinct needs of the new venture. In some cases, experts are asked to serve as advisers, as when music producer and entrepreneur Phil Ramone was signed to promote Lucent's Epac audio coder software, designed to offer CD-quality sound over the Internet. In other cases, entire management teams are brought into the new company. When Lucent formed Lumeta, a company offering software safeguards against cyberterrorism, hackers, or disgruntled employees, the core of the technical staff transferred from Lucent's Bell Labs where the technology had originated. But the remainder of the management team—especially marketing, sales, operations, and finance—were imported from outside the company.[3] Lumeta was cofounded by professional venture capital investors, bringing that experience to the company as well.

Support Infrastructure: Financial Resources

Most technology-based companies provide seed money for developing new ideas and a process for integrating them into their mainstream businesses. Seed capital for new ventures, however, proves more difficult, both for the providers of funds and for their recipients. We will examine the provider's perspective in a subsequent section on management of corporate venturing. But from your perspective as a corporate entrepreneur, simply note that the provision of seed capital can become caught up in the internal politics of the company. You must learn to play this game, as there are many claims against the revenues of the company, but few are chosen for actual funding.

The Launch Platform: A Cultural Collision

For all the benefits conferred by the parent, corporate entrepreneurs also face challenges unknown to their nonaffiliated brethren. Most of these derive from the culture of the parent firm, the unstated mechanics of personal conduct that drive the collective behavior of the organization. Whether your have entered corporate entrepreneurship through the acquisition of a company that you built or as a founding member of the corporate team, you should understand these cultural distinctions. They make a difference in how you can operate.

Time-driven vs. Event-driven

A football game is time-driven. Predictably, the players take a break at the end of fifteen minutes of clock time so that copious beer commercials can be shown. By contrast, a baseball game is event-driven. The inning is not over until the team on the field meets its milestones—three outs—no matter how long it takes.

A publicly traded corporation operates much like a football team (presumably without the beer commercials): an annual calendar of events, especially financial reports, drives the planning and budgeting process. In many cases, corporate entrepreneurs must synchronize their financial requests with this annual budgeting and disclosure cycle. By contrast, events tend to drive decision making in an independent start-up, and achievement milestones substitute for the calendar in marking progress.

Income-orientation vs. Value-orientation

The share price of common stock in a publicly traded company becomes the ultimate economic measure of management's stewardship, and share price is closely tied to earnings. Stock markets punish announcements that earnings per share will fall below the expectations of analysts, while the converse is greeted with exuberance, sometimes even rationally.

Now consider what it takes for a new venture, say iBiquity Digital, to bring a penny a share to the bottom line of Lucent Technologies. As of the spring of 2002, Lucent had about 3,427 million shares of common equity outstanding. To make a penny's difference, Lucent's share of the iBiquity bottom-line profits would have to exceed $34 million.

Profits on this scale will not be possible for an extended time, and so the economic value of a start-up venture must derive from its balance sheet—what the company *can* be worth—not from its income statement (see Chapter 7). Earnings will be predictably negative for an extended period. The parent company must accommodate this reality within an earnings-oriented culture, and corporate entrepreneurs must understand how their ventures look to the flint-hearted budget cutters from the comptroller's office.

Key to Success: Promotion vs. Wealth Building

Promotion rewards success in a corporate environment. Promotion, however, has less relevance in an enterprise with perhaps a dozen or so people, especially in contrast with the financial rewards that can accrue from appreciation in the value of one's ownership stake in the company. The cultural gap looms equally large—promotion is conferred on you by a pleased boss. Wealth accrues from a pleased market.

The Safety Net

Many companies provide a safety net for employees willing to join the new venture—either some separation allowance or return to a position in the company in the event of failure. In contrast, the independent entrepreneur and management team rarely enjoy a fallback position. For them, failure causes financial losses that are direct and personal, hitting much harder than mere corporate embarrassment. The motivational aspects of financial survival require no further explanation. And for just that reason, professional venture capital investors like Nth Power's Maurice Gunderson will not fund start-up companies that provide any kind of fallback position for the team. They expect you to walk the wire without a net.

Managing Corporate Venturing

From the bridge of the mother ship, managing an internal start-up raises issues not found elsewhere in the organization. These management considerations include the following:

Multiple Ends and Means

Start-up ventures often serve multiple purposes in an established company, and so challenge the thinking of strategic managers to sort out their true priorities. In addition to the expected financial return, the purposes of corporate venturing can include:

- Building new lines of business;
- Exploring markets and/or technology opportunities that do not fall within the purview of one of the operating divisions;
- Filling strategic gaps in ongoing business lines or extending core businesses in logical directions;
- Creating demand for the company's mainstream products, as Intel attempted with its investments in ventures that built demand for bandwidth and processor speed;

- Importing unique technological and/or business capabilities into the firm; and
- Providing an outlet for the intellectual property created in the company's laboratories and for creative talent that the company seeks to retain.

At the same time, corporate entrepreneurship programs have multiple tools available to achieve these strategic ends, including:

- Venture capital investment in enterprises originating outside the company;
- Start-up, incubation, and funding for internally generated ventures;
- Licensing the intellectual property to others, possibly including competitors; and
- Strategic partnerships.

The large matrix formed by this set of ends and means plainly offers too many possibilities for all to be pursued at once. Indeed, this proliferation of choices contrasts sharply with the single focus of venture capital investors like Nth Power—return on invested capital. Thus, the leadership of any company considering an entrepreneurship program must first focus on the limited set of possibilities that meshes best with its own strategic objectives. A recent McKinsey study of thirty new venture units (NVU) in major corporations showed that success more readily followed programs with a few focused goals and well-chosen tools. Those that attempted to achieve too many objectives with too many tools found themselves without critical mass in any area and unable to balance the conflicting operational requirements (Coveney et al. 2002).

The McKinsey researchers then identified three focused strategies that were practiced by the most successful NVUs: building entirely new businesses; building businesses for eventual integration with the mainstream offerings of the parent company; and building new business from the intellectual property generated by the firm.

First Strategy: A Whole New Ball Game

Many established companies find their growth slows with maturity because of market saturation. Some retailers, like McDonalds, the Gap, or Home Depot, find that they have occupied all the best store locations after an extended period of growth. In other cases like that of Nike, the number of feet available for new shoes eventually comes to limit growth (Garvin 2002). Many of these companies find it appropriate to seek growth in related, but unsaturated markets—the first of the strategies suggested by the McKinsey analysts.

One note of caution, however—if growth is the objective, then the new venture managers must seek that 1 percent of all opportunities likely to provide meaningful growth from a base that is already large. A collection of profitable but small businesses will not accomplish this, and could even distract from the needed focus.

Second Strategy: Back to the Mother Ship

The second successful strategy uses new ventures to enhance the core businesses. The McKinsey evidence suggests this to be more difficult to execute well because it requires that the new venture establish a relationship with the ongoing lines of business. Three special challenges derive from this relationship. First, all the cultural mismatches discussed earlier must be overcome—they cannot be circumvented. Second, venture program managers should avoid excessive reliance on the current business units for ideas, which could vitiate one principal advantage of corporate venturing—the ability to fill strategic gaps in ongoing businesses. And third, the venturing process should be organized in a way that facilitates the political credibility of the new enterprise within the corporate structure. Lacking this credibility, the new venture might not be able to achieve the desired synergies within the parent company.

Third Strategy: Building from Intellectual Capital

The third successful strategy identified by the McKinsey analysts would build additional value from intellectual property already owned by the parent. Consider, for example, Delphi Corporation, a first-tier automotive supplier spun off from General Motors in 1999 with a portfolio of patents now numbering around 7,000 and a rate of new inventions averaging two per week. At the same time, a distinct NVU, then called Delphi Technologies, Inc. (DTI), was formed to create, manage, protect, and leverage Delphi's intellectual property.[4]

DTI has a dedicated management team and a distinct set of profit goals. As "owner" of the intellectual property, DTI began by licensing to third parties and strategic partners of Delphi Corporation in exchange for a stream of royalty payments. The consequent profits would be returned to the parent, Delphi, for redistribution to the operating units to reinforce its strategic objectives.

A pure licensing model faces an inherent limitation, however. The licenser must find a company with a business model that meshes well with the offered technology. Where the technology is very advanced for the market or where it would be disruptive to established competitors, potential licensees can be hard to find—a bit like searching for unicorns, which are hard to find because they don't exist.

To draw full value from its intellectual property, DTI has added to its licensing operation internal capabilities in mergers and acquisitions, new market analysis, business case development, and venture negotiations. Externally, partnerships were formed with business incubators to identify target markets, and to provide management and investment partners for the new ventures. Delphi seeks to build a complete commercialization capacity from what had once been a simple strategy of enhancing income with licensing revenues. Its business model now includes the creation of new wealth, even in markets unrelated to the corporate mainstream, based on new applications of the technologies developed by those mainstream businesses.

Building Externally: Corporate Venture Capital

Corporate venture capital funds provided about $5.7 billion to start-up ventures in 2000, dropping to $4.8 billion in 2001 according to The MoneyTree™ Survey of PricewaterhouseCoopers, Thomson Venture Economics, and the National Venture Capital Association. These funds resemble their independent counterparts with two exceptions. First, many of these enterprises serve purposes that are "strategic" in nature, addressing subsets of the multiple purposes discussed earlier. Thus a lower return can be rationalized if the other strategic objectives are met. And second, the compensation system sometimes treats the corporate investment group (and even the entrepreneurs) like employees whose salary and benefits do not depend on the success of the venture—a practice no professional venture capital investor would tolerate. For that reason, such a compensation plan will make the enterprise less attractive to outside investors.

Little systematic evidence shows how well or how poorly companies are meeting their strategic objectives. Regarding financial objectives,

---

Lycos Ventures: A Corporate Seed Fund[5]

Lycos Ventures was formed in July 1999 by the Internet portal, Lycos, Inc. (which merged in October 2000 with Terra Networks). Its purpose is to make early-stage investments in companies involved with Internet infrastructure, wireless data, on-line media, and e-learning. The fund seeks underserved markets where an opportunity to establish leadership exists.

Terra Lycos expects to capture promising new concepts and turn them into practical businesses that relate well to the parent's own portal and Internet business. In addition, Terra Lycos seeks a preview of Internet technologies and business models likely to be of strategic importance. Long-term capital appreciation is a third goal.

Lycos Ventures acts as a full-service incubator rather than simple funder, using the connections and resources of the parent company to provide industry expertise and distribution outlets for its portfolio companies. Joining Terra Lycos in the first $75 million fund were Bear Stearns, Mellon Ventures, Inc., Sumitomo Corporation, Vulcan Ventures, and others. Lycos Ventures is located in Pittsburgh, Pennsylvania.

---

however, the outcomes are mixed. Studies suggest that companies with reward systems similar to those of the independent venture capital firms achieve results comparable with those firms. But those with corporate compensation schemes or strategic objectives that work against the financial often fail to achieve the revenue goals set for them, whatever other benefits they might confer on the parent (Gompers and Lerner 2000: 95–121).

In any case, independent entrepreneurs seeking funding for businesses that appear to mesh with the interests of established corporations would do well to open the dialog early in their search. Despite their newfound entrepreneurial spirit, it sometimes takes a big company a long time to make up the corporate mind.

Building Internally: It Takes the Right Stuff

Companies seeking to launch corporate ventures in pursuit of some strategic goal must create an internal culture that challenges, nurtures, and rewards their internal entrepreneurs. These persons, often called "champions," pose an unusual management challenge. On the one hand, they are caustic to the established order. The best of them practice constructive insurrection, which despite being constructive nevertheless remains insurrection. The human fondness for stasis causes the established order to resist these revolutionaries.

On the other hand, the business environment—especially markets and technology—changes at an accelerating rate. Corporate ventures can be thought of as limited experiments with an unknowable future, seeking to discern opportunities and dangers that await them. They must therefore differ from what has gone before if they are to serve this purpose.

And so the management challenge is to distinguish the champions with vision and capacity from those who are merely sociopaths, and to guide, focus, and empower the former. The story of how a traditional, professional midwestern engineering company became a launch pad for new ventures illustrates the range of the possible.

Black & Veatch: An Entrepreneurial Engineering Company

The next time you drive past a nuclear power plant or step into an elevator from the eighty-second floor, give some thought to the engineers who designed these structures. Would you feel more comfortable knowing that they were designed by a methodical, conservative engineer or by an entrepreneurial spirit? The answer to that question speaks volumes about the internal culture of Black & Veatch, a worldwide engineering, procurement, construction, and consultation firm headquartered in the suburbs of Kansas City. Yet that properly conservative culture also spun out two enterprises of unexpected imagination and daring. One succeeded and one failed, and the story of how that happened can help us understand the process of corporate venturing.

The success, the Black & Veatch Solutions Group (BVSG), developed in overlapping stages, the end of which could not have been foreseen from its origins. Rather than following a master design crafted by some corporate mandarin, BVSG evolved from a matrix of ideas and internal champions. It began with a market insight that was powerful but limited to the electric power industry. The solution to this recognized market need then became the foundation idea for a core of related information technologies. As the power of these technologies became apparent, the market concept grew beyond the electric power business. And finally, as the technology and market concepts matured, so did the organizational structure that would enable Black & Veatch to capture the value that had been created.

In contrast, the failure, *EHSmanager*, began as a powerful market idea but ended badly, the result of an agreement that apparently failed to align the interests of the individual partners with the interests of the partnership. Together, their story illuminates the world of corporate entrepreneurship.

BVSG: The Original Market Insight

The electric power plants of the 1970s and 1980s were hot (meaning high-energy densities), heavy (meaning big industrial facilities covering hundreds of acres), and complex (meaning multiple, interactive systems for energy delivery and control). But most of all, they were expensive, with final costs usually exceeding estimated costs and measured in the billions of dollars. Their design and construction required large teams of engineers generally organized in ways that the builders of Pharaoh's pyramids would have recognized.

The hot, the heavy, and the complex seemed at the time unavoidable, but considerable savings might be achieved if costly delays and rework could be reduced. Many on-site changes were a consequence of the complexity—miles of pipe and hundreds of miles of wire ran through these facilities, often and inadvertently seeking to occupy the same space at the same time. A better way to integrate the disparate design decisions and identify these interaction problems before the concrete was placed would save large sums in later construction. Black & Veatch took up that challenge in the late 1970s.

Late 1970s: The Technology Idea

P.J. Adam, head of Black & Veatch's power division and later its chairman, recognized that any engineering firm with a design tool that addressed this integration problem would enjoy a significant competitive advantage. Not only could problems be reduced during construction, but the design process itself could be made more efficient, cost estimates more accurate, and procurement more timely.

At about the same time, a young mechanical engineer named John Voeller became head of Black & Veatch's information technology group. Voeller had been working with various automated design and visualization tools as well as relational databases—essentially software that links a variety of once-disparate data sets into an integrated information tool. And as is so often the case, the combination of top management support and grassroots talent would prove uncommonly potent.

Voeller organized a project team with many members coming from disciplines traditional in a large engineering firm—electrical, civil, mechanical, and so forth—rather than from the computer sciences. Hence, they were naive regarding their task, initially underappreciating both its complexity and its duration. But Voeller, ever the visionary, did appreciate the value of the goal and recognized the ultimate power of information technology to achieve it, even if the means at hand—mainframe computers fed data on punch cards—were still primitive.

They were setting out to make a single-entry database that would link all elements of building a large, capital-intensive facility—design, engineering, procurement, and construction. This would be coupled with three-dimensional graphics, in effect lifting the construction business off the flat plane of the two-dimensional drawing. Through the relational database, Black & Veatch engineers would have access to the same design information that, in principle, had always been available to them—but now available much faster, with much less labor, and continuously updated.

Adam's intuition proved correct. When the first version of the new system, called *PowrTrak*, was rolled out in 1983, Black & Veatch did indeed gain the anticipated advantage over competitors. *PowrTrak* enabled the company to cut the time from contract to first power as much as 50 percent. This saved the owner from accreting interest charges during construction, one of the costliest elements of any new power plant. Overall, the cost per kilowatt of a large, new coal-fired power plant fell by about half by the early 1990s.

PowrTrak required continuous investment, however, both to broaden its use as computer hardware shifted from the mainframe to the PC, and to give it new capabilities in advance of imitators. One senior executive estimated that Black & Veatch had invested over $30 million in *PowrTrak*, a considerable sum for a company with sales of around $300 million at the start of the campaign.

An Expanding Market Concept

As the reputation of *PowrTrak* grew, Black & Veatch found itself providing information technology (IT) services to its customers in addition to its traditional engineering services. At the same time, the customer base for these IT services expanded to include such nontraditional players as General Electric, IBM, General Motors, and the United States

Department of Defense. These IT projects expanded the scope of the work as well. The original *PowrTrak* concepts of 3D design and relational databases became a core technology that served management systems in general, each project drawing upon these core capabilities and, in turn, enriching them.

Two elements of the external business environment provided a strong following wind for Black & Veatch. First, the dispersion of computing power made possible by the transition from mainframes to minicomputers and then from minicomputers to the PC began to build a demand for networked IT systems. Black & Veatch had developed the necessary IT skills through its expansion into international power plant markets in the late 1980s. The design and construction of new power plants around the world required the kind of networking capabilities that would soon be demanded in many other markets.

And second, by the 1990s the IT market was in full cry for integrated solutions to the "stovepipe" problem—individual systems for payroll, inventories, and the like, which worked reasonably well in isolation but were generally incompatible with each other. Thus, they were unable to address the most important management challenges, which cut across these functional areas. The integration issues arising in power plant design provided a physical metaphor for these cross-cutting management issues, and the skills that Black & Veatch had developed seemed to translate naturally.

Over the 1990s, the realization grew that these nontraditional IT projects could become more than a mere supplement to the current lines of business—indeed that they could be packaged to become a distinct business line by themselves. And so the internal controversies within Black & Veatch turned on how this value might best be captured.

Capturing the Value: Origins of BVSG

Historians have observed that the genius of England in the halcyon days of the British Empire was its ability to call forth the leadership best suited to the crisis at hand. The same might be said of companies. And in the case of BVSG, it was indeed true. If John Voeller was the technical visionary behind BVSG, Gerald White was to become its business leader and the driver of BVSG's quest for an independent role.

White joined Black & Veatch in 1980, a young mechanical engineer newly graduated from Purdue. His first boss was John Voeller. White appreciated technology, but his real skills lay in management. In an engineering company, led by people whose first love is technology, White soon found himself the "go-to guy." When a difficult management challenge arose within the IT group, White was the one most capable of response. All of this business prowess was self-taught—skills learned from reading, observation, and benchmarking. As a result, Gerald White came to lead what would later be called the Information Services Group of the Power Division by sheer force of aptitude for the task.

It was generally recognized within Black & Veatch that these new IT services were becoming quite unique. First, as the Information Services Group grew, its customer base increasingly diverged from that of the mainstream engineering business—IBM and General Motors didn't build many power plants. Second, the gross margins (revenues from services sold less the direct cost of providing those services) began falling in the engineering business from 1996 onward as competitors installed their own versions of *PowrTrak* and as power plant construction shifted from the relatively complex coal or nuclear plants to the relatively simple combustion turbines. That trend to commodity engineering—simplicity, cost competition, and lower margins—soon carried over into Black & Veatch's other construction markets. By contrast, margins in the IT services business remained high. And third, customers began coming to Black & Veatch's IT group with open-ended design questions directly analogous to the physical plant questions once posed to the engineers— how can we improve, say, manufacturing productivity by 2003? Thus, the IT services business plainly was beginning to diverge from the mainstream at Black & Veatch by the mid-1990s. It was less obvious what to do with it.

No Pain—No Gain

Gerald White became chief among a group of advocates for an independent BVSG and ultimately its spin-off from Black & Veatch through a public stock offering. The first step was taken in 1997 when the Information Services Group of the Power Division became a separate divisional partnership within the Black & Veatch corporate family. Then in 1999, BVSG was spun off from Black & Veatch with its own board of directors, though still wholly owned by the parent company. An initial public offering (IPO) of BVSG stock was planned for late 2000, but subsequently postponed.[6]

These transitions, however, caused much internal pain, which was exacerbated by the slow decision-making process at Black & Veatch. This was a matrix organization built around a strong professional ethic. Though highly effective in marshaling the intellectual resources to design and build major infrastructure facilities, the matrix thinking also influenced business decisions because these too were reached through a consensus process. This process, often long and untidy, tested the advocacy skills of White, Voeller, and the other proponents of the spin-off.

Some argued that the transition should not occur at all, that the company should not provide engineering competitors with a service that had become a key market discriminator for Black & Veatch. These objections were overcome by the observations that most competitors had their own systems and that design was taking on the economic characteristics of a commodity anyway.

Pricing became a more difficult issue. Even in 1999, the bulk of BVSG's business was internal to Black & Veatch. Should the highly profitable BVSG price its services to internal clients at cost as it had in the past? Or, should internal clients pay market rates? And if so, would they be required to buy from BVSG? Positioning BVSG for an IPO provided a powerful argument for market rates, which would make the new stock more attractive to investors. This argument prevailed, and for an extended period the internal Black & Veatch units would be required to buy their IT services from BVSG.

Another set of issues grew up around who would be on the new team. When the IT business was a part of the Power Division, people flowed in and out as is typical in a matrix organization like Black & Veatch. But then the music stopped, and those on board at the time found themselves in a classic confrontation with greed and fear. On the greed side, the dot-com market bubble of 1999–2000 and the prospect of a public stock offering had many of the group's members checking the availability of Porsches. But on the fear side, many had also become accustomed to a compensation package with life insurance, health insurance, four weeks' vacation, and a modest but dependable salary. Porsche or no, they were much less comfortable with life in a fast lane propelled by stock options.

Gerald White and his lieutenants recognized these competing influences as they chose the team that would go forward. At the same time, the corporate leadership became aware of the dangers to morale of seeming to create a caste system—an elite set of high rollers in BVSG and the drudges in the mainstream businesses. Formation of an Employee

Stock Ownership Plan helped mitigate these perceptions by giving all participants at least some stake in the success of BVSG.

But most important, Black & Veatch management sought to make entrepreneurial opportunities widely available so that the BVSG experience could be replicated elsewhere. Gerald White noted the importance of simply teaching engineers that a successful business model requires more than technology—it must also include an understanding of market value and the way that value can be captured. He observed that the example set by BVSG would provide motivation for this way of thinking throughout Black & Veatch.

Buoyed by early success, the company sought other markets where spin-off enterprises might provide growth opportunities for staff and parent company alike. One of these was environmental compliance with burgeoning regulation at all levels of government concerning the environment, worker health, and safety—known collectively by the acronym EHS.

Nobody's Perfect: EHSmanager

Compliance with federal, state, and local EHS regulations appeared to offer leverage for information systems to both reduce costs and improve effectiveness. For the most part, Black & Veatch approached this market through extensions of its traditional engineering services. But one segment seemed especially well suited to a new venture.

This start-up—initially called EHSmanager.com, and later just EHSmanager after "dot-com" became more of an epithet than an accolade—would address an unserved sector of the environmental market, small and mid-sized businesses. By the late 1990s the Environmental Protection Administration had begun to shift the focus of its enforcement actions from major polluters to smaller but more numerous businesses. These were poorly prepared to understand the new requirements, let alone manage them successfully. Independent estimates placed the potential size of this market at $4 billion and growing at an annual rate of 30 percent. Despite its size, however, the market remained underserved because of its dispersed nature, which made traditional channels impractical.

John Voeller, ever the polymath, saw in the still-developing Internet the channel to reach this market. With the right technology, a comprehensive knowledge base of regulatory requirements at all levels of government could be kept up to date, and specific problems matched with solutions known to be acceptable. But as with BVSG, the leadership that was needed to make an idea into a workable business model came not from the top but from the engineers themselves. An internal group of engineers led by David Guyot (another of Voeller's "go-to guys" with whom Black & Veatch seemed so richly endowed) researched the opportunity and brought it to the company's management. He received the go-ahead in 1997.

This time, however, Black & Veatch reached outside the company to bring in entrepreneurial leadership and external partners. When EHSmanager was finally launched in 1999, Black & Veatch owned one-third of the enterprise in partnership with two software companies. EHSmanager became the first application service provider software management program to consolidate the multiple requirements of environmental, health, and safety management into one comprehensive solution. It was provided through Internet subscription and linked interactively to federal and state regulations. The president of the new venture explained its value in a Black & Veatch press release of January 2000:[7]

"When we looked at the complexities and expenses faced by owners of small and medium-sized businesses through conventional compliance programs, we recognized a need for a management tool which would provide a *comprehensive, user-friendly, and affordable* solution," said Patrick Pfeifer, president and CEO of EHSmanager.com, LLC. "Every business owner is faced with EHS compliance issues, as well as risk management concerns; understanding those issues and appropriately dealing with them can be challenging.

"The WorkSafe System is more than an Internet-delivered software product," continued Pfeifer. "It offers additional resources, including on-line consulting and expertise, help-desk assistance, quality EHS training modules, bulletin board discussions, and EHS product guidance services. WorkSafe offers these resources in a customized application for every business owner. You purchase only what you need."

Sounded good, and it probably was. But one does not have to observe the entrepreneurial scene long before reaching the sad, but true, conclusion that more things ought to work than ever do work. This proved to be the case with EHSmanager. After a promising beginning that included venture capital investment and a prospective Canadian merger, the company ceased operations in early 2002. The software platform, Worksafe, became the property of the erstwhile merger partner, and the company's creditors sued for involuntary bankruptcy.

The root causes of this collapse remain obscured by litigation, but some conclusions can be inferred from press accounts (Roth 2002). EHSmanager apparently put its Worksafe platform in escrow to the Canadian merger partner, whose financial backers then invested in the joint enterprise. These backers, however, were unwilling to support another round of funding because it would dilute their ownership. Having gained possession of the software platform through the escrow agreement, they had much less need for EHSmanager as a company. Their technology needs met, the Canadian partners resisted the attempts of the original owners, including Black & Veatch, to infuse more capital, terminated the merger, took their escrowed software platform, and set up the business in Canada. And so the Black & Veatch enterprise failed—not the result of unworkable technology or of market failure, but rather the consequence of an ill-constructed partnership. It is unclear whether the purloined Canadian business will survive in the hands of its new owners.

Patrick Pfeifer may have summarized it best when he told a reporter, "It was so close to being a huge success story for Kansas City and for us. . . . It's just a real shame" (Roth 2002).

Lessons Learned

Successful corporate venturing arises from a combination of factors. Two components, however, seem essential. The first is a corporate culture that encourages the pursuit of new value, a willingness to trade increased risk for the prospect of capturing that value for the firm, and appropriate rewards for those who succeed. The second is a set of individual champions who can muster the vision, energy, and intellectual capacity to take on new venture creation—and the wisdom to know their limits.

In the case of Black & Veatch, John Voeller observed how the best members of the technical staff sought projects that they believed would be exciting and adventuresome. The matrix organization allowed internal mobility so that these intellectual resources could be focused without resistance from the line units. Further, Black & Veatch encouraged a professional engineering culture where an individual's status depended as much on his or her skills with technology as on mere rank. Thus, the technologists felt quite secure in bringing their ideas to the company's management, who in turn participated capably in the debate. A matrix of ideas was thus generated that might have been foreclosed in a more hierarchical organization.

Equally important, champions, the "go-to guys" in Voeller-speak, arose who were capable of giving substance to the ideas thus generated. Top management supported these champions, both culturally and with real resources. Thus the *combination* of a favorable culture and special individuals yields a greater likelihood of building a successful corporate entrepreneurship program than either does in isolation.

The Black & Veatch story, however, also suggests a note of caution. It is one thing to start new companies bright with promise, but quite another to nurture them successfully through their subsequent growth phases. Demonstrated skill in the former does not ensure success with the latter. In the final analysis, a company's stakeholders will measure the success of the corporate venturing program more by its ability to bring income to the bottom line than by its cleverness in the art of new-company formation.

10

The *Real* New Economy

Our journey began with the observation that "the new economy" is indeed a reality—just not the reality envisioned by some during the frothy years of the dot-com mania. This chapter seeks to identify the economic realities now emerging and describe what can be known of their salient characteristics. It does not presume to forecast the future, thereby joining a lengthy tradition of failed technology forecasts, because the future is never discovered—it is made. The real makers of the future, the entrepreneurs who bring new technologies and services to a free market, will choose the path forward.

A Perspective on the Future

We humans live under the strong influence of things seen now, and when we think of a technological future, it tends to look a lot like the present, only better. I recall, for example, the science fiction magazines, which I read assiduously in my youth. The cover illustrations often showed handsome, fit people in skintight suits with jet-packs on their backs zooming effortlessly to schools, libraries, and shopping. Much of that has come true today, though not as originally imagined. Today, people can indeed learn, access literature, and shop—not with jet-packs, but through the far richer environment of the Internet, moving virtually and instantaneously from place to place. And they don't have to wear skintight suits.

Figure 10.1 illustrates the human tendency to project the present in linear fashion into the future. In contrast, the real technological future tends to follow an S-shaped trajectory. This causes most analysts to overestimate the economic and societal impact of new innovations in the near term and to underestimate their impact in the long run. When the

Figure 10.1   **Pathways to Change**

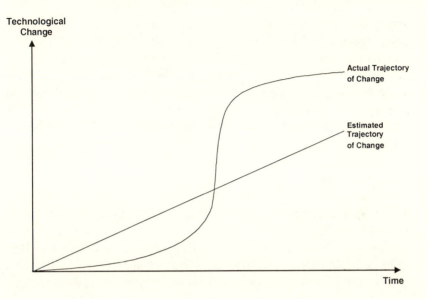

linear view fails to meet expectations, many then falsely assume that nothing at all has changed. It has, but the change is invisible until the technology reaches the inflection point of the curve—and then it becomes unstoppable.

The electric utility industry offers a case in point. When the Nth Power founders, Maurice Gunderson and Nancy Floyd, thought about the deregulated future, they envisioned a nonlinear change—a competitive business environment in which energy services could be delivered through nonutility business models that would deploy advanced electric generation equipment near customers' premises. These smaller generating plants would provide learning curve economies in manufacturing rather than the static economies of scale from larger, custom-built plants. We cannot, of course, know the minds of the utility executives who rejected this vision. But from their actions, we might infer a linear view of the future in which the only technologies of interest were those fitting the vertically integrated utility model.

Most reasonably astute observers can see where the current competitors position themselves in the marketplace. By contrast, the future offers no facts, but only the challenge of analysis, reasoned supposition, conjecture, and error. In an opportunity-driven business environment, effective listening and rapid learning become the most essential skills. Carver Mead, doyen of the computer revolution, once observed that "the first and most crucial step [is] usually to think about what the problem is trying to tell you, rather than tell it what you know already." In his own quest to understand the ramifications of advanced computer technology, he found it essential "to sort out what the thing was really trying to tell me from the things that the experts were telling me" (Guilder 1989: 39). Beyond this kind of thinking, reliable guides into the future cannot be found. Do not bother looking for them.

Elements of the *Real* New Economy

The incipient transformation replays a story as old as economic man, but one that offers lessons for the future. Consider, for example, the new economy that emerged from the widespread electrification of the U.S. economy, which the National Academy of Engineering ranked first among the great technological achievements of the twentieth century. Electricity allowed the benefits of energy services to diffuse widely, and in doing so upset incumbent industries from kerosene lamps to manufactured ice. The effects on manufacturing, for example, were profound.

The minimum efficient size of the steam engine, electricity's predecessor, effectively kept power tools from small manufacturers; and where steam power was employed, a complex system of belts and shafts transmitted the energy throughout the plant. This proved clumsy, inefficient, and a constant maintenance problem. By contrast, electric power made fractionalized energy services available throughout manufacturing plants, and these could be switched on and off at will. Thus, the organization of work could be rearranged, and techniques for mass production enabled. The swiftness of the change is striking, even by contemporary standards. By 1900, only about 5 percent of manufacturing horsepower derived from electricity. Ten years later, electricity's market share had increased to 25 percent. By 1929, electricity had essentially swept the manufacturing market, and led to the sharp rise in the productivity of American industry after World War I (Rosenberg 1972: 162). These changes opened profound opportunities, which entrepreneurs like Henry Ford and George Westinghouse recognized and built upon. The next "new economy" will surely offer the same.

The most interesting question, of course, is not where the economy has been but where it might go. Some distinguishing characteristics of the emerging new economy can indeed be discerned—not because they can be forecasted, but because they are manifest right now as persistent elements of the business environment. These include:

- The rise of knowledge as the chief source of economic value, and especially the increased pace and intensity of competition;
- The potential for privatization of many markets for public goods;
- The convergence of scientific disciplines once thought distinct and their rise as the key source of opportunity; and
- A set of emerging societal issues, the resolution of which will shape the competitive environment for entrepreneurs.

The Rise of Knowledge as Value

Knowledge is rising to become the canonical source of value in the real new economy. Not that previous economies held ignorance in high regard—brains and skill in abundance enabled the design of a steam locomotive, the production of a barrel of oil, or the harvesting of a bushel of wheat. The difference is that previously the knowledge with the greatest economic value concerned how to *make* these useful things. Increasingly, the source of economic value is the knowledge itself—a gene sequence, a compelling scene in a film, lines of music, or lines of software code. In such an economy, physical goods will not disappear; but they will be valued more for the weightless ideas they contain than for their ability to lift and move some things, give shape and form to others, and so forth (Coyle 1998).

Information Science and Technology: Driving the
Knowledge-Based Economy

Scientific advances tend to occur in waves during which one sector—say nuclear physics during the late nineteenth and early twentieth centuries—advances rapidly to outpace the others. When societal conditions permit, invention and innovations translate this knowledge into economic reality. Today, we are at the beginning of such a revolution, led by profound advances in every aspect of information science and technology:

- *Computers*: High-speed computation and massive data storage that multiply the data available for any purpose;

- *Advanced Communications*: Networks that can move these data swiftly, economically, and—increasingly—securely; and
- *Advanced Software*: Capacity to link computers and telecommunications to help build insight out of data.

The information revolution has strongly influenced progress in every field from genomics to medicine to nanotechnology. Consider biotechnology, for example. Computer simulation of complex living systems enables biologists to shift their focus from the individual components to the ways that those components work together in networks. This enables a more complete understanding of the performance of entire systems, progressing from the regulatory mechanisms of genes, cells, and tissues to an ability to model entire organs—and ultimately a fully functional model of the entire human body. Computer simulations of these systems will eventually overthrow conventional biomedical research by improving the design of drugs, the engineering of specific tissues, and perhaps the design of special bacteria for industrial purposes.

The pace of this information revolution, documented in Chapter 5, shows no signs of abating. And yet, the effects of these gains in information technology are distributed unevenly across the U.S. economy. Take productivity, for example, a widely cited but one-dimensional metric of technology's usefulness in creating economic progress. Studies by the McKinsey Global Institute reveal that 76 percent of the productivity gains that attended the boom of the 1990s occurred in only six sectors of the U.S. economy; and these six sectors accounted for less than a third of the nation's total gross domestic product. Further, the McKinsey studies showed no correlation between investment in information technology and productivity gain (Farrell 2003).

In part, this derives from a misunderstanding of the way that knowledge creates value within an enterprise. Consider the case of General Motors and its lurch into (and out of) automation (see text box, pp. 179–180).

The Economic Structure of Knowledge

A rich literature on the economics of knowledge has grown up over many years, and I cannot hope to do it justice here. Instead, I will focus on those few elements that offer the most insight for the creators of new ventures.

General Motors and the Plunge into Automation

The case of General Motors's bold plunge into automated manufacturing, summarized from an account in the *Economist*, illustrates well how a misapprehension of the way that knowledge adds value can lead to difficulties.

It was once noted that General Motors (GM) did not make cars—it made money, and prior to the 1970s that was generally true. It made its money in the classic manner of the mature business—by sheer size. Lacking motivation to innovate, its well-depreciated equipment was perfectly adequate to the tasks of mass producing standard cars of indifferent quality. With the 1973 energy crisis and a growing perception of inferior quality and performance, customer preference began to shift away from GM's offerings. By 1980, the company had posted a loss of $763 million, its first loss since 1921 (*Economist* 1991).

Roger Smith became GM's chairman in January 1981, and immediately sought to reverse the situation. "Technology leadership is what will keep us ahead in world competition," Smith declared shortly after taking office (*Economist* 1991). The showpiece for this strategy, would be the automation of GM's Hamtramck plant in Detroit.[1]

Recall from Chapter 4 the difficulties faced by a mature business in adopting any kind of radical innovation. But in 1981, GM had no capability at all for high-technology automation, and not enough time to gain experience the old-fashioned way. So it sought to purchase the skills. Electronic Data Systems (EDS) was soon acquired for $2.5 billion, and Hughes Aircraft for another $5.2 billion. With the EDS purchase, GM hoped to graft on the automation and computer skills needed for plant modernization around the world, and with the Hughes purchase to inject aerospace technology into the cars themselves.

GM intended the Hamtramck plant to demonstrate advanced robotic technology that would later be used throughout its global empire. The plant opened in 1985 with a complete array of automated devices—260 robots for welding and painting cars, 50 automated guided vehicles to ferry parts around the plant, laser measuring devices, television cameras, and, everywhere, computers (*Economist* 1991).

The new technology soon proved disastrous. The software contained a plethora of bugs that revealed themselves only when operations began. With each new discovery, the entire line had to be shut down for reprogramming. The automated vehicles often refused to move, even though they were nonunion. The robots crashed into the cars they were building, and even into one another. A year after opening, quality problems abounded, and the Hamtramck plant produced at only 50 percent of its intended capacity.

In the end, much of the automated equipment had to be scrapped and replaced with human workers. Though the plant remained highly mechanized, its complete reliance on advanced robotics proved unsustainable and was eliminated. In the place of radical innovation with advanced automation technology, GM finally succeeded with disciplined, incremental innovation and a relatively labor-intensive technology. And five years after

(continued)

its ill-starred opening, the Hamtramck plant won the coveted Malcolm Baldrige National Quality Award.

The GM experience illustrates the problems that arise when information technology is misapplied, at once overreaching and underachieving. GM overreached by seeking to replace so much of its line workforce. To be sure, these workers brought with them all the needs and foibles of human-ity—subject to fatigue, mistake prone, expensive, and requiring continual attention. But they also brought to the job tacit knowledge, "know-how," that could not be programmed into the robots. By contrast, the robots were indefatigable, not prone to random errors or inattention, and never out on strike. But without the tacit know-how of the workforce, the plant could not function. Information technology is better employed to reinforce and en-able these basic human skills than to attempt replacing them entirely.

At the same time, the information technology underachieved because it would not have conveyed a lasting competitive advantage even if it had been successful. Rivals could also invest in the same technologies and systems, which vendors like Itran (Chapter 2) or even EDS would be only too happy to provide. For information technology to create a sustainable competitive advantage, it must connect with and reinforce some distinctive competence already in place, or it must enable the using company to con-nect with some unreached element of customer value—an ability to order a car with exactly the performance and options desired, for example.

In contrast, the kind of systems adopted would address only a limited set of issues. To be sure, many standard, repetitive operations can be auto-mated, and this can serve the cause of efficiency well. But if we think in terms of competitive leverage, then advanced information systems serve best when they build flexibility into a production process rather than perform standard, repetitive operations. The automated delivery vehicles, for example, would have replaced the forklift operators, but would not have addressed more basic issues like reducing inventory to its lowest possible level.

And so information technology can indeed drive the value of knowl-edge in the emerging new economy. But to accomplish this, its designers must think in terms of the efficient and timely flow of relevant knowledge that connects well with some sustainable business advantage. They are unlikely to succeed by simply automating what already exists.

What Is Information Worth?

Many years ago, economist Kenneth Arrow noted the paradox of infor-mation value: a prospective purchaser cannot know what to pay for in-formation until he or she knows its content; and once the content is known, there is no longer any need to make the purchase. Thus, pro-spective readers cannot know whether the content of the next issue of, say, MIT's *Technology Review* will be worth the $5.00 cover price until they have read it. As a result, they must base their purchasing decisions on the general reputation of the publication for accuracy and relevance—in effect, a brand-based decision. This makes it difficult for entrepreneurs to enter information markets once an incumbent brand becomes established.

Further, the established brand can raise its value by providing information storage and retrieval services for its own content. For example, the *Wall Street Journal* once offered[2] subscribers to its Internet edition several features not found in print: custom highlighting of articles in categories of special interest to the reader; the ability to store articles in a set of files stored on the *Wall Street Journal* Web site but organized by the reader; retrieval of additional materials from past editions (at an additional price). All these made the Internet edition more valuable to scholars and researchers. And unlike the information content, these Internet-based services can be valued readily by customers—at the cost of the time that customers save when they seek specific information. This, in turn, raised the cost to the customer of switching to a different newspaper, and hence built a powerful barrier to entry for new competitors.

Cost and Value Structure

Knowledge products—a movie, a song, a book—are costly to produce but quite inexpensive to reproduce. In the presence of competition, this quickly drives the price down to the marginal cost of production, which can leave unrecoverable the fixed cost of creating the knowledge in the first place. Indeed, this cost structure will pervade much of the new economy and confront entrepreneurs with special opportunities and challenges.

In the resource-based sectors of the economy, an upward-sloping supply curve means that the next increment of production will be more costly than the last. This rising cost acts to dampen demand, and the downward sloping demand curve means that customers value the next increment purchased less than they did the last. The demand and supply curves intersect where the marginal cost of that next increment equals its marginal value to customers.

These basic rules of economics arrange themselves differently in the knowledge-based sectors of the economy. There, the supply curve is essentially flat, especially when the knowledge is available over the Internet where the marginal cost of additional users is essentially zero. For example, you and I (and many other subscribers) can read the on-line *Wall Street Journal* at the same time without affecting each other's consumption of the product. But if I buy a shoe or eat a hamburger, these resource-based products become entirely mine, and you cannot readily share what I consume. In the case of networked products, my value in use actually increases with your use of the product, as discussed in Chapter 5.

Market Growth

The cost and value structure of knowledge-based markets suggests that market growth will be more rapid for new products and services than for resource-based counterparts. This, in turn, holds several implications for entrepreneurs. Most obviously, declining costs and increasing value should multiply the opportunities for successful new enterprises to achieve the exponential growth so prized by venture capital investors.

But this door swings both ways, and scale will be vigorously pursued by all competitors who seek a larger market base over which to distribute the inherently high fixed cost. Since larger markets are better markets, and the largest markets are found in global trade, competition will turn international more quickly in the new economy.

Knowledge-based markets will tend to concentrate more quickly, reducing the number of competitors to a very few large companies while the smaller firms are confined to defensible niches. This means that entrepreneurial ventures competing in the early stages of a knowledge market must secure enough working capital to endure this inevitable consolidation.

The leaders in this rush to oligopoly do not necessarily offer the most advanced information product but rather the one closest tailored to the characteristics of knowledge markets. For example, many users of word-processing software (including your author) had long thought WordPerfect to be superior to Microsoft's current Word. However, Microsoft displaced WordPerfect as market leader by packaging its word processor with other desirable applications. When large software-using organizations sought standardization, the Microsoft products enjoyed an advantage because they all worked together and because they could be priced as a package. Here the network economies were sufficient to overcome the superiority of any individual application.

Segmenting the Market

The new economy will provide entrepreneurs seeking to build high-growth ventures with improved opportunities for market segmentation, another consequence of the cost structure of knowledge products. Once the basic product has been created, then variants can be tailored to specific markets at little additional expense, especially when the new version can be "dumbed-down" for a set of customers who cannot use all the features demanded by the premium users for whom it was introduced. This practice, common in software, allows the vendor to follow the market's demand curve far down into the low-value segments.

Human Capital

The scarce resource of the new economy is already evident—the time and energy of the most talented people. Ultimately technology does not reside in books or software, but rather in the minds, attitudes, and cultural propensities of its practitioners. Your challenge will be to attract to your venture those armed with the requisite intellectual skills and the nerve to apply them. Increasingly, technology companies are outsourcing their technical talent from countries like India. Access to such highly talented, motivated, and low-cost human capital can become a salient advantage of the established firm in competition with a new venture.

Business Models for Knowledge

Many companies in the first wave of the knowledge economy were able to create customer value with information products and services. The difficulty arose when they tried to capture enough of this value to generate a return for their investors. For a brief time, this failure of value-capture could be disguised as an investment in market share. But with the 2000 crash of the NASDAQ, that illusion could no longer be maintained. The return to reality brought a search for knowledge-based business models that could capture as well as create value. That search presents one of the salient challenges to entrepreneurs offering knowledge products. Consider the case of the encyclopedia, an example of the ongoing search for a business model that links the capabilities of the technology and the delivery platform into a unified and profitable whole (see text box, pp. 184–185).

The New Market in Public Goods

Economists define "public goods" as services we all enjoy—clean air, parks, national security, and so forth—but cannot purchase as individuals.

Knowledge in Search of a Business Model

The venerable *Encyclopedia Britannica* published its first edition in 1768 during the flourishing of letters and arts in Scotland, and from that time has been irretrievably identified by the adjective "authoritative." Britannica became an American company in 1920 but continued to build its legend of intellectual rectitude. It entered the 1990s a clear market leader, and no stranger to technology. *Encyclopedia Britannica* had created a digital version for the Lexis-Nexis service in 1981, and the first multimedia CD-ROM encyclopedia under its Compton's brand in 1989. Its hardbound set, redolent with authority, still sold for $1,600; and *Encyclopedia Britannica*'s revenues for 1989 were estimated at $650 million, gained largely through a worldwide sales force numbering 7,500. Yet this happy condition was not to continue.

By the early 1990s, marketplace demand for the traditional, hardbound encyclopedia as a knowledge platform was vanishing at an astonishing pace. Revenue plummeted, and by 1994 had shrunk to a level between 50 percent and 80 percent of its 1989 value. (Contemporary news accounts present differing estimates because Britannica, a privately held company, is not required to disclose financial data, and so does not.) The company was put up for sale and finally purchased in 1996 by a Swiss entrepreneur, Jacob Safra.

The source of the difficulty was competition from an unexpected source: information packaged in a new technology, the CD-ROM, and offered through an entirely different business model. On October 12, 1992, Microsoft announced its entry into the knowledge market with its own encyclopedia, *Encarta*, essentially a digital version of the old Funk and Wagnalls encyclopedia that once shared supermarket checkout lines with the tabloids. Microsoft improved the presentation enormously, adding some new content but mostly graphics, film clips, music, a host of special effects, and even games. Initially Encarta was sold as a stand-alone CD, but Microsoft soon bundled it with its other applications that personal computer makers included with their products.

Like many disruptive technologies—manufactured ice, for example—the new encyclopedia was inferior in many ways. The limited storage capacity of the CD in the early 1990s did not permit extensive text or visuals, and so the market was focused on school-age children—or, in reality, guilt-ridden parents who sought to increase the constructive uses for the home computers they had bought (Mossburg 1993). As the technology improved, so did the offering. Over the next ten years, the information content doubled, and the encyclopedia was renamed the *Encarta Reference Library*. Customers could find it in DVD and CD versions as well as on-line.

A newer, leaner *Encyclopedia Britannica* fought back after its 1996 purchase. Its North American sales force was disbanded, and a CD-ROM edition produced. But here, limitations on the technology constrained the company's ability to compete. With 44 million words, in contrast with the 7 million or so in the early *Encarta*, the CD format would not permit copious visual and audio effects, and so it did not compete well in the youth-oriented market held by *Encarta*. Further, *Encyclopedia Britannica* initially bundled its CD with its thirty-two-volume, hardbound set, which offered

(continued)

little additional value beyond a more efficient search algorithm. The stand-alone CD cost $1,000, a strong disincentive to separate purchase. Lowering the price, eventually by a factor of ten, helped somewhat, but *Encyclopedia Britannica's* infirmities in the home-computer market remained a disadvantage. This business model failed.

On October 19, 1999, *Encyclopedia Britannica* announced a radically different business model. It would make its entire content available on the Internet for free. The notion was that the on-line content would "deliver the eyeballs" of a set of affluent readers whose attention would be valuable to advertisers. A news service and on-line shopping mall were added, and *Encyclopedia Britannica* effectively became an Internet portal for a range of general information resources. Though it began with great promise—the first-day flood of Internet traffic causing the site to crash—this model also failed. Revenues from advertising simply could not support the operation, and Britannica lacked the cash to continue in this low-margin, high-competition business. In March 2001, the company laid off a third of its dot-com workforce and began to charge for its on-line content. Rival *Encarta*, which had also offered free on-line content, restored charges, too. Currently all encyclopedia purveyors offer wide-ranging educational content, all emphasizing homework assistance, and at a cost that is roughly comparable.

None of this experience gives evidence of any business model likely to dominate the market for knowledge products through the kind of virtuous cycle noted in Chapter 2. Plainly, this model remains to be invented.

Therefore the government purchases these for us, either directly as in national defense or through regulation as in environmental quality. In the case of environmental protection, especially against global threats like disruptive climate change from the buildup of heat-retaining gasses in the atmosphere, several forces are converging that might establish a private goods market to accomplish these public purposes in the new economy. Such a market would provide attractive opportunities for entrepreneurs astute enough to recognize them.

The first force is a general discontent with the limitations of command-and-control regulation—that is, regulatory mandates for the installation of specific technologies like scrubbers on coal-fired power plants or specific standards like radiation limits on their nuclear cousins. While these can ensure compliance, they do not align the interest of the public with that of the regulated entity. And so compliance is grudging and performance along dimensions of public interest goes no further than the mandate requires.

The second force is the difficulty in reaching any international agreement on environmental standards, either to ensure trade equity among nations or to reduce pollutants of common concern. Some market mechanism, however, might replace political agreement in allocating the cost of and responsibility for cleanup—and do so in a more efficient manner than regulation could.

And the third force springs from a dawning awareness that the accumulation of greenhouse gasses in the atmosphere does indeed pose a threat to human welfare around the world. Hence, the will to act might be marshaled in spite of the difficulties above.

Lacking effective command-and-control regulations, nations might well seek more market-focused policies to better align public needs with private markets, allowing the societal preferences for clean air to be expressed as customer preferences. Consider, for example, a mandatory cap on carbon emissions enforced by a requirement that suppliers and users of fossil fuels hold tradable rights for each metric ton of carbon they produced—the "cap and trade" approach. This would have the effect of placing a price on carbon emissions that would eventually be included in the price of all goods and services. Technologies that are environmentally benign would thus gain an advantage over those that are less benign. Taxes on the burning of specified fossil fuels would have the same effect. In either case, resort to these market incentives could allow a vital societal need to be expressed in the marketplace—and in doing so, open new kinds of opportunities for entrepreneurs.

Convergence

The natural world does not partition itself by scientific discipline, and neither do the entrepreneurial opportunities that derive from the sciences. Instead, the most powerful opportunities in the new economy will arise at the intersection of the traditional engineering and science disciplines. Consider, for example, the synergistic combination of four distinct fields of science and technology, each of which is progressing at a rapid rate individually:

- *Nanoscience and Nanotechnology*: technology at the atomic, molecular, and supermolecular scale that can build from blocks of matter well below the range of human experience;
- *Biotechnology and Biomedicine*: technology addressing the self-replicating structures of matter, especially through genetic engineering and often using the investigative methods of the information and nanoscale technologies;

- *Information Science and Technology*: as described earlier; and
- *The Cognitive Sciences, Including Cognitive Neuroscience*: technologies for improving human cognition and intellect.

At the very small scale, 1,000 nanometers and below, these separate fields achieve a material unity, and from that unity springs hope for a new golden age of human development. This scientific progress, however, cannot fulfill its promise for human betterment unless entrepreneurs, operating either independently or from a corporate platform, find a way to bring it to market in a timely and cost-effective way. This is the excitement of the emerging new economy—and the entrepreneurial challenge.

Technological opportunity and societal need come together at the point of the convergence of these technologies, more popularly termed the "Nano-Bio-Info-Cogno," or NBIC technologies. J. Spohrer has organized this opportunity set in one area where need quickly translates into market—improved human performance. Table 10.1 summarizes his thinking (Spohrer 2002).

The first row shows the arena of human performance most familiar to us, the environmental context in which people perform life's daily tasks. The artifacts of performance improvement are familiar: our tools, a computer, for example; airplanes; buildings; automobiles; and the like. Much of human progress has focused on this environmental context for performance. And it is here that the impacts of the great convergence will be most familiar—new materials that change shape and color; intelligent robotic agents to assist us; a digital world for games; and so forth.

The second row of Table 10.1 concerns personal technologies, which operate outside the human body but are personal in that they will become as omnipresent with us as the six-shooter was with the cowboy in the old western movies. These are called "mediators" because they connect individual humans with other humans and with information from and about the external environment. Contemporary examples include PDAs and cell phones. In the future, wearable information systems might provide any person access to any fact (or opinion) at any time and at any location.

The third row of Table 10.1 moves inside the human body to familiar and temporary ingestibles such as medicines or foods. An ongoing flood of innovations continues to improve these. The fourth row also

Table 10.1

Opportunities for Improved Human Performance

Relative position	Improvement possibility
External (outside the body), environmental	New products: materials, devices and systems, agriculture and food New agents: societal changes, organizations, robots, chat-bots, animals New mediators: stationary tools and artifacts New places: real, virtual, mixed
External, personal	New mediators: mobile/wearable tools and artifacts
Internal (inside the body), temporary	New ingestibles: medicines, foods
Internal, permanent	New organs: new sensors and effectors, implantables New skills: converging technologies, new uses of old sensors and effectors New genes: new genetics, cells

Source: Spohrer (2002), 91–98.

concerns performance innovations inside the body, but permanently emplaced. Contemporary examples include artificial limbs and the artificial heart, and the NBIC technologies promise an enduring flow of sustaining innovations to extend the progress achieved thus far. For example, even the improved artificial hearts discussed in Chapter 4 can still be rejected by many patients' immune response, which is triggered by molecular and cellular reactions at the newly introduced surfaces. NBIC technologies could yield implant materials that are custom designed to mesh with the unique immune response of individual patients (Connolly 2002). With regard to prostheses, recent advances in the NBIC technologies might enable direct links between the human brain and machines. This would enhance an individual's ability to directly control mechanical, electronic, and even virtual objects as if they were extensions of his or her own body (Nicolelis and Srinivasan 2002).

But the most exciting, and for some the most potentially frightening, applications of NBIC concern the human brain and its potential interaction with the computer. Even as the size and cost of computers have plunged, their computing capacity has accelerated (see text box, p. 190). And every step along this path brings us to the time when computers reach such a size and capability as to be implantable in the human body. We already implant electronic devices in people: pacemakers for the heart, cochlear implants, and the like. An implantable computer could extend these artificial aids to the brain. Unless ethical issues intervene, such devices might be feasible within twenty years.

One could easily imagine significant medical benefits from implanted computers monitoring a host of vital signs from blood pressure to brain chemistry. Blindness or deafness might be cured through electronic sensors. And the consummate tragedy of aging, the decay of a fine mind, could be relieved.

Yet the application of technology is never easily confined. Recall the sixteenth-century efforts of the church, first to ban the crossbow, and later (after it proved very effective against the Turks) to restrict its use to killing non-Christians. Neither worked. Similarly, a computer implant could extend human intellectual powers as easily as it could ameliorate their decay. Imagine, for example, the ability to download information—this book, for example—into a chip and absorb it into your brain as you sleep. That possibility, however, carries with it a set of heavy ethical baggage and reaches deeply into what it means to be human—and besides, you would miss the literary enjoyment I have

---

The Incredible Shrinking Computer

The science fiction movies of the 1970s illustrate where the computers have come from. Recall that the computers of the time were portrayed as room-sized devices with blinking lights, chirping sounds, and a cadre of worried-looking acolytes in white lab coats and carrying clipboards—an accurate reflection of the reality of the time. Even HAL in the futuristic movie, *2001: A Space Odyssey*, looked a lot like big iron.

Today, computers are powerful, ubiquitous, but invisible—the acolytes and clipboards presumably finding work elsewhere. In terms of power, recall the Furby—that little owl-like interactive toy that was popular a few years ago. That toy has more computing power than was onboard the Apollo command module during the lunar landing. In terms of ubiquity, the average automobile contains a dozen or so computers, all out of sight. And the computers embodied in the greeting cards that play little ditties for us usually get thrown away shortly after the occasion. Computers have thus joined the throw-away society.

No physical laws appear to stand in the way of further reductions in size and cost. Soon everything will be able to offer services that are as intelligent as they need to be. And even we humans might gain intellectual powers beyond our present comprehension.

---

worked so hard to provide. We shall address the ethical issues that will accompany the new economy next.

The New Social Issues

Free markets are never really free, and that is probably for the best. Rather, they operate inside the legal, ethical, and moral context of their time. And so it shall be for the new economy. To be sure, growth and convergence in every field of science and engineering will offer unprecedented possibilities; but with these will come unprecedented societal issues to challenge our collective wisdom. Three stand out: privacy, ownership, and the nature of life itself.

Privacy and the Right to Self

Consider the possibilities for market segmentation discussed earlier. As information systems grow in capacity and scope, progressively finer segmentation becomes possible, ultimately leading to products and services that can be entirely personal and offered at a price that can be entirely personal. In effect, each customer becomes a contestable market. As with much of the new economy, this will prove a mixed blessing.

At one extreme, we would surely want medical service providers to have complete, accurate, and timely information about us. And in those circumstances, medical ethics would prohibit the selling of this information, even though inadvertent release or theft remains possible.

But commercial transactions enter a separate ethical regime. Customers are already asked to exchange personal data for some service. For example, I enjoy a "subscription" to the Internet edition of the *New York Times*, delivered every morning to the e-mail address that I have provided. This marvelous service costs me nothing, but does require that I register with the *Times* providing my zip code, age group, and gender. With this information and knowing the articles that I and others select to read, the *Times* can then tailor its content to the demand. The modest revelation seems small to me in comparison to the benefit.

But now consider Amazon, which pushes the envelope a bit farther. Because I purchase books there, Amazon holds on file my credit card, which contains much more detailed information. In addition, Amazon tracks my purchases, and, taking full advantage of my book addiction, offers suggestions for books I had not known I wanted. This begins to build the positive feedback loop of Chapter 2: the more I use the site, the better its service, and the better its service, the more I use the site. Aggregate that over a large customer base, and you have a business model of extraordinary power. Again, Amazon claims to safeguard this individual information—a claim that I readily believe, because selling it would cost Amazon its powerful competitive advantage. But what further rights might I have regarding that information once I have revealed it either deliberately or through my actions?

Finally, consider what can be known by aggregating data at the lowly point-of-sale terminal. A complete economic demography of an individual could be assembled with technology at hand today, probably a more detailed and accurate picture than each of us has of ourselves. And so the issue becomes ownership—who *owns* the data, especially the patterns of knowledge that can be built from the aggregation of isolated factoids? The resolution of this issue will exert a powerful influence on the emerging new economy.

Property and the Meaning of Ownership

The good news of the knowledge economy is the ability to disseminate products of the mind widely. This is also the bad news, at least for the owners of that property. As long as intellectual property had to be bound up in a physical product—a book, a film, or a record, for example—the opportunities for illicit copying were limited. To be sure, anyone could share the content, say, by inviting friends over to listen to a record collection, a practice that seems charmingly quaint now. But those who wished to duplicate the content had to duplicate its physical embodiment as well, and in most cases the reward was not worth the effort.

That union of the physical and the intellectual broke apart in the digital revolution. As a result, intellectual products from a Van Gogh landscape, to a Bach fugue, to this book can be digitized, stored on a variety of media, and shipped anywhere in the world almost instantaneously. And in technology, what can be done generally is done.

The resulting challenge to property rights has been felt most famously in the music business. Traditionally, the large recording companies for popular music sold their products through physical objects: first vinyl albums, then cassette tapes, and now the CD. To buy the object was to buy the product. But now popular music can be found in digital form on the Internet, downloaded from a proliferation of file-swapping services, and either stored digitally or returned to the world of objects as a locally "burned" CD. The recording companies blame this "piracy" for their recent decline in sales—681 million CD albums were reported sold in 2001, compared with 785 million in 2000.

Stopping this, however, has proven difficult. The record industry successfully sued Napster, the progenitor of the file-swapping services; but by the time Napster closed in September 2002, others like Morpheus and KaZaA had already replaced it. These later entrants configured their business models to avoid successful lawsuit, and file-swapping continues apace. Some estimates suggest that one-third of all music in use has been illegally copied, and in countries like China, the figure is probably closer to 90 percent. In Germany, for example, about 160 million prerecorded CDs were sold in 2002. In contrast, Germans bought 500 million blank CDs that year. The record industry has countered with: a fee-based Internet service for on-line music, which has proven unpopular; a technology initiative to physically prevent copying, which proved to be a hackers' delight; and well-publicized lawsuits against the customers who copy music files, which unleashed a torrent of bad publicity.

The difficulties of the recording companies will soon arrive for the movie producers as technology begins to cope with their much larger file size and DVD formats. The resolution of these issues of intellectual rights will shape knowledge markets in the new economy.

Life and the Meaning of Humanity

Most people can readily imagine the compelling benefits from the convergence of NBIC technologies, especially around human performance. But these technologies also lead us into unexplored areas of ethics and even of religion, because they allow humankind to manipulate the very essence of our humanity, and perhaps also our spirituality. Take the potential for computers implanted in the body to significantly enhance intellectual performance of the recipient. The appellation "cyborg" comes readily to mind, and opportunities for demagoguery abound. But for thoughtful persons, the technical possibility raises a host of ethical questions without immediate answer. Who should receive these? Those most able to pay? Those with the greatest need? And what constitutes a compelling need?

In other arenas, our nascent ability to engineer the genetic codes of animals, plants, bacteria, and other life forms raises concerns about the release of new biota into the living environment with unknown consequences. Witness the resistance, chiefly in Europe, to genetically modified agricultural products. For the present, demagoguery trumps thought—the pejorative label "frankenfoods," for example—but the issues raised are real, despite the name-calling.

Yet other advances raise issues of the nature of life itself. Consider the accelerating advances in computational power discussed in Chapter 5. In his provocative on-line essay, entrepreneur Ray Kurzweil suggests some possible consequences of the accelerating growth in capability (Kurzweil 2001). He begins by noting the capacity of the human brain, which contains about 100×10^9 neurons, give or take a few. Each neuron has about 1,000 connections, each of which can perform about 200 calculations per second (CPS). Multiply these out, and you discover a human performance capability of about 20×10^{15} CPS. By contrast, IBM's "Blue Gene" computer is expected to achieve about 5 percent of a human brain's capacity, 1×10^{15} CPS, by 2005. So far, so good.

But Kurzweil goes on to estimate the implications of the exponential acceleration of computing power. Using a simple curve-fitting model, he projects that:

- by the year 2023, computers will be able to provide the equivalent capacity of one human brain (20×10^{15} CPS) for an investment of $1,000,
- by 2037, the equivalent computational capacity of one human brain for $0.01, and
- by 2049, the equivalent of the entire human race for $0.01.

It is immaterial whether Kurzweil's model misses the mark by a few years or a few decades. The fact remains that computer science and technology are following this trajectory, and we should explore where it leads.

Kurzweil then speculates on the use of this massive computing power. Nonbiological devices could be built to replicate in great detail the functioning of clusters of human neurons. These clusters might then aggregate to perform human and societal functions creating a kind of artificial intelligence truly beyond our present imaginings. Highly speculative? Of course. But already we can observe the beginnings of this in the current concepts of Web services and grid computing. Only the computational power is lacking, and that is on the way.

The point, however, is not to make a technology forecast, but rather to suggest how technology advances occur in the context of societal and moral questions that cannot be addressed with the intellectual tools of economics. Yet humankind must resolve these if progress is to continue. By raising these matters with you now, I hope to alert you that inventing the future will not be all about economic value, compelling as that might be; rather it will also require social innovations of equal power. And, that will not be a task for sissies.

11

Toward a Personal Entrepreneurial Strategy

> . . . there are those sublimely cursed by discontent,
> and to them happiness comes only when they push their
> brains and hearts to the farthest reaches of which they
> are capable. Nothing is more rewarding than the effort a
> man makes to matter—to count, to stand for something,
> to have it make some difference that he lived at all.
> — *Leo Rosten,* Captain Newman, M.D., *a novel (1961)*

We turn now from the economic to the personal, and so close our journey through technology and entrepreneurship with some reflections on the larger themes that will influence your success. Entrepreneurship with technology presents a complex and sometimes contradictory picture—here we focus on the primary colors.

Time Flies: Whether or Not You're Having Fun

Every aspect of new company creation will take longer than you think for reasons that you cannot envision at the outset. Sales and revenue seem especially perverse in their capacity to elude forecasts. This has several implications.

First, you must maintain a sense of urgency as a matter of personal habit. Bob Shaw, president of Areté Corporation[1] and a highly successful venture investor, seeks an urgent dissatisfaction in the entrepreneurs he funds. During the process of getting to know an entrepreneur in whom he would place his trust (and his money), Shaw occasionally asks the prospect to drive him someplace. If the entrepreneur shows discontent with the slow lane and the pace of traffic, even to the point that the drive scares Shaw, then one important personal trait has been demonstrated—perhaps also a need for life insurance.

This visceral sense of urgency would seem well warranted by the realities of technology and capital markets. We observed in Chapter 5 that the first technology to capture a significant market share can sometimes be difficult to dislodge, even by a demonstrably superior competitor. In such cases, the advantages of the new technology cannot overcome the switching costs that would be borne by customers. To be sure, first to market does not guarantee long-term success—just ask the folks at WordPerfect. Rather, you should consider it just one more weapon in your competitive arsenal, placing you ahead of those second-entry competitors who must find a way to reduce the costs of switching. In addition, technical obsolescence can overtake a delayed market entry in these times of rapid advances in every field of science and engineering.

Finally, and most commonly, your enterprise can simply run out of working capital before revenues arrive or milestones can be met. In that case, the next round of financing, if it can be gotten at all, is sure to come at a share price low enough to thoroughly dilute your ownership. A skilled early-round investor, who also does not wish to have his or her value diluted, can be your best guide to the amount of working capital that you will need—just do not let that reliance dilute your own sense of urgency. Just as you can never be too thin or too rich, neither can you have too much working capital.

The Learning Entrepreneur

It is not the learned who prevail in the marketplace but those who can learn. Nobody can see enough moves ahead on the competitive chessboard, and in many cases the only way to elicit new information is to take action. Learning from the consequences of those actions lies at the heart of any competitive strategy. The learning process has several dimensions.

Listening to Technology and Markets

Spend your time listening to the markets and the technology rather than rushing to tell them of your clever inventions. What we might call "Lapidus's law" can be inferred from the story told in Chapter 3—that the resources devoted to understanding your intended market should be about twice the resources devoted to technology development. The strongest business models integrate this clear understanding of customer value with technology suited to the task and with a delivery platform that enhances both technology and value.

To accomplish this, you must first listen to real customers and learn what holds value for them and what does not. Beware of broad market studies, which often miss customers in niche markets because they lack both the interest in these niches and the special discernment required to recognize them. Such discernment can be the chief advantage of the entrepreneur, and customers in niche markets might well offer you insights that are not obtainable from mainstream market studies. Recall that Apple introduced the Mac personal computer in a niche considered too small to be of interest to the larger competitors. By contrast, the mainstream market tends to be the province of these established competitors who understand very well how to please their current customers.

Second, you must develop an instinct for the cheap experiment, the ways that special market insight can be gained through simple tests like the one Amar Bose conducted in the stereo store (Chapter 4). And third, you must remain alert to unanticipated market opportunities made possible by tectonic shifts in the nature of science and engineering. In many cases—the Internet, for example—technology leads customer expectations by many years. Entrepreneurs add value by anticipating what customers will find valuable before they know it themselves.

Context Counts

Every technology market has a unique culture and set of economic characteristics. These cultural rigidities are among the principal forces resisting the convergence discussed above. You must learn the specific characteristics of your chosen market and distrust reasoning by analogy with other technology markets.

When to Fold

Successful entrepreneurs tend to be incurable optimists, believing not only that a better world awaits but also that they can help create that better world. Indeed, no other attitude will allow an entrepreneur to succeed, independent of whether that degree of self-esteem can be justified by the facts.

Too often, however, a strong will and a winner's attitude act as barriers to learning. Self-confidence does not require omniscience, and you must be willing to change course when circumstances require it. For example, the Nth Power team of Gunderson and Floyd changed course several times as they learned what would and what would not work to secure their first fund. Recall the blindness that Sherlock Holmes noted in Watson when he said, "You see, but you do not observe."

A Team Sport

Throughout the book we have observed how team building becomes an essential skill for the technology entrepreneur. Indeed, a management team that investors view as incomplete can pose a major obstacle to venture capital funding.

Technology entrepreneurs seem especially vulnerable to building a technocentric team and neglecting the marketing function. A study of high-technology start-ups in the Boston area found that very few companies presented themselves to venture capital funders with a deficiency in technical capability. But in 40 percent of the cases, marketing and sales skills were entirely absent from the team.[2] Neither can you get away with the facile assertion that you will hire a marketing person once the technology development is complete. Experienced investors know that market planning has got to be built in at the beginning to guide technology development (Roberts 1991: 202–3).

The way you build your team will depend on your own unique circumstances and strategy. For example, the initial management team at EnerTech Environmental (Chapter 1) consisted of Kevin Bolin and his family. Such a team might have been adequate had the company retained its original business model as a licensing operation—recall that Bolin's wife, Laurel-Ann, is an attorney. But for the more aggressive business model that EnerTech later adopted, persons deep in the specific context of the sludge disposal market were needed. This pathway to team building—a lead entrepreneur with other key team members added subsequently—is quite common.

In contrast, the core management team at Nth Power Technologies—Gunderson and Floyd—was formed as a unit of two. To be sure, other partners have been added, but the culture of the firm continues to be set by the founding team. And in further contrast, the entire management team at BVSG was in place when it became an independent operating unit.

Whichever pathway to team formation is taken, trust and respect among team members must be nurtured. Prior experience working together almost certainly helps, but does not seem essential. In addition, intellectual diversity should be sought. If the rest of the management team simply replicates the skills and propensities of the founder, the sort of obliviousness noted above can occur. On the other hand, too much diversity can lead to conflicts among team members. As with all matters entrepreneurial, judgment and balance win in the end.

The Intentional Entrepreneur

In closing, we note that entrepreneurship is a life choice, not an accident: hence our title, *The Intentional Entrepreneur*. But we would also commend another important choice to your attention—the decision to enjoy the process. St. Thomas Aquinas once remarked that nothing is done well that is not done with joy. This is especially true of entrepreneurship. If you do not find your desire to change the world a sublime curse, then perhaps entrepreneurship is not for you after all.

When you become the intentional entrepreneur, you set before yourself a grand adventure. Nothing afterward will ever be the same. Gunderson and Floyd note that their entrepreneurial experience has ruined them for anything else in life. And Kevin Bolin, asked if he would do it all over again no matter what the outcome, replied with a single word, "Absolutely."

Notes

Chapter 1

1. For a complete discussion of the SBIR program as a means for technology financing, please see Chapter 7.

2. "First closing" is a term of art describing a key milestone in the life of any venture capital company. It means that the company can call in the capital commitments of its limited partners and begin to invest. In most cases, the partnership agreement allows further investors to join the fund up to a year after the first closing. Then comes the second closing, and further fund investors are admitted only upon an affirmative vote of the partners already on board.

Chapter 2

1. F. Lee Van Horn, president of Palomar Consulting, demonstrated the power of graphically representing the business model in a series of lectures to the Executive MBA program at the University of Missouri (Kansas City). The figures presented here were inspired by those lectures.

2. We cannot, of course, know the minds of the competitors of the day. Therefore, we must be content to interpret their actions and infer intent from them.

3. Game-changing technologies, also termed disruptive technologies, are discussed at length in Chapter 5.

Chapter 3

1. The author appreciates the mentoring of Jordan J. Baruch, whose teaching at the Harvard Business School in the 1970s inspired this parable.

2. In fairness, environmental advocates point out that the price customers pay for grid-generated electricity does not reflect its true cost, and so the market is biased against solar electricity. This is generally true. A marginal kilowatt-hour generated when the electric grid operates near peak capacity, say at 4:00 PM on a July afternoon, costs significantly more than a kilowatt-hour generated in the middle of the night. The consequent pollution is much higher, too. However, the pricing structure in most regulatory jurisdictions does not reflect this physical reality. In a better world, it would, but you must work with the realities that exist, not with those that should exist.

3. Lapidus's figure of merit, the ratio of market research to engineering research, does not include sales and promotion in the numerator. Cytyc now trades on the NASDAQ under the symbol CYTC, and Exact Sciences under the symbol EXAS.

The concept originated with a marketing innovator and teacher, Ralph E. Grabowski, of Andover, Massachusetts.

Chapter 5

1. TIBCO Software is a global provider of business integration solutions. It serves companies with incompatible software systems, a legacy of the single-purpose systems of the past. The core of the business model is to enable real-time processes, improved performance, and enhanced business visibility by integrating previously incompatible applications and systems. Further information is available at: www.tibco.com.

Chapter 6

1. An advisory board can help your new enterprise gain entry into the venture capital community. These members do not have legal liability (which they appreciate), but simply advise you, oftentimes out of personal interest. Their contacts with the venture capital community, however, can be of great value.

2. These criteria are adapted from the Nth Power Web site, which is available at: www.nthfund.com.

3. One can only observe the financial performance of the publicly traded Nth Power portfolio companies. Any conclusions about the private portfolio must be inferred, not observed. The ticker symbols for the publicly traded companies are: Capstone Turbines, CPST; Proton Energy Systems, PRTN; and Evergreen Solar, ESLR.

Chapter 7

1. The developmental activities of a technology start-up can be sorted into four types: (1) early technology development, the process of proving that the advanced concept will actually work; (2) product development, packaging the technology in a platform usable by customers; (3) market development, building enduring market interest in the product; and (4) company development, creating the organization needed to capture the value. These do not take place in sequence, but rather tend to proceed in parallel processes, each with an emphasis appropriate to its time.

2. The Central Intelligence Agency supports In-Q-Tel whose mission is "to deliver leading-edge information technologies to the CIA and the Intelligence Community." More can be found at the In-Q-Tel Web site at: www.in-q-tel.com. The U.S. Army operates from a not-for-profit investment platform, OnPoint Technologies. It seeks to "discover, invest in and support companies and programs developing innovative mobile power and energy technology for the commercial market with potential application to U.S. Army needs." OnPoint Technologies can be accessed at: www.onpoint.us.

3. The GeneTrace story suggests the disproportionate effect of societal influences on start-up technology companies. Monsanto will survive the currently fashionable protests over genetically modified crops. GeneTrace did not.

4. The term "angel" as a description of an investor has its origins in theater. Early in the 1900s, risky Broadway plays were financed by high-net-worth

individuals, who gained the sobriquet. Today, an angel is formally accredited under SEC Rule 501, which requires a net worth of at least $1 million, or annual earnings of more than $200,000 for the two most recent years, or if the earnings are joint with a spouse, $300,000.

5. Estimates of venture capital placements vary widely, in part due to different accounting methods and in part due to differing conceptions of the scope of the venture capital industry. As it has grown in size, venture capital has also changed in character. It has become more international with some overseas investments being placed directly, others through U.S. affiliates. It has become more corporate, with large, established companies like Intel, Dell, Merck, and Johnson & Johnson investing for strategic growth as well as financial return. Depending on which of these are included in the accounting, the estimates of the size of the industry vary enormously. Here I use the estimates of The MoneyTree™ Survey by PricewaterhouseCoopers, Thomson Venture Economics, and the National Venture Capital Association. These offer a mid-range set of numbers, but are consistent across time. The data can be found in the *MoneyTree Report* available at www.pwcmoneytree.com/moneytree.

6. One of the most comprehensive is: Copeland et al. (2000).

Chapter 8

1. Richard Marczewski proposed the sword and shield metaphor and is the source of many of the insights offered in this section.

2. Knowledge products—books music, software, and so forth—are usually protected by copyrights, not by patents. However, the general principles underlying that protection are the same for both.

3. The author is grateful for the time taken by Light Cicle founder Dianne Syme in providing background information and for the *Wall St. Journal* article that called attention to this unusual enterprise (Coleman 2000).

4. To win a judgment is one thing, but to actually collect quite another, especially when the counterparty is a foreign firm. In principle, any company can file a complaint with the International Trade Commission (ITC), an arm of the U.S. Department of Commerce. The ITC actually follows up these cases, though the wait can be up to fifteen months and the filings expensive. In Light Cicles' case, the company was assisted by Sears, which had stocked the copied product on its store shelves. Sears directed the Taiwanese company to pay or lose its entire Sears business. The check followed.

5. When filed, a patent must include complete specification of the manner and process for using it. This must be sufficient for a person "skilled in the art" to understand how to make the invention work. However, this disclosure reveals only the best mode of implementing the invention at the time of filing. The shortcuts, improvements, and efficiencies that you discover later are all yours.

Chapter 9

1. Recall from Chapter 5 that network externalities are the reinforcing effect that large numbers of users have on the propensity of additional users to employ the same technology. The more users a system has, the more valuable the system becomes to those users. The fax machine is the classic example.

2. In recent days, competition has emerged in the form of Motorola's "Symphony" system. This approach does not require a digital broadcast system, but rather converts the standard analog broadcast to digital within the radio. This spares the broadcaster the need to adopt a digital signal technology and the customer a monthly subscription fee. The history of iBiquity Digital Corporation can be found at: www.ibiquity.com.

3. Detailed information regarding Lumeta is available at: www.lumeta.com.

4. The author appreciates the insights contributed by Atul Pasricha, vice president of Mergers, Acquisitions and New Markets and Michelle Drage, director of Commercialization and Licensing, at Delphi Corporation. Further developments are available at: www.delphi.com.

5. Press releases and the Lycos Ventures Web site are available at: www.lycosventures.com.

6. As of this writing, the public stock offering remains on hold awaiting a more favorable economic climate.

7. Black & Veatch press releases are available at the company Web site at: www2.bv.com.

Chapter 10

1. The Hamtramck venture was part of a three-front modernization drive. In addition, GM formed a joint venture with Toyota in 1983—the New United Motor Manufacturing, Inc. (NUMMI)—at an old GM plant in California. Through NUMMI, GM sought to introduce Japanese-style production efficiencies into U.S. auto making. And the third was the Saturn project. This new, relatively autonomous division would design and build small cars to compete with the imports that were taking market share from GM.

2. In a late 2003 decision, the *Wall Street Journal* ended its storage and retrieval service, thus reducing the distinction between it and other business newspapers.

Chapter 11

1. The Web site for Aretê Corporation is at: www.arete-microgen.com.

2. Surprisingly enough, production skills were absent in 35 percent of the manufacturing start-ups included in the study. Worse yet, 60 percent of the business plans for manufacturing companies did not even discuss production (Roberts 1991: 203).

References

Abernathy, William J. 1978. *The Productivity Dilemma: Roadblock to Innovation in the Automobile Industry*. Baltimore: Johns Hopkins University Press.

Abernathy, William J., and Kenneth Wayne. 1974. "Limits of the Learning Curve." *Harvard Business Review* (September–October): 109–19.

Abiomed, Inc. 2004, data available from Web site at: http://www.abiomed.com/abiocor/faq.html

Anderson, Oscar Edward Jr. 1953. *Refrigeration in America: A History of a New Technology and Its Impact*. Princeton, NJ: Princeton University Press.

Arthur, W. Brian; Y.M. Ermoliev; and Y.M. Kaniovski. 1987. "Path-dependent Processes and the Emergence of Macro-Structure." *European Journal of Operational Research* 30: 294–303.

Beardsley, Scott; Andrew Doman; and Par Edin. 2003. "Making Sense of Broadband." *McKinsey Quarterly*, no. 2. Available at: www.mckinseyquarterly.com/home.asp.

Black, Bernard S., and Ronald J. Gilson. 1998. "Venture Capital and the Structure of Capital Markets: Banks vs. Stock Markets." *Journal of Financial Economics* 47: 243–77.

Buffett, Warren, and Lawrence A. Cunningham. 1998. *The Essays of Warren Buffett: Lessons for Corporate America*. New York: Cunningham Group.

Business Week. 1982. "Even Sony Can't Avoid the Price War in VCRs." September 6: 33–34.

Center for Women's Business Research (CWBR). 2002. *Women-Owned Businesses in the United States, 2002*. Available on-line at: www.womensbusinessresearch.org.

Christensen, Clayton M. 1999. *Innovation and the General Manager*. Boston: Irwin/McGraw-Hill

———. 2001. "The Past and Future of Competitive Advantage." *MIT Sloan Management Review* (Winter): 105–9.

Chartrand, Sabra. 2003. "Protecting Ideas in the Insurance Business." *The New York Times*. Internet Edition. June 23.

Coleman, Calmetta. 2000. "Family Duo Develops Famed Icicle Lights, but Rivals Filch Idea (and Profits)." *Wall Street Journal*. December 21, p. B-1.

Connolly, Patricia. 2002 "Nanobiotechnology and Life Extension." *Converging Technologies for Improving Human Performance*. National Science Foundation and U.S. Department of Commerce. June, pp. 162–69.

Cook-Deegan, Robert M., and Stephen J. McCormack. 2001. "Patents, Secrecy, and DNA." *Science*, July 13, pp. 217.

Copeland, T.; W. Foote; J. Murrin; and T. Koller. 2000 *Valuation: Measuring and Managing the Value of Companies*, 3d ed. New York: Wiley.

Coveney, Patrick F.; Jeffrey Elton; Baiju Shaw; and Bradley Whitehead. 2002. "Rebuilding Business Building." *McKinsey Quarterly*, no. 2. Also available at: www.mckinseyquarterly.com.

Coyle, Diane. 1998. *The Weightless World: Strategies for Managing the Digital Economy.* Cambridge, MA: MIT Press.

Cringely, Robert. 1992. *Accidental Empires*. New York: HarperBusiness, HarperCollins.

Davis, Randall. 200(. "The Digital Dilemma." *Bridge* 30, no. 2, pp. 12–20.

Drucker, Peter F. 1985. "The Disc pline of Innovation." *Harvard Business Review* (May–June): 67–72.

Ealey, Lance, and Glenn Mercer. 1999. "Telematics: Where the Radio Meets the Road." *McKinsey Quarterly*, no. 2: 6–17. Also available at: www.mckinsey quarterly.com.

Economist. 1991. "Management Brief: When GM's Robots Ran Amok." August 10, pp. 64–65.

———. 2001. "Patently Absurd?" June 21, pp. 40–42.

———. 2002. "Incredible Shrinking Plants." February 23, pp. 71–73.

Farrell, Diana. 2003 "The Real New Economy." *Harvard Business Review* 81, no. 10, (October): 104–12.

Foster, Frank H., and R.L. Shook. 1993. *Patents, Copyrights, and Trademarks.* 2d ed. New York: Wiley .

Foster, Richard G. 1986. *Innovation: The Attacker's Advantage.* New York: Summit Books.

Fox, Stephen. 1998. "The Strange Triumph of Abner Doble." *Invention and Technology* (Summer 1998): 34–44.

Freiberger, Paul, and Michael Swaine. 2000. *Fire in the Valley: The Making of the Personal Computer.* 2d ed. New York: McGraw-Hill.

Garvin, David A. 2002. *A Note on Corporate Venturing and New Business Creation.* Boston: Harvard Business School Teaching Note 9–302–091.

Gompers, Paul, and Josh Lerner. 2000. *The Venture Capital Cycle.* Cambridge, MA: MIT Press.

Guilder, George. 1989. *Microcosm.* New York: Simon and Schuster.

Halberstam, David. 1986. *The Reckoning.* New York: Avon Books.

Jones, Joseph C. Jr. 1984. *America's Icemen.* Humble, TX: Jobeco Books.

Katz, Donald. 1996. "Rise of the Silicon Patriots." *Worth* (December/January): 87–146.

Kirsch, David A. 2000. *The Electric Vehicle and the Burden of History.* New Brunswick, NJ: Rutgers University Press.

Kunze, Robert J. 1990. *Nothing Ventured: The Perils and Payoffs of the Great American Venture Capital Game.* New York: HarperBusiness.

Kurzweil, Raymond. 2001. *The Law of Accelerating Returns.* Available at: www.kurzweilai.net/meme/frame.html?main=/articles/art0134.html.

Lasica, J.D. 2002. "Why the Wired West Still Matters." *Online Journalism Review.* Annenberg School of Journalism, University of Southern California. Available at: www.ojr.org/ojr/lasica/p1020203502.php.

Leonard-Barton, Dorothy. 1992. "Core Capabilities and Core Rigidities: A Paradox in Managing New Product Development." *Strategic Marketing Journal* 13 (Summer): 111–25.

Lerner, Josh. 2000. "The Problematic Venture Capitalist." *Science*, February 11.

Liebowitz, Stan J. 2002. *Re-Thinking the Network Economy.* New York: AMACOM Books.

McGahan, Anita M., and Brian S. Silverman. 2001. "How Does Innovative Activity Change as Industries Mature?" *International Journal of Industrial Organization* 19, no. 7 (January): 1141–60.

McGee, Suzanne. 2000. "Cache Flow: The Life Cycle of a Venture Capital Deal." *Wall Street Journal.* Internet Edition, February 22.

McWilliams, Gary. 2001. "Compaq Shifts Toward Computer Services, Software." *Wall Street Journal.* Internet Edition, June 25.

Miller, R., and D. Sawers. 1970. *The Technical Development of Modern Aviation.* New York: Praeger.

Moore, Geoffrey A. 2002. *Crossing the Chasm.* New York: HarperBusiness.

Mossberg, Walter S. 1993. "Parental Guilt Sells Encyclopedias on CD-ROM Too." *Wall Street Journal.* April 29, p. B1.

Murtha, Thomas P.; Stefanie A. Lenway; and Jeffrey A. Hart. 2001. *Managing New Industry Creation.* Stanford, CA: Stanford University Press.

Narayanan, V.K. 2001. *Managing Technology and Innovation for Competitive Advantage.* Upper Saddle River, NJ: Prentice Hall.

Nicolelis, Miguel A., and A. Srinivasan. 2002. "Human-Machine Interaction: Potential Impact of Nanotechnology in the Design of Neuroprosthetic Devices Aimed at Restoring or Augmenting Human Performance." *Converging Technologies for Improving Human Performance.* National Science Foundation and U.S. Department of Commerce. June, pp. 223–26.

Ollivier, Joe. 2000 "Never Keep the 'Angels' Guessing," *Desseret News* (Salt Lake City). October 15.

Oviatt, Benjamin M.; Patricia P. McDougall; Rodney Shrader; and Mark Simon. 2000. *Heartware International.* Available on-line from McGraw-Hill at: www.mhhe.com/primis.

Pfeiffer, Eric W. 2002. "Discount Daze." *Red Herring* (San Francisco). January, pp. 57–59.

Pool, Robert. 1997. *Beyond Engineering: How Society Shapes Technology.* New York: Oxford University Press.

Pooley, James, and W. Bratic. 1999. "Why Trade Secrets Can Be So Valuable." *Nouvelles* (Journal of the Licensing Executives Society) (December): 163–66.

PricewaterhouseCoopers. 2001. MoneyTree™ Survey. Limited data available from: www.pwcmoneytree.com.

Regalado, Antonio. 2000. "The Great Gene Grab." *Technology Review* (September–October): 48–55.

Roberts, Edward B. 1991. *Entrepreneurs in High Technology.* New York: Oxford University Press.

Roberts, Michael J.; Howard H. Stevenson; and Kenneth P. Morse. 2000. *Angel Investing.* Boston: Harvard Business School Teaching Note 9–800–273.

Roth, Stephen. 2002. "Tech Firm Leaves Unpaid Bills, Untapped Potential." *Kansas City Business Journal,* American Cities Business Journals, Inc. March 15.

Rosenberg, Nathan. 1972. *Technology and the American Economy.* New York: Harper and Row.

Schindehutte, Minet, and Michael H. Morris. 2001. "Pricing as Entrepreneurial Behavior." *Business Horizons* (July/August): 41–48.

Sechler, Bob. 2000. "Angel Investor Ranks Grow, Boosted by New Tech Wealth." *Wall Street Journal.* Internet Edition, August 16.

Senge, Peter M. 1990. *The Fifth Discipline.* New York: Doubleday.

Shapiro, Carl, and Hal R. Varian. 1999. *Information Rules.* Boston: Harvard Business School Press.

Spohrer, J. 2002. "NBICS Convergence to Improve Human Performance." In *Converging Technologies for Improving Human Performance: Nanotechnology, Biotechnology, Information Technology and Cognitive Science,* ed. Mihail Roco and William Bainbridge, pp. 89–102. Arlington, VA: National Science Foundation.

Stalk, George, Jr. 1988. "Time—The Next Source of Competitive Advantage." *Harvard Business Review* 66 (July/August): 41–51.

Thomke, Stefan, and Eric von Hippel. 2002. "Customers as Innovators: A New Way to Create Value." *Harvard Business Review* 80, no. 4 (April): 74–81.

Timmons, Jeffrey A. 1994. *New Venture Creation.* 4th ed. Chicago: Irwin.

U.S. National Science Foundation (U.S. NSF), Division of Science Resource Studies. 2001. *National Patterns of R&D Resources* (May).

———. 2002. *Science and Engineering Indicators.* Available at: www.nsf.gov/sbe/srs/seind02/start.htm.

Utterback, James M. 1994. *Mastering the Dynamics of Innovation.* Boston: Harvard Business School Press.

van der Heijden, Kees. 1997. *Scenarios: The Art of Strategic Conversation.* Chichester, UK: Wiley.

von Hippel, Eric. 1988. *The Sources of Innovation.* Oxford: Oxford University Press.

Waite, Thomas J.; Allan L. Cohen; and Robert Buday. 1999. "Marketing Breakthrough Products." *Harvard Business Review* (November).

Weber, Thomas E. 2001. "Intangibles Are Tough to Value, but the Payoff Matters in Dot-Com Era" *Wall Street Journal.* Internet Edition, May 14.

Wetzel, William E. Jr. 1997. "Venture Capital." In *The Portable MBA in Entrepreneurship,* 2d ed, ed. William D. Bygrave, p. 186. New York: Wiley .

Wong, Henry. 2001. *Why Seed? Why Now?* Available from Artemis Ventures or from the company's Web site at: www.artemisventures.com.

Zook, Chris, and James Allen. 2001. *Profit from the Core.* Boston: Harvard Business School Press.

Index

David L. Bodde holds the Charles N. Kimball Professor of Technology and Innovation at the University of Missouri in Kansas City. His doctorate is from the Harvard Business School, and he holds graduate degrees from M.I.T. He serves on the Board of Directors of several energy and technology companies, and advises many others on technology-based business strategies. Dr. Bodde has a wide range of executive experience in both government and the private sector, including the Midwest Research Institute, the Congressional Budget Office, the Department of Energy, and TRW. He was once a soldier and served in the Army in Vietnam.

Fully capable of folly, he is restoring a pre-Civil War house in Kansas to National Historic Register standards—but in doing so has gained an appreciation for the skill and ingenuity of those innovators long dead. They too built a new economy, and we are the beneficiaries.